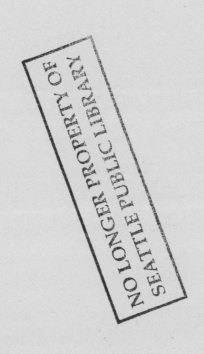

WITHOUT A PRAYER

WITHOUT A PRAYER

THE DEATH OF LUCAS LEONARD AND HOW ONE CHURCH BECAME A CULT

SUSAN ASHLINE

PEGASUS CRIME
NEW YORK LONDON

WITHOUT A PRAYER

Pegasus Crime is an imprint of
Pegasus Books, Ltd.
148 West 37th Street, 13th Floor
New York, NY 10018

First Pegasus Books hardcover edition August 2019

Interior design by Sabrina Plomitallo-González, Pegasus Books

ISBN: 978-1-64313-072-9

10 9 8 7 6 5 4 3 2 1

Printed in the United States of America
Distributed by W. W. Norton & Company, Inc.

This is a true story. Some names have been changed to protect the privacy of individuals. Those names are indicated by an asterisk. Excerpts from written material appear in italics and are reproduced exactly as they originally appeared, as far as spacing, spelling, grammar, and punctuation. The exception is Sarah Ferguson's text messages and emails that were read aloud in court, during her trial. Those messages appear in italics but have been edited for an easier read.

For Lucas Benjamin Leonard, who deserved to live free.

CONTENTS

Name References   *xi*

PART ONE: ORIGIN OF A CULT   1

Don't Go Inside   3

Smooth Pebbles in a Stream   11

Genesis   31

The Gospel According to Jerry   37

Children of the Flock   61

Demon Strongholds   73

Sarah Ferguson   89

Resurrection   95

The New Senior Pastor   105

They Could Leave   127

Exodus   139

A Shaking Is Coming   145

Repent   169

Break Away   177

PART TWO: THE CRIME   187

Crapstorm Coming   189

Code Blue   209

Scrambled. Dead. Period.   221

Unveiled   263

Building a Case   273

Trial   295

Sentencing   349

Bruce Leonard Reflects   369

Afterword   377

Acknowledgments   379

Source Material   383

NAME REFERENCES

IRWIN FAMILY

Jerry Irwin — Word of Life Christian Church (WLCC) founder
Traci Irwin — Jerry's wife
Tiffanie, Naomi*, Daniel/Dan,
Joseph/Joe — Jerry and Traci's children

MOREY FAMILY

Linda Morey — WLCC loyalist
Kathleen/Kathy*, David/Dave — Linda's children

LEONARD FAMILY

Bruce Leonard — Luke's father
Kristel — Bruce's daughter
Deborah/Debi (Wright) Leonard — Bruce's wife
Sarah, Jayden* — Debi's children
Gabriel*, Ada*, Noah*, Ivy* — Sarah's children
Lucas/Luke, Christopher/Chris, Grace, Ezekiel* — Bruce and Debi's children

WRIGHT FAMILY

Rick Wright — former WLCC pastor, Debi's brother
Seth* — Rick's son
Jeff Wright* — Rick and Debi's brother

Rich Dibble — Anglican priest who befriended Bruce
Brooke Bowden* — WLCC loyalist

WLCC NEIGHBORS

Stacey Brodeur,* Meredith Brodeur,* Tara Litz

LEONARD FAMILY NEIGHBORS

Frances Bernard*, Cindy Kellam, Brenda Livingstone*,
Frank Livingstone*, Pamela Murphy*, Olivia*

PART ONE
ORIGIN OF A CULT

I feel for these people that I'm about to tell you about, but you gotta listen to me. It's like the person who comes out of a cult—the bitterness, and the anger, and the resentment they feel toward those who lied to them, especially when they find out it was a lie, and they got out of it. But if you look at it from the truth's point of view, you've got an individual came over, knelt down in front of somebody and said, "Beat me. Please beat me. I wanna be beat." Now, in light of that, you know, what right do they have to be bitter and resentful of the people they told to beat 'em after they beat 'em?

—PASTOR JERRY IRWIN
TO THE CONGREGATION ON NOVEMBER 10, 1996

DON'T GO INSIDE

Halloween—the nightmares it represents—came early for Chadwicks, New York, in 2015. It was three weeks before little devils and monsters would march the neighborhood carrying treat bags. A warm breeze was blowing orange and yellow leaves down Oneida Street. The sun was baking carved pumpkins on porches, turning their insides black and collapsing them into oozing messes, filling the air with a pungent odor. Temperatures hit an unseasonable seventy degrees at noon, allowing folks to revel in the light and warmth before an approaching long, dark winter. They were outside in T-shirts and shorts, playing kickball in the yard, walking the sidewalks with no destination. The joie de vivre was out of place against the backdrop of macabre neighborhood decor: foam tombstones, inflatable witches, giant cobwebs.

There, at the intersection of summer's life and fall's death, one building was unadorned. The Word of Life Building stood out on the block as having no Halloween decorations, yet a real horror story was playing out behind its walls.

There was a strange aura around that place. That's what neighbors said of the old redbrick building after people moved there in the early 1990s and stamped "Word of Life Building" over the front door. Another sign pronouncing it a Christian church added to the mystery. Those words appeared to be the only indication of godliness. The people at the Word of Life Christian Church didn't welcome others. They shut them out.

The building and its new occupants became quite the curio. Many were saying it was a cult. Everyone was talking, and the rumors were more than small-town chitchat. It was intel gathered through personal experiences and grassroots espionage.

Stacey Brodeur's* home acted as a lookout for her visiting aunt from Florida, who was constantly entertained by the comings and goings across the street. She would peek out the windows and shout, "Quick! Come look!" They'd watch a parade of cars pull into the church driveway. Someone would get out. Unlock the gate. Open the gate. Go inside. Close the gate. Disappear.

A Catholic church was on one side of the Word of Life Christian Church, and Tara Litz was on the other side. She rented the first floor of the house next door. Admittedly nosy, she was always watching from her window. From her backyard, she would climb the picnic table to peer over the wooden picket fence that her reclusive neighbors had put up along the property line.

There were German shepherds on a platform off the third story, and dogs on the roof that no one could see, only hear. Fireworks exploded from the roof at times, and there were bonfires on the asphalt shingles. One produced an odor so foul it made neighbors sick. Children could be seen in the parking lot, walking in a line. Cars pulled into the church at the same time each night, well after dark. And there was bizarre chanting. It wasn't language, but noises—weird noises. And there was an inexplicable, deafening *whoosh*, like a jet, and flames were involved.

The Word of Life Building was never a tired topic among the locals. They spoke of men, beefy and intimidating, walking the grounds in black trench coats even in the middle of summer. But what was actually playing out over many years behind those walls was far more sinister than the story line written in neighbors' imaginations.

A colossal, three-story structure, the building was conspicuous in the row of residential homes on Oneida Street, the main road running through Chadwicks, located in central New York, outside the metropolitan area of Utica. The community isn't even large enough to constitute a village. It's technically a "census-designated place," documented purely for statistical purposes. Simplified, it's a community with a recognized name. And until Columbus Day 2015, Chadwicks was invisible to the rest of the world.

What became the Word of Life Building at number 3354 in the 1990s was built in 1916 as a public school occupying almost two acres. The rectangular building had wings on either end that contained stairwells. An aerial shot would show that, with a flat roof and those wings, the building was shaped like a capital letter "I." It got an add-on in the 1970s, a large gymnasium built in the rear, attached by an indoor ramp. The gym, which could not be seen from the road, would eventually be converted to a church sanctuary.

The path leading to the front door was a concrete sidewalk, same as you'd see at any school. At one time, hundreds of students, teachers, and parents walked the concrete slabs to the school entrance, but not long after the real estate transferred to the WLCC, no one went in that way. Few outsiders were allowed in the building at all. The new owners installed a locked metal gate at the head of the driveway. They planted a hedgerow of fifteen-foot trees on one side of the building, and there was that fence they built on Tara's side. Sauquoit Creek acted as a natural barricade across the back property line.

Stacey's mother, Meredith*, was pleased when the church bought the building. Of course, they called it a church, and Meredith thought that was good. The grounds had become an eyesore, but when folks moved in, the lawn started shaping up. That was refreshing. So was the idea of new friends on the block. All that, in the beginning, seemed promising. A middle-aged man mowed the lawn and trimmed the shrubs. Meredith's husband would go over for a chat. *What a nice guy*, he thought.

"But nobody else we saw there ever spoke to you," Meredith later said. "We realized after—they weren't a friendly bunch."

It didn't take long for Stacey to experience her first eyebrow-raising incident with the newcomers. It was before they erected the head-high swing fence across the driveway. She was on her way home and had just turned onto Oneida Street from Elm Street, which is a few doors away from the church, when she saw a little boy waddling shoeless in the road. He couldn't have been more than three years old.

This wasn't long after the 1993 disappearance of twelve-year-old Sara Anne Wood, who had lived in the nearby hamlet of Sauquoit. Wood was presumed kidnapped and murdered, and the crime caused fear around the country, particularly this close to home in Chadwicks. People were hesitant to approach a child who wasn't their own. Stacey wasn't about to pick up the boy and take him home. She rushed to her house, but her parents weren't there. Keeping her eye on the wandering baby, she went next door and rallied one of her aunts who was living in town. Together, they ran down the driveway of the church in pursuit of the child who'd just toddled down there. But he'd vanished. All they could hear was the rushing waters of the creek. They swallowed, and searched the property with just their eyes, fighting a sickening hunch.

A door creaked. The boy was crawling out of a parked sedan. They took his hand and brought him to the church door, where they knocked and knocked.

After some time, an older woman appeared. With a yank, she pulled in the boy and slammed the door. No words were exchanged.

Emergency responders got the same reception. Alarmed by the sound of sirens one day, Stacey and Meredith ran to the front of their house to see firefighters pounding on the church door. They watched them scrambling to find a way in. State troopers arrived. One wound up on the Brodeurs' doorstep.

"Do you know these people over here?" he asked. "We've got an alarm going off and can't get in."

But the women had no influence over there. No one did. Parishioners of that peculiar church did not interact with the neighbors—not anymore. Things had changed.

Positive brushes with the churchgoers were minimal and sporadic but had happened, mostly when the group had first moved into the building. A couple of years in a row, the church held a rummage sale. They set up tents on the lawn and, along with bric-a-brac, sold homemade breads. Stacey went over to shop. They sure were friendly then.

Tara moved next door in 2004, a single mom with a four-year-old boy and a daughter on the way. Every Sunday, WLCC members would pull into her driveway and give away cakes, breads, and doughnuts. She would take some for herself, some for people at work. Other neighbors came. They were getting freebies, and they were grateful. But it lasted only a couple of seasons.

Tara noticed teenage girls in the church parking lot but never saw them leave. When she heard her son chattering from her bedroom, she investigated and found his imaginary friends were very real. He'd been talking with the girls through the window. It was odd, she thought, teenage girls befriending a preschooler. But Tara believed the girls were glad to have someone on the outside to talk to, so she allowed it.

One teen from the church did reach out to Tara. Her name was Naomi*. She gave Tara her phone number and made her promise to call if she needed anything. Tara made that call in 2008, after she'd had surgery and needed a favor. The single mom wouldn't forget the act of kindness, and Naomi wouldn't stop being considerate. She eventually noticed Naomi leaving the property, and whenever a car she was riding in would pass through the gate at the Word of Life Building, Naomi would wave to Tara. She was the only one. All other contact from behind those brick walls was frosty.

No one could delineate when the total shut-off occurred or figure out what prompted it. Tara believed it might've happened when she called animal control after hearing dogs barking all hours of the day and night. She discovered the church was running a puppy mill.

"They would drive their van outside the gate and park it there. And then people would come. And I realized—they're selling dogs," she later recalled.

Someone from the church erected a "Jesus Saves" sign for an audience of one. It was a giant, handmade billboard of wood painted black with letters of bright white. Angled to face Tara's apartment, it could be seen from only her backyard.

The strangeness increased over time. The daily car parade began happening much later at night. At one point, it appeared the cars were entering the building itself, as if into an underground garage. The vehicles would drive around back and vanish. Someone would hurry and lock the gate. Later, the vehicles would emerge at the same time and form a single file. One by one, they would exit, and again someone would hustle to the gate and lock it.

At Halloween time, building number 3354 was especially spooky. Each year, Chadwicks had a Halloween parade, and families would line Oneida Street—except for the spot in front of the redbrick building. People from the church would chase them off the lawn. Though Oneida Street was a typical stream for trick-or-treaters, no one knocked on door 3354. The men in trench coats would hide in the bushes. Other men would pace the roof, patrolling, guarding their domain. It was the scariest thing on the block.

Like a scene out of a Halloween thriller, kids would ride their bikes past the secretive church, screaming, "Don't go inside! You'll never come back out!"

How prophetic that would be.

Nineteen-year-old Lucas Leonard would go inside on October 11, 2015. He would never come back out alive.

Some of you still think that your mind is your own, to think whatever you want to think, whenever you want to think it. And you don't have a right. That's just the seed of sin that'll lead—eventually—to death.

—Pastor Jerry Irwin

to the congregation on August 18, 1996

Clayville, in upstate New York, was named after Henry Clay. It is, perhaps, fitting that Lucas Leonard was raised there. Clay was a three-time failed presidential candidate but a master at conciliation. The once Speaker of the House of Representatives was a negotiator in the peace treaty that ended the War of 1812. He motivated his followers with these words: "An oppressed people are authorized, whenever they can, to rise and break their fetters."

Clayville is about halfway between Syracuse and Albany, dead center of the state, and looks like an impoverished community you'd find nestled in a remote camping area. Most annual family incomes didn't top $40,000 when Bruce and Deborah Leonard took up residence near Church Road (appropriate, given their reverence for God). Their house was at 2347 Main Street, bought in 1993 with a price tag of $28,000. The population was 464.

The Leonard home was built in the early 1900s, but age was no excuse for its ramshackle appearance. The colonial's baby-blue color was clouded by mold and mildew. Fingerlike black stains crept over the rain gutters. A $2 patriotic pull bow served as the rusted storm door centerpiece, and next to it was a handheld-size American flag, the kind given out free at Independence Day parades. Whirligigs hung from the porch roof, spinning in front of the paint-chipped window trims. Items from teapots to drink bottles lay scattered across the porch, forever left where they'd been set down.

The exterior of the homes it was sandwiched between were in similar decline, so the Leonard place didn't stand out in that regard. But neighbors would one day feel it necessary to make a point: the

Leonard children were always clean. They emphasized—*always* clean.

Main Street in Clayville had a college-dorm-living feel in the sense of neighborhood intimacy, both geographically and socially. It was barely wide enough to make a three-point turn. On the side of the street where the Leonards lived, there was but a step or two of grass from one front door to the other (across the street, houses had slightly more yardage). Neighbors would walk their dogs and get stopped by a neighbor, then two. Eventually a group would form, and people would catch up on news and gossip. Everyone knew one another's names and business—except that of the Leonards.

There was Frances Bernard*, a grandmother with a yappy miniature lapdog whose bark competed with Frances's stories, told with anima-tion and the raspy voice of a chain-smoker. She was tenderhearted yet held nothing back. She'd birthed and raised seven children. For twenty-three years, she lived near the Leonards in a cigarette-smoke-filled house with a clock that gonged loudly on the hour. The coffeepot was always on. She considered Debi Leonard her friend.

Pamela Murphy* lived with her daughter next door to the Leonard home. Because they were on different schedules, interactions were brief—mostly small talk or Pamela saying hi in passing. All but one would return her greetings. The patriarch, Bruce Leonard, would make a beeline for the house.

About a half-dozen doors down is where the Livingstones* called home. Frank* and Brenda* were the neighborhood givers. Brenda would come home from garage sales with bags of clothes for children who needed them. You'd find the clothing clean and neatly folded inside paper bags on a chair in the entryway, awaiting distribution. Pictures of family, and some of the neighborhood kids, covered the walls and shelves. Theirs was a cozy home, compact and lived-in. It was open to everyone—always. Over the years, their kitchen table seated many visitors. They even invited strangers inside, four-legged ones included. Brenda would feed the wild cats that seemed to instinctively know hers was the place to go for caretaking. Frank, a senior citizen, had a neighborhood paper route. He would one day drop a Sunday paper dated October 11, 2015, on the Leonards' porch. It would sit for years unread.

The Leonards found themselves lucky to have a thrift store right across the street. The fire department was a two-minute walk in one direction, the library a two-minute walk in the other. Cindy Kellam was a librarian there. She also spent time at her in-laws' place, next to the thrift store. She'd been friends with Debi back when they were kids in the same youth group, but they lost touch with each other when Cindy went to college. Sometime in the late nineties, while at her in-laws' house, Cindy spotted Debi in her front yard across the street. It was a complete surprise. Cindy gave a single-armed wave as broad as her smile and shouted, "Hello!" But Debi wasn't the same. She was standoffish. She gave no indication of wanting to resume a friendship; quite the opposite. Debi had always been somewhat quiet, thought Cindy, but not cold.

Debi was born in Springfield, Massachusetts, in 1956, the oldest of Richard and Nancy Wright's four children. Her brother Rick was born the following year, followed by Jeff*, and then Susan, who was twelve years younger than Debi. In 1969, Richard moved the family to New Hartford, New York, just outside Utica, and took a job as an accountant at Duofold, Inc., a maker of thermal underwear. Debi's family was loving and supportive. She and her siblings attended public schools, and the extent of their worship, for a while, was going to church once a year on Easter.

Debi acted as a mother to her youngest sibling after illness forced their own mother bedridden. She took on the role with a loving hand and heart. Coming of age was difficult for Debi. She was more insecure than the average high school girl and didn't stand up for herself. She got through her teenage years a little more scarred than the rest of her peers and fell into a volatile relationship with a longtime friend. Debi ended up marrying that friend, and they had two children. Tragically, their third child, a boy, died of sudden infant death syndrome. After some years, Debi fled the marriage with her children and returned to live with her parents, who had moved to Clayville. Her brother Rick lived next door, and he'd become heavily involved in a local church run by a man named Jerry Irwin. Rick persuaded Debi to try it out. She didn't have a job, or a focus, except her children. Debi was a stay-at-home mom at the time she began attending the church around 1986, not long after Jayden* was born, and when Sarah was three or four years old. Just a few years later, she would meet Bruce Leonard.

Bruce was born in 1950 and grew up near Cooperstown, home to the National Baseball Hall of Fame. He spent time working at the Cooperstown Farmers' Museum and labored on a nearby dairy farm owned by his family.

Bruce met his first wife, Ellen*, when they were both students at the State University of New York at Oneonta. He married her in 1973, after graduating with a degree in education. It was around that time Bruce landed a position as a high school teacher for a small school district, Owen D. Young Central School District in Herkimer County, east of Clayville. His mild manner made it difficult for Bruce to keep control in the classroom, so he left the job after a short time and went on to pursue a master's degree in plant and soil science.

In 1979, Ellen gave birth to Kristel.

Though Ellen was a firm believer in God, Bruce wasn't particularly religious. He started attending church with his wife and began showing more interest over time, eventually being seated on the board of directors.

In December 1987, with problems plaguing their relationship, Ellen left the marriage after fourteen years, taking their only child with her. The divorce summons came just four months after Ellen's abrupt departure. His wife was awarded custody of Kristel. Bruce's future had been ripped away, and now he didn't know where his life was headed. That's when Bruce met Jerry Irwin.

Bruce later reflected on his frame of mind. *I was at a very low point and had stopped attending the local Methodist/Presbyterian church. It was too depressing to go without my wife and baby girl.*

A family friend took a lost, lonely, and broken Bruce to Pastor Jerry's fledgling congregation, operating out of the basement of a home in Bridgewater, New York.

It was just in a living room with some friends, Bruce recalled. *[Jerry] said something to me, (I forgot the specific) regarding my situation which there was no way for him to know so it got my attention, as to "hey, maybe God is showing him things."*

Bruce began regularly attending Jerry's services in 1989. That's when he started interacting with Debi. At first, she was just one of the new friends he'd met. But three years later, Bruce and Debi married in the church, a move that more firmly established their roots with Jerry's flock.

When the couple moved to the Clayville neighborhood, Debi brought her two children from her interracial marriage, now ten-year-old Sarah and seven-year-old Jayden. Bruce came with thirteen-year-old Kristel, the daughter he affectionately dubbed "The Eldest." By this point, Kristel was back to living with her father full-time.

Bruce and Debi, exceedingly God-fearing and dedicated to Jerry's congregation, which would later be named the Word of Life Christian Church (WLCC), naturally expected their children to attend the church and develop the same covenant to God. Bruce formed a positive connection with the group, because it was small and comprised mostly of family members. He was also beguiled by the pastor's messages.

I was very impressed with Jerry Irwin's preaching/teaching. He stuck to the Bible, pointed out what was plainly written and also noted things which sometimes people assume but which are not written. Many of the messages were tough—He started preaching years ago about having our thoughts under control, specifically under God's control, being renewed in the spirit of mind.

Only Jerry heard from God. His followers did not. Leaving Jerry's group meant losing their cherished link to God. Bruce and Debi would do anything to keep in God's favor. Capitulation to the one who ruled over you demonstrated faithfulness to God. Deeply loyal to the Word of Life, the couple honored Jerry with complete submission because Bruce considered faith and loyalty as one and the same.

The Leonard children spent inordinate amounts of time at the church. Sarah was eventually pulled from Sauquoit public school to complete her education in the Word of Life Building, followed by Jayden. Though she'd been attending public school and doing quite well, Kristel also went on to be schooled inside WLCC. Eventually, the Word of Life Building would be not only Kristel's school but also her home.

The kids were restricted by the parameters of their parents' faith but were allowed some typical childhood experiences. They could watch certain movies, play video games, and listen to the radio.

Bruce was a patient man who could tune out the chaos of the house if the kids got to acting crazy. He spoke slowly and measured his words. He put so much thought and time into making decisions, it became a running joke in the family: ask Bruce if he'd like a cup of coffee and guess how many minutes it would take him to answer. It drove Kristel nuts. If she asked for help with a decision, he would have her create a list of pros and cons.

Kristel wouldn't learn the value of carefully weighing decisions until later in life, when she was old enough to appreciate it, but other lessons she cherished from the start, like when her father gave impromptu science lessons wherever, whenever. Any plant they came upon was an opportunity to learn how light affects growth, or which plants rely on insects to spread their pollen or seeds—anything biology related. Bruce was an excellent teacher who enjoyed sharing his enthusiasm of nature. He took his children on outings once or twice a month to the farm that had been in the family for decades. It was there that Kristel received a lot of her lessons. Sometimes, they'd bring city friends, prop them on horses, point out indigenous plants and wildlife, and teach them about cattle and farm machinery. Bruce engaged with those around him, and with gusto.

Bruce had come of age in the hippie era. When Kristel was a baby, Bruce wore the classic long seventies sideburns with a mushroom top cut of brown hair. As Kristel grew, so did her father's hair, slightly curling over the ears. He added a mustache. As time went on, he grew a beard. As he aged, it stayed that way—overgrown hair, full beard and mustache—but the brown locks gave way to sheer white, an unkempt, mountain-man look that didn't help the community's later perception of him. He stood five foot nine and had a slender frame he maintained through the decades.

Debi was a gentle person and a nurturing and caring mom. As for child-rearing, her biggest fault seemed to be that she was not a good housekeeper. Dinner would often be late, and clean dishes were hard to find. Debi was poor at delegating chores and enforcing the rules. Other than the occasional grounding or light spanking that led to tears, neither she nor Bruce was a disciplinarian. It was a common scenario: before going to work, Bruce would leave a chore list for each child, only to return and find it undone. The Leonard patriarch would call family meetings, usually about pitching in.

"The meetings were basically a combination pep rally and light chiding with a few scriptures to fortify his points about keeping up on responsibilities," Kristel would later recall. "Everybody was quiet generally, biding their time until the snack cakes at the end. Dad never got angry, though he was certainly frustrated."

Two adults and the three children of their blended marriage was the family makeup for several years, and then came the first child of their union: Lucas Benjamin Leonard joined the world on November

8, 1995. He arrived looking like an artist's rendering of a cherub, with blue eyes; delicate, straw-colored hair; a complexion of milk; and cheeks accented by perfect pink circles. Like his personality, there was a shock of uniqueness in his features. It was the hint of strawberry sheen to his hair, the bit of wild stallion that set him apart. No one could yet know the fight he would put up, refusing to be broken.

In 1998, Bruce and Debi welcomed their second son, Christopher. Grace was born in 2000, and Ezekiel* arrived three years later.

"The kids were adorable," recalled Frances with her husky voice, strongly accenting the word "adorable."

By the time the littlest was born, Kristel had long been gone from the Leonard household, having moved in with the Irwins, who headed the Word of Life Christian Church. Sarah flew the nest when Luke was about seven, and her brother Jayden followed. The family unit that remained, for many years, consisted of Bruce, Debi, and their four younger children: Luke, Chris, Grace, and Ezekiel.

The clan's quiet was noted by the community. The Leonard children didn't mingle much. Their escape was the backyard and just beyond. Their back lawn was a small patch of grass and weeds that sloped down sharply, ending at a railroad bed, where the track ballast was piled at a steep incline, like a wall. But it wouldn't keep the kids from climbing the tumbling gray stones, kicking up white clouds of ballast dust that had a slight smell of rotten eggs. They would cross the tracks to get to Sauquoit Creek. *Sauquoit* is a form of a Native American word that means "smooth pebbles in a stream."

Of the seventeen miles of creek, three flowed south directly from the Leonards' backyard in Clayville to the backyard of the Word of Life Christian Church in Chadwicks, all the way, the gritty waters wearing down the unique facets of each stone in the creek bed, molding a foundation of rocks that were all the same. It was a fate similar to what the Leonards would experience in their church environment. The children often swam in the stream that smoothed pebbles.

They stuck to their own neighborhood, and though trite and cliché, it was true of the Leonards: they kept to themselves. Bruce was a mystery, fodder for gossip. He was termed an "odd duck" by one neighbor, seen as unfriendly by others. When out in the community, he would not make eye contact. Everything in the family had to be cleared by him. The children often called him Father and used the word "obey" when speaking in terms of what they were and were not allowed to do ("We have to obey the rules"). Debi had to run everything by him. Cindy Kellam watched with interest one day at the library when Debi had to make a decision and called Bruce to get his permission.

The Livingstones wondered why Debi stayed with Bruce. If Debi was outside talking to Brenda, one only had to count to ten before Bruce arrived. With his eyes solely on Debi, he would tell her, in a calm and barely audible voice, "Okay, you've talked enough. Time to come in."

Debi would leave.

Occasionally, Brenda would be able to coax Debi inside to sit at her kitchen table for a cup of coffee. Frances had tried that, too, though it only worked once, and didn't go well. It started with Frances and Debi talking outdoors.

"Come on in, Deb." Frances motioned toward the house. It would be so much more comfortable. "I'll make some coffee or tea."

It was only a few minutes after they crossed the threshold that Ezekiel, his face framed by a home haircut, came knocking. "Father wants to know what you're doing."

"We're gonna have coffee," Debi told her youngest.

Ezekiel left. The coffee began brewing. Sarah, who had returned home to live, was next to knock on the door.

"Come on in, Sarah," Frances greeted her heartily.

"Oh, I can't stay," she replied politely. "Father wants us home." Then, after a pause, added, "What are you doing?"

"We're havin' a party!" joked Frances. Her voice put strong emphasis on certain words, pausing almost theatrically, as if for effect. But it was clearly just her style and not intentional. "Come on in!"

But she wouldn't. Sarah left, and Debi followed.

Debi and Frances's friendship developed another way. Because Frances didn't have a car, Debi would offer to drive her to the grocery store, or Frances would call and ask, "Deb, could you take me to Reilly's?" That was the gas station and convenience store down the road.

"Yeah," Debi would respond reflexively. Then, as a quick afterthought, she would add, "Let me ask Father first."

Frances would walk to their house and knock on the door. "Deb, I'm ready," she'd say through the screen, bringing her face close so as to be heard. But she wouldn't go inside.

Always, Ezekiel would travel with them. Frances adored him. She would lean over and look Zeke in the eye, her stiff, double-handled handbag hanging from her forearm. "You want some doughnuts or ice cream? Whatever you want, get it. I'll get it for ya."

He would usually pick out a box of different kinds of doughnuts.

"Zeke," she thought she was whispering, "there's not enough doughnuts in that one box. You got a big family. Get another one."

Though she was fond of Debi, Frances thought of Bruce as domineering. His word was law. Those in the community used attributes like "controlling" to describe him. Add to that "strange" and "weird."

The Leonard kids were extremely quiet, well-mannered, and respectful. Almost without variation, those were the adjectives most everyone used to describe them. And some would say "socially behind," "sheltered," "loners." They weren't allowed to play with other children.

"Luke was happy-go-lucky. Smiling. All he had was a bicycle," Brenda Livingstone reflected. "Didn't go anywhere. Never drove a car. Never had a girlfriend. Playing in the yard, throwing stones all the time."

They weren't allowed to celebrate holidays. When Frank mentioned Christmas to the littlest one, Ezekiel told him, "Oh, Christmas is bad. Real bad."

We were encouraged to be scriptural, Bruce later explained, *shy'd away from the pagan trappings of Christmas and Easter, live holy, obey those who have the rule over you, etc.*

The Leonard kids took trips to the thrift store across the street, the town park, the fire station for special events, and the library, where Cindy never saw them with any friends. In that confined area of their neighborhood, within just a few dozen feet, they would stick together as a family.

Then, there *was* someone else. A little girl moved to the neighborhood a few doors down. She would ride by on her bicycle, and the older Leonard brothers would say hello. They were friendly. She didn't know they didn't play with other kids. She didn't know their parents were considered different. She didn't care. She was ten. Luke was a year older, Chris a year younger. And with the naivete and persistence of a child, the raven-haired little girl pushed her way into the lives of the Leonard children. She saw what others didn't: there was so much more to Luke than his silence.

"He was supersmart, but no one really knew it because he was quiet," Olivia* later shared.

He spent his days turning nothing into something. He once made a hoverboard out of a tarp and a piece of wood. He could rewire things to make anything he needed. He was smart in the way tinkerers are, their brains constantly turning, taking apart machines and electronics, trying to figure out how things worked. He always wanted to be outdoors, building or fixing things. He would build tents in his backyard with sticks and trees. He would cut down trees, build fires. He and Chris once built a bridge so they could walk across Sauquoit Creek. Ezekiel would snap up the remnant twigs and whittle them down to make bows and arrows. Luke would fish in the creek and clean his catches. In the winter, he liked to ice-skate.

Olivia was right there, all the time. When she got home from school, she would go see them. They would ride bicycles and skateboards,

Rollerblade. Just being kids. Debi would take her children to the nearby park in the town of Paris to play at the playground, and Olivia would go with them.

Luke had a great talent and enthusiasm for art. One year, the town of Paris chose him to represent them in a countywide sidewalk chalk competition. He won first place.

The town park was also where Debi put each of her kids through swimming lessons. All the Leonard children were skilled swimmers. Olivia had a pool, and they would go to her house to use it, part of the lure being the implicit promise of treats. They would sit on her porch and talk—and eat. Because the Leonards received donations from the local food pantry, a program that provided food to the needy, the kids rarely got snacks. Olivia's mom would make them meals and spoil them with junk food. They would go nuts over a bag of chips and salsa.

Luke and Chris were respectful to Olivia. "Complete gentlemen," she later recalled.

Luke had inherited his father's way of carefully thinking through his words and often paused while speaking. But he did not hold back when it came to joking with loved ones. Luke would laugh—all the time—and it was a laugh that shook his whole body, even if one couldn't hear it. They were more like single, isolated laughs, in succession, each one producing what looked like a muscle spasm in his chest cavity. His grin shared the spotlight with his sarcastic wit. He had unparalleled, robust joy and a teasing nature.

He was funny—and fun. And quite the daredevil. In winter, with a barely measurable amount of snow on the sidewalk, Luke would climb out the second-story window of his house, onto the porch roof, and do a full flip in the air, coming to a solid landing on his feet in the street below.

Chris went on to prove himself more of a cook than adventurer. He was quieter than even Luke, but once he got comfortable around someone, he would open up and let his sense of humor shine through. He had a big heart. Olivia found him lovable and called him a "big teddy bear," because he put everyone else's needs before his own.

"He wanted to make sure everyone was okay all the time," she later recalled. "If I came over, and I looked sad, he'd be the first one to ask if everything was okay and what was going on. He wanted to talk. And if his sister was sad, he'd want to make sure everything was okay and see what he could do."

The Leonard children attended school at the Word of Life Christian Church until Luke was fourteen. Then, Debi started homeschooling them, each year submitting curriculum proposals to the school district. About a year and a half later, they joined a homeschool co-op that met on Wednesdays at Crosspoint Church in nearby Whitesboro. The other moms liked Debi. Aside from being a sweet woman, she was talented with arts and crafts, so they appointed her instructor for it. Through the co-op, the kids got homework once a week, instruction in music and art, and had science labs, field trips, and sports. Luke and Chris joined the soccer program and came to love it. But even surrounded by kids their own age, their social interactions remained minimal. The entire Leonard family would go to the kids' soccer games but barely interacted with the other families, if at all.

At home, the kids would cross the street to the thrift store nearly every day; usually with their mother, until they got much older, and then only as long as they had permission. The clerks would sell them books for just a dime or sell Debi clothing for a quarter. They would also send her home with freebies. The kids went to the library daily. Sometimes, they would get books, but they always got movies. Chris would place holds on material and call each morning to see if it had arrived. If it hadn't, he would stop in anyway, sometimes making several trips a day. The kids watched movies when they lay down to go to sleep at night.

The house next door to the Livingstones' sat vacant for about a decade, but the door was unlocked, so the Leonard boys, Grace, and Olivia would go in and play. (Being the youngest, Ezekiel would often get left out). They would step without caution on the broken glass, the sound of it crunching under their feet breaking a quiet otherwise only punctuated by an occasional piercing giggle. They would press their palms on the wooden windowsills, on top of the peeling paint, careful to avoid the dead flies, and lean out the windows. They could see the Livingstones were home next door and smell the hamburgers cooking. One by one, or all at once, they'd climb the fence into the Livingstones' yard, where they would invite themselves into the kitchen to talk—"stupid, foolish kids' foolish talking" Brenda would later call it—and eat.

Brenda would find odd jobs for excuses to give the kids money. "Olivia," she'd say. "I've got five dollars for you if you want to clean the bottom of the chair legs." And then she'd tell her husband to turn off the TV. He knew the Leonards weren't allowed to watch it.

The kids were at the Livingstones' just about every day. That probably had something to do with the fact that Frank and Brenda stocked their house for them—cupcakes, pretzels, chips, popcorn, and soda. They would hunt yard sales for clothes to give the Leonard children, because they often saw them wearing the same clothes every day. The kids spent time at the Livingstones', playing and eating ice cream, usually right up until Brenda's early bedtime.

"It's eight o'clock. You're going now," she would have to tell them. But they didn't want to leave.

Olivia was at the Leonard house every day, but for years, she wasn't allowed to go inside. She also was not allowed to go to their church, a church they did not speak of to their neighbors. The kids moped about having to go to church. That wasn't unusual to Olivia. It was church, she thought—who would want to go to church? The Leonard kids would ask their parents if their friend could go along, but the answer was always no. They would have to wait to see her when they got home.

Finally, one day, Olivia was allowed inside the Leonard home. The only room off-limits was the parents' room, but she did peek inside to see the floor covered with mounds of clothing. There was a bed that only Bruce used. Everyone else slept downstairs on couches in the living room. They had a lot of animals but had been taking good care of them. Except for the living room, the rest of the house was a dump. Olivia led a clean-up effort, and they tackled Luke's bedroom first. It was a project the kids enjoyed. Luke ended up with a dresser and a bed and began sleeping there instead.

Olivia was privy to things outsiders did not see, like the method of discipline in the Leonard household. When Bruce was upset about something, he'd walk away, or call the kids into another room. "The kids never came out and had been beaten," she later reflected. Nor did they speak of having been punished. And they likely would have told her, she believed. They seemed to trust her and confide in her most everything, like their dissatisfaction with the restrictions placed on their lives.

They began acting out in small ways. Grace was swearing a lot. Brenda's sister had to scold her for using the f-word. Out of sight of their parents, all the kids swore. They wanted to act like other kids. They wanted to be normal teenagers. They began pressuring their parents for permission to do forbidden things, like attend public school. Olivia overheard their parents tell them they could not go to public school because they didn't want them around people who were swearing. The boys were constantly asking Olivia what public school was like. They told her they wanted to go. They wanted to drive. They wanted to have girlfriends.

With a wink and a grin, neighbor Frances Bernard would gently rib, "Hey, Lucas. You got a girlfriend?"

Luke would look serious as his cheeks flushed and, characteristic of his long, well-thought-out replies, would eventually vocalize a sheepish no.

They also wanted to work. Luke got his parents to agree to let him work as a lifeguard at the town of Paris pool when he was fifteen. His application was given priority status because he'd gone through the town's swim program. But the boy also proved his skills in the water, having taken lessons all the way up to level seven, the town's most challenging course. Swimmers had to prove their mettle by mastering skills such as taking off their jeans in the water and turning them into a flotation device, and being able to tread water for thirty minutes without touching the wall. After he completed all skill levels, Luke took and passed the American Red Cross lifeguarding course.

The Leonards attended swim classes as a family. Sometimes, Bruce would be there, but mostly it was Debi. Regardless, they did not engage with those around them unless someone approached them first. That stood out to Paul Harris*, an employee of the town parks and recreation department. He found Luke to be introverted and socially delayed. He figured it was because of limited social interactions due to his homeschooling. Paul hoped the job would help Luke step out of his comfort zone and make friends, but that didn't happen. Paul couldn't think of a single time that Luke started a conversation, and he did not look others in the eye. But he impressed as an exceptionally polite young man who acknowledged anyone who spoke to him.

Curiously, the first season of Luke's lifeguard employment was also his last. Paul was surprised the following year when he didn't see an application from Luke. When he saw Debi at the pool with Ezekiel the first week it opened, he approached her. "I didn't see Luke's application this year. Did I miss something?"

She didn't give a reason but vaguely suggested Luke was busy with studies or schoolwork.

Though he hadn't earned their friendship because of what appeared to be shyness, Luke's work ethic earned the respect of the other lifeguards. He was out on the deck doing everything required of him. He'd proven his reliability in his own neighborhood, too, by rushing to help single mom Pamela without invitation. He would shovel out her car if it got stuck in the driveway in winter. It was this level of dependability that prompted the Livingstones to hire Luke for dog-sitting.

By this time, Luke had established his place in the family as an inventor and repairman. At seventeen, he acquired a broken blue minibike. In the spring of 2013, he sat in his backyard, on a lawn that was more crabgrass than anything else, and took it apart. He torqued this, ratcheted that. As he worked, tiny twigs poking out of the lawn left lines of red on his arms that stung but didn't bleed.

When he finished putting the bike back together, he pushed it up to the street, over a curb, and between two parked cars. He flipped open the choke, jumped on the kick-starter, and gave it a shot of gas. The bike zoomed into the path of an oncoming SUV, T-boning its passenger side. Brakes squealed. Luke hollered. The crunch of his knee was loud enough to be heard by others. He'd broken it. The bike was totaled.

Over the next two years, the injury would cause problems for Luke. The pastor of his church, self-proclaimed prophet Tiffanie Irwin, would eventually consult God and deliver a prophecy about the affliction. And it would be jaw-dropping.

In the year or two leading up to October 11, 2015, Olivia had a bonfire at her house. She invited Luke and Chris, of course, along with her friends from school. But it proved to be disastrous. Olivia's school friends told the Leonard boys to get lost. Crushed by it, one of the brothers called Olivia the next day and told her they no longer wanted to be friends. She and the Leonard children separated. Though the Leonards' markedly changed behavior would soon be the talk of Main Street, at the time Olivia parted with her friends, the Leonard boys were no different than they'd always been, and "Grace was still the same old Grace."

Olivia moved on, took a job, and got busy with life. The boys' lives remained stalled, despite their constant yearning to get out into the world.

Meanwhile, thirty-one-year-old Sarah, now with four children, moved back into the Leonard home. Bruce allowed it on the condition that she attend church at the Word of Life. It was meant to be temporary, just a few months. Sarah took over Chris's room in the attic, forcing him to share a room with Luke, something that became a source of contention among the siblings. The big sister's presence was like a shadow, monitoring the others' behaviors. She also helped Bruce keep tabs on Debi's communication with outsiders. She began going to the library, Chris's favored hangout, to use their computers and printers, where Cindy Kellam once overheard her chiding Chris for trying to borrow an R-rated movie.

In the year leading up to Luke's death, those around the Leonards began to notice a distinct difference in Debi's personality, as well as the personalities of the children. Bruce remained aloof, but the rest of them got quieter. The thrift store clerk saw they'd become mysterious, their heads bowed all the time, as though they were under hypnosis. Debi stopped going into the store altogether.

Something, surely, wasn't right.

The library director would later tell police that Luke had always gone to the library and seemed happy, except in the year before his death: "He wasn't friendly. He wouldn't say hi or talk to me anymore." He went in less frequently.

Sarah's temporary arrangement grew permanent. She remade the attic into an apartment, and, after some time, Grace moved up there, too.

Then . . . Grace vanished.

"Grace, toward the ending, you never saw her," Brenda later recalled. "She never came out of the house. She started hiding in the house."

"With the babies," Frank added. "Sarah's babies."

Her absence led to wild speculation, and a rumor circulated that Grace might be pregnant. Brenda and Frank drove to the Leonard home to investigate, planning to drop off a newspaper when the boys were outside.

"Where's Grace?" Brenda asked when they got there. "Where's she been lately? We haven't seen her in a long time."

The boys went to get her, and she emerged, showing no sign of pregnancy.

"She was holding one of the kids like she was the mother taking care of all the little kids—Sarah's kids," Brenda later recalled. "She come out, and she said hi and smiled."

"Nice-looking girl," added Frank.

"A little lady now," Brenda interjected.

Grace was fifteen, petite, all of five foot one and barely more than a hundred pounds. She had braces and big blue eyes framed by glasses, with full, wavy brown hair past her shoulders that she often draped to one side. The older Leonard brothers were turning into men. Luke had grown to five foot eight and 130 pounds. He talked of wanting to join the army. His strawberry blond hair was darkening and thinning. He grew a chin strip and a barely evident mustache. Chris was short and slender, with wavy dark brown hair that sometimes hung in his eyes, or was sometimes gelled into a deliberate sloppiness. As he had since childhood, Chris wore glasses. He had added an earring in each ear.

The Leonard children were beloved to those who lived on their close-knit street, people who would defend their honor to the end, and beyond.

Sarah had settled in with her young children. There were now eleven people in one household. The new dynamics were about to change everything, and one person would wind up dead.

"She was my friend," Frances would one day tell a news reporter of Debi. "May they burn in hell."

The first couple years I was serving God, going to this Bible study in somebody's house—I went to a lot of Bible studies in people's houses. And I just quit doing it. Because it was just a futile waste of time. I began to learn just to do what God was telling me to do. And sure, God would send me some places and want me to attend services and get involved in home groups, and I've done it. But you just don't go floating around to every invitation you're given. It's just a waste of time. . . . And I remember at the end of this Bible study—last time I ever went to this house that I can remember—the teacher, I'm pretty sure, was giving a reading about wives submitting to their husbands, reading out of Ephesians and other places in the Scripture. And as we walked to the door, this spiritual woman—I'm being very cynical. She was just a downright butch of a woman. She shoulda changed her name—she walked to the door, and she said, in about this tone of voice [deep and at earsplitting volume], 'I let my husband wear the pants in the house, just so he wears the ones I tell him to!' as we're walkin' out the door. Stupid. Fools."

—PASTOR JERRY IRWIN
TO THE CONGREGATION ON AUGUST 18, 1996

GENESIS

In the beginning, what would become the Word of Life Christian Church was a Bible study group in Richfield Springs, New York, southeast of Utica. It was the early 1980s, and a man known as Pastor Reggie was in charge. He'd previously been pastor of nearby Cherry Valley Assembly of God. Two other former pastors of the Cherry Valley church—Mark Russ, and then John Mutchler—succeeded Pastor Reggie in Richfield Springs.

Jerry Irwin took over in 1984.

Jerry Dean Irwin was born in Erie, Pennsylvania, on April 22, 1957, the son of Charles and Judith Ann (Gardener) Irwin. He and his three sisters were raised just outside of Erie, in a home their family built next to a cow pasture. When Jerry was eight years old, he carried buckets of cement and mortar so his father could set blocks for the foundation. Though his parents were not churchgoers, they sent their children to Sunday school at a Baptist church. Jerry believed it was to get the siblings out of their parents' hair. When he was eleven, he listened to an evangelist guest speaker who asked if anyone wanted to receive Jesus as their savior. Despite having no idea what that meant, Jerry walked to the front and kneeled. The preacher laid hands on him and prayed. Jerry would later say that from that moment, he felt different.

Jerry recalled his home as one of abuse, his parents continually calling him stupid and no good. He would never amount to anything, they told him. His grandmother would remark how well behaved he was, and his mother would declare, "That's because he knows I'll beat him if he acts up." His father would ridicule him in front of people for not doing something correctly or fast enough. Jerry spoke of it in email years later, to the daughter he would never raise. He complained of getting hit over and over in unbridled rage, rather than being dealt a focused spanking for discipline. His family, he relayed, showed little encouragement and even less affection. Jerry suffered low self-esteem and fear of rejection. Decades later, the pain still fresh, he would describe his childhood woes to his disciples as a knife stabbing him through the heart and ripping him open, only to callus over, causing him to hate his parents. He would rebel against them. He would resent them.

When he was sixteen, Jerry was convinced a police informant was setting him up for an arrest, so he smashed out the windows of the informant's house with a baseball bat and fled town. Hitchhiking landed him in a small town in Ohio, where he met a man with a fish tale: he'd reeled in copious cash working as a deckhand on boats in Florida. Jerry convinced the man he was eighteen and traveled south with him to Port Canaveral, where he got a job on a sixty-five-foot scallop boat. Five days a week, Jerry would leave dock before sunup and unload just before midnight. On the weekends, he would get drunk and do drugs. It was during one of those benders he met Robin* at the Pillow Talk Lounge in Cocoa Beach. Two weeks later, he asked her to marry him. He still hadn't revealed his real age.

Jerry rented a trailer near the port and switched to a job on a swordfishing vessel destined for the North Atlantic. Robin went along, and it was during this time the two began having disagreements. In a 2005 email to his daughter, Jerry claimed that occasionally something would come over Robin, as if she became a different person who was mean and hateful. She would say some of the cruelest things, he wrote, and he usually responded with hurt and anger. Like his parents, he felt that she never encouraged him and was quick to put him down in front of others.

Always on the move, the couple hitchhiked to Jerry's parents' house, and then to Robin's hometown, and married in November 1974. Jerry joined the air force, and they settled at Chanute Air Force Base in Illinois. He and Robin decided to have a baby. As time went on, tension increased, and he felt there was nothing he could do to meet her approval.

They relocated to Griffiss Air Force Base in central New York in September 1975, and Mark* was born that December. Their relationship continued to erode when Robin befriended a couple who lived in a trailer a few lots away. Jerry became convinced they were speaking critically of him. In response, his wife encouraged him to seek out his own friends, but Jerry's opinion about friends was that they deliberately interfered with family relations and caused trouble between spouses. He refused to have a social life and pressured Robin to end hers. He started college but dropped out.

In 1977, Robin became pregnant with their second child. Their relationship strained, Jerry and Robin decided to seek counseling. Robin went to the base psychologist's office for help, and soon after, Jerry was called in. He claimed that the psychologist remarked endlessly about Robin's beauty in an elaborate charade to elicit jealousy. The couple went from one counselor to another, but it never got them anywhere. Jerry stopped talking his wife out of leaving and one day drove her to the airport. The event branded in Jerry a memory of Mark's pained expression when he realized his father was no longer walking with them.

Jerry was not present for the birth of his daughter Serena*. Robin took both kids and moved to Colorado, where her parents lived. Jerry believed that Robin had arranged to have his career counselor spy on him. He became depressed, his life spiraling into a seedy world of bars and constant partying. In May 1979, he resolved to kill himself.

"What is love? And who loves me?" Jerry spoke out loud, alone, on the way to get it done. He believed at that moment, the road he was walking disappeared in front of him, and he was weightless in a sky of not azure but rose. He saw God sitting on his throne with Jesus at his side and felt the presence of the Holy Spirit as he had the day he went before the altar as a child. The revelation changed his life.

In 1980, Jerry went to Colorado to find his children. He ended up living with them in their grandparents' home for a short time, but Robin eventually took the kids and left with another man. Their daughter would later write Jerry and tell her mother's side of the story: Robin thought Jerry was insane. He would stare at her just to make her crazy. He would talk to demons and paint weird stuff on the walls. Robin had said she'd left to protect the children. She feared Jerry's parents, claiming his mother had once tied Mark to a tree while babysitting. It was after they moved to New York that Jerry got mean, Robin had told her daughter.

It was all so confusing to Serena, because her maternal grandparents had always said Jerry was "really nice, gentle, and soft spoken."

In 1984, Jerry met another woman.

Traci Prim was raised with her two younger sisters on a farm in Richfield Springs, where she was a hard worker, up with the roosters and then to school. She helped her mother birth and doctor animals. She was gentle-voiced and obedient, a follower.

Traci was book smart, a gifted learner and voracious reader, but lacked common sense. She got good-natured teasing for thinking there was a paint color called camouflage that came out of the can multicolored. She was gullible, for sure. And, her mother, Diane Griffith, later said, "She was the best kid in the world." Mother and daughter had a special bond, so close that Traci's sister was jealous of their relationship. Despite that, the middle daughter, who shared a room with Traci, considered Traci her best friend.

Traci was raised a devoted Christian. She was active in church and busy with school, where she was involved in sports and played clarinet in the band. She had a close group of girlfriends and was popular with the boys.

Diane once took her eldest daughter on a road trip a half hour east to a large dairy farm in Sharon Springs. She was delivering a Jersey cow and would get a horse in return. A guy Diane had gone to school with happened to be on the farm—with Jerry. Jerry, who was almost ten years older than Traci, exchanged his address with her, and the two became pen pals, getting to know each other through letters. In one letter, Jerry wrote that God told him Traci was going to be his wife. Only about two months after meeting, they married. Traci was eighteen. Jerry started his church on their wedding day.

Jerry was cool to Traci's family, who had visited his church in Richfield Springs a couple of times. When Diane talked to Jerry, he wouldn't look at her. "He'd look down. He'd look away. He'd look next to me," she later said. "He'd look every place but me." She noticed he didn't do that with others.

Jerry told Traci that her middle sister was a bad influence on her because she watched TV. Neither attended that sister's high school graduation in 1986.

But Jerry's new bride was interested in connecting with family—Jerry's. Traci, and the children who came of her marriage to Jerry, would spend a decade searching for Jerry's children Serena and Mark. When they finally found them on a reunion website, it took a lot of coaxing to get Jerry to reach out to them. He was not happy—rather, downright upset. Traci's children would exchange pictures and emails with them, but it was only after persistent nudging, and the passage of many months, that Jerry would follow suit. In the end, Mark and Serena chose not to reestablish a relationship with their biological father.

Maybe because people are self-deceived, they have this thinking, brother. They think that I don't see it, and I don't know it. And they think they can act one way in my presence, but I don't know how they really act when my back is turned, when they're someplace else. I *know* it! It's just uncanny ability. It haunts me sometimes. I know what people think. Say, "Why would God tell you what I'm thinking and tell you what I've said to my wife or my husband when you're not around?" It's because I'm the pastor of the church, and I need to know."

—PASTOR JERRY IRWIN
TO THE CONGREGATION ON AUGUST 18, 1996

Jerry moved the Bible study into the basement of his home. There were just a handful of participants now, down from the early days of "twenty-five or thirty disgruntled people," as he later characterized them. He once used these words to tell his congregation the attrition was due to an ineffectual pastor: "We had a real compromiser for a pastor at the time who had some real hypocrites for the music leaders and, you know, they lived disgustingly ever after until he didn't see any more glory, and then he tried to dump it on me."

Years later, Jerry complained that the pastor sent preachers who tore him apart and told him the congregation would be sunk with him at the helm. Now, here it was, the group a Noah's Ark in its own right. They were a chosen people, part of something special, building from the ground up. Carving a path to God was in their hands. They invited pastors from other communities to speak. Enhanced by cellar acoustics, these evangelical preachers electrified the room with their fast-paced talking, voices rising as they spoke of everlasting life, of who would be given passage and how they would get there.

One such spellbinding speaker was the Reverend Peter Puleo, from Mount Zion Ministries in Herkimer. His arms would whip around in time with his preaching, his hands outstretched until the webs of his fingers showed. When listeners were desperate for the next word, his voice would hush. They would hold their breaths to gain the silence needed to hear it—that one word that could mean their salvation.

Jerry was so impressed with the traveling minister that he named his congregation City on the Hill: Mount Zion Ministries. Perhaps following the lead of that pastor, he adopted preaching methods to gain center stage, though he fell short. He had the quality of a preaching voice but a backwoods vernacular, using "set" instead of "sit" and a lazy pronunciation of "to," instead saying "tuh." He would chop off the last letter of words ending in "ing." He wasn't the most fluent speaker, prone to using fillers like "um" and cutting off his own sentences while searching for the correct word or thought. He would ramble in spots where he'd lose his train of thought and have to stop speaking until he figured it out.

But he did have an advantage over the other preachers: he knew the intimate, behind-the-curtain details of his parishioners' lives, and the information was coming from the Lord God Almighty himself.

"I know," he told his flock, drawing out the second word, making it seconds long, and he waited before emphasizing the next line: "I do." The rest was a continuous thought. "I know how you live in your house, and I don't even have to call you. Sometimes it's a plague for me, and sometimes it's a curse for me. But I know how you live."

His was a mostly monotone voice until the jolting "hallelujah!" that made babies cry. He sprinkled his sermons with "Are you hearing me?" And when he prayed, his body moved a lot, his head bobbling. He would close his eyes just enough so his lashes acted as drapes, and his eyelids would flutter rapidly, as though receiving a divine message. His body would twitch, like muscle spasms all over. He would clench his teeth, causing his jaw muscle to swell and release, swell and release. Add to the intrigue, Jerry could speak in tongues; a holy language with no discernible words but sounds that listeners could interpret for themselves.

The man was a mystery, heaven-sent. Members of this tight group felt a spiritual awakening and, perhaps more importantly, a sense of belonging. This was their place.

Jerry, at this early stage, came across as kind; his second wife, Traci, kinder still. She was attractive, though more on the cute side, with porcelain skin and cheeks like an adolescent still hanging on to baby fat. She had deep brown, shoulder-length curly hair and hazel eyes. She presented as wholesome, in modest outfits and simple makeup. In her girlish voice, she would open each sermon with a prayer and a request for money in the collection plate. Each service would end with a call for the sick or injured to come forward for healing. Jerry would lay hands on them and pray.

On New Year's Day 1986, the pastor and his wife had a baby they named Tiffanie. Jerry would one day believe his daughter to be his spiritual shadow, and Tiffanie would see herself akin to God's right hand. At the age of thirteen, in a diary, she would retell her own birth as a miracle, claiming she was stillborn, her face blue. Someone hung her upside down and hit the bottoms of her feet and, supernaturally, she spit out a substance, took her first breath, and lived.

After Tiffanie's birth, Traci cut off all ties with her family. Her mother, Diane, had no idea why. She contacted her daughter every way possible, even reaching out through mutual friends, but there was dead silence—for almost thirty years.

Though he'd had no relationship with them, Jerry referenced Traci's parents a decade later in one of many sermons about women needing to submit to their husbands. "Some husbands are afraid if they don't go along, they're gonna get killed in their sleep. I truly believe that about my wife's parents." He told the congregation his father-in-law went along with whatever his mother-in-law said, out of fear for his life. "There was that fear inside that, 'I might not wake up tomorrow if I don't do what she says.'"

It was, Diane's family later said, completely made up. Jerry often urged men to take control of their wives under the threat that if they didn't, their salvation was in jeopardy. This message was taken seriously, like everything out of Jerry's mouth. Because Jerry said so, it came from God.

Jerry was big not just in divine presence but in girth. He stood over six feet tall, and in later years, his words were sometimes separated by deep puffs of breath, a result of the growing belly fat impacting his lungs. His larger-than-life appearance made him seem just that—greater than earthly. He exuded control. It wasn't until years later that some of the congregants came to realize a more malevolent control, though by then, they'd been eased into accepting it. In a sermon from the nineties, Jerry talked about his desire for overarching control: "You can set there, and then when the service is over, there's this intimidation and manipulation from some of you, where you just wanna push your will. It's like some of you set through the service and don't hear a thing that's said. You don't hear a thing, don't learn a thing. And then you get over [to me] and you're, 'Oh yeah, by the way, I wanna talk to you about something.' I wish I knew how that worked. How to maintain that control after the service is over."

Early on, there was the occasional missed red flag that Jerry wanted to be more than just a shepherd, like when he got into a rift with the Mount Zion pastor and severed ties. But in the 1980s, control appeared more as guidance to members of Jerry's flock. He met a need, and in some cases, as with Debi Wright and Bruce Leonard, a critical one.

I started going regularly to this living room/basement church meeting and considered it as my God provided safety net, Bruce recalled.

He would bring along Kristel when he had visitation. She was ten when Bruce began attending regularly in 1989. That was also the year Traci gave birth to her second daughter, Naomi, who would come to call herself "the rebel child."

The congregation eventually settled into 3354 Oneida Street, the former Chadwicks Junior High School. By this time, it hadn't been a school for many years. At first, the church shared the building with other businesses. There was a karate studio in the front and a gymnastics training center in the back. The parish rented out what used to be the school's home economics room. Jerry was sold on the idea of using

Sauquoit Creek for baptisms. The church was open to the public and welcoming. They did outreach (all but Jerry, who claimed knocking on doors would only make him "more miserable" because it took time away from studying Jesus) and invited speakers. Attendance was booming. It was thrilling. Jerry's charisma attracted people. A former member later spoke of Jerry in the early years as "humble and loving"; another described him as "a caring man."

Jerry had a beard and mustache, but the beard was sparse on his cheeks, so from a distance it could look like a goatee. Facing him head-on, near the peak of his head, at the one-o'clock mark, was a white streak of hair. Jerry, with his fuzzy face and black, slicked-back hair, was gentle-voiced and thoughtful. But after a time, his mannerisms more often resembled a grizzly, violent and unpredictable. Without warning or provocation, he would verbally attack individuals with a rainbow of colorful insults, or all of the parishioners at once, using creative one-liners: nasty, miserable, rotten people, no-good flesh-eating sinners, goofy-acting jerks.

"Some of you I've watched over the years, and you're so arrogant," he once told them. "You're totally off the wall. You're half dead in your thinking. Because you're filled with the devil of strife and arrogance and pride. And this is a mistake that I've made—because, to be honest with you, in the past, some of you just weren't worth my time, and my feelings, and that was wrong—but I just let you do your arrogant, self-righteous, evil things."

He talked openly of wanting to take some of his parishioners, pull out their hair, and throw them up against the wall "because of the way they acted."

"Some of you act so pious," he spat. "You're so full of it."

Jerry's congregation began to fear him, never knowing whether to expect the brute pastor or the temperate one. But they checked themselves with reminders of the pastor's influence over their passage to heaven. And they held out hope that things would get better.

In 1990, they got their wish. Jerry packed up his family and moved to Rochester, New York, to pastor at a church as part of the "deliverance movement," a group of traveling ministers who practiced deliverance ministry: a belief that every ill in a person's life was from being possessed by a demonic spirit. They performed cleansing rituals to cast out demons in people. It could look like a scene from a horror movie, with someone on a bed, fighting and writhing, as ministers prayed, speaking in tongues.

In Jerry's stead, Debi's brother Rick Wright took over services in Chadwicks. Under new leadership, the group breathed freedom. With Jerry's departure went the oppressive air. Laughter returned. Good things were happening, and parishioners were content. Children of the church joined in social events inside the building. Pastor Rick allowed it, whereas Jerry viewed socializing as "empty chatter."

In 1992, Bruce and Debi went from being friends to spouses. Kristel moved in with her father full-time, and the church became the nexus of her life.

At the wedding rehearsal dinner, Bruce declared himself "happy, happy, happy," his bride beside him with a gap-toothed grin. Debi kissed him on the cheek. They simultaneously reached for each other's hands and clasped them, and Debi showed off the engagement ring, her pale finger tucked in her beloved's hand. In the era when softball-size eyeglasses, mullets, and perms were cool, dozens of church members filled the Sauquoit Pizza Cafe with bursts of laughter as they ate pizza and wings, leaving behind stacks of empty paper plates. Babies babbled and whined. Kids played pinball and playfully teased one another. This was family.

There was a flashing of cameras like the paparazzi, and someone went around with a video recorder. A chorus of "in Jesus's name" filled the room as the group wound down the night in song. Pan to Bruce. Cut to black.

On his wedding day, wearing a white tuxedo juxtaposed with a bloodred bow tie and sash, Bruce gave a tap dance and took a bow. He followed that with a prewedding pep talk before the roomful of guests, who clapped and shouted, "Amen!" as he spoke of a second-chance God, one of love and mercy. "With him, we don't have to be bound."

Rick Wright performed the ceremony. "If any of you had known Debi or Bruce just a few short years ago, you would've seen a lot of heartache. You would've seen a lot of struggling. You would've seen two people who were, at one time, about ready to quit." Before them at the altar were two changed people, said Pastor Rick. And there was a reason for that. "They decided, in the midst of that struggle—when they couldn't get out, and they tried everything in their own power to do it—they couldn't see the light at the end of the tunnel until they gave their lives to Jesus." No more dwelling on past failures.

Sarah was the flower girl, in ruby-red slippers. Jayden carried the rings on a shiny pillow. Kristel trailed behind in a long bridesmaid dress with puffy sleeves, holding a bouquet of flowers. In a white bridal gown with a train, Debi took a vow to love and "submit" to her husband for the rest of her life. She turned to Kristel and, reading from a piece of paper, said, "Kristel, in my heart, you already are my daughter. And my promise to you is to be the mom to you that God wants you to have. You are very precious to me, and I love you." In front of the large gathering of people, she kissed Kristel on the cheek.

At the reception, just before they cut the wedding cake, Bruce and Debi were asked to leave words of inspiration they could be reminded of when watching their wedding video one day far into the future. They faced each other briefly, then looked forward and said in unison: "'The blessing of the Lord, it maketh rich, and he add no sorrow to it.'"

Jerry was at the wedding and gave a prayer. In situations like Bruce and Debi's wedding, where everyone else had reason to smile, Jerry's eyes often looked sad, or empty. He had been visiting the Chadwicks church every month or two as a guest minister and was uncomfortable with what he saw. He didn't talk about it then, but during a service in 1996 he recalled, "Every time I came to this church, you'd all play stupid . . . you know, a lot of you, you got so loose with one another, got so familiar with one another, just really stupid. But I walk in the room, you all shut up. Now, either you despise me, or you know what you're doing is wrong. You know—what is it? So what are we doing? We're just playing games here with one another?"

While in Chadwicks, Jerry alleged his supervisor at the Rochester church was a pervert, liar, and thief, eventually telling his congregation that the man "realized that he couldn't totally dominate and control me, so he kicked me out." Jerry stayed in Rochester a little while longer and began delivering sermons in his home to a group of about forty faithful.

In his absence from Chadwicks, Jerry got the idea there'd been a conspiracy to get him out of town so another pastor could destroy Jerry's church and move everyone to a different one in Utica. It prompted Jerry to return to Chadwicks permanently in 1993. He and his wife had added two more children: Daniel, who was two years old, and Joseph, born that year.

Rick Wright continued as pastor, but Jerry, as founder, was still overseer of the church. At his behest, members started a school to educate their children within its walls. The contract to start the school cost about $3,000, and Bruce Leonard offered up the financing. The Agape Christian Academy acted as a typical kindergarten-through-twelfth-grade school, except the teachers were simply church members who worked for free. They were not required to have any degree or specific level of education. For several years, Debi was the school's kindergarten and first-grade teacher. The school followed the Accelerated Christian Education (ACE) homeschool curriculum, a Bible-based education.

Jerry had his hands in everything, and in 1993, he facilitated the sale of the Chadwicks building to the congregation, who paid for it with $175,000 in contributions. It was now a vibrant congregation that had ballooned to as many as seventy or eighty members under Pastor Rick's leadership.

The sale came one month after the congregation took another name: Word of Life Christian Church. Members were instructed to make out their tithing checks to "WLCC." The Word of Life designation earned jeers from the community and beyond, because it was the same as a Christian fellowship in the Adirondack region. Jerry said he'd heard a religious radio show calling him a name stealer. He told his followers he wouldn't go to ministers' meetings out of dread, because he didn't know what they'd been told about the name, which he claimed was a member's idea. He swore he'd never heard of the Bible camp in Schroon Lake.

Word of Life in Chadwicks was not affiliated with any church. Denominational religion, Jerry preached, was "to keep you in a back-slidden state. To keep you in a ineffective, ignorant place."

Jerry preached that other churches had doctrines from Satan and molded Scripture to meet their own agendas: "You can prove just about anything you want by using these Scriptures. You can take these out and make them say just about whatever you want." His church, he claimed, was the only one that provided the true word of God. "You wanna walk in the Spirit, then you need the accuracy of the word of God controlling you. If you wanna walk in the Spirit, then you need the accuracy of the word of God leading you and illuminating your path. You might say, 'Well, I hear what you're saying there, but I can turn in this place in the Bible and it seems to be saying something different, or it says this. And so, I decide that I'm gonna hold on to what I see here and reject that part over there.' That's just as big a mistake as any other thing you can do in Christianity."

Jerry needed a place for his family to live, and in October 1993, he had Pastor Rick apply for building and zoning permits to build a fourteen-hundred-square-foot parsonage for the Irwin family on the church's third floor. The cost: $45,000. Rick filled out the application and listed Jerry Irwin as the contractor.

It was around this time that WLCC members prepared a document called the Constitution and Bylaws of the Word of Life Church. Traci Irwin was appointed treasurer. The constitution listed requirements of members, such as attending both the Wednesday and Sunday services, subscribing to the beliefs of WLCC, contributing financially through tithes and offerings, and submitting themselves to the church and its leadership. In return, members would receive certain benefits, among them, *the best possible spiritual care.* They would have access to *pastoral counseling at no charge.* The primary benefit and privilege of membership: *While it is one thing to know a shepherd, it is quite another thing to have one. Each member receives the privilege of knowing that Pastor Rick is their pastor.*

Under Article II, Section 1 (THE LOCAL CHURCH, Leadership): *The spiritual leadership of the local assembly is vested in the Pastor and Elders whom the holy spirit has made overseers of the flock.*

The document gave the pastor ultimate authority over everything.

Jerry bided his time but didn't end his meddling. He'd been pairing existing church members through marriage with so-called words of God, supposedly directly from the Lord himself. He brought a teenage girl, Helen Lehrer, into his office and told her she would facilitate another member's divorce. Helen was horrified. Jerry was seated at his desk, cocksure and resting back. She was alone and shaking.

"I . . . I can't do that," she stammered.

Abruptly, Jerry grabbed a phone book and stood, leaned into her face, and told her in a smooth and icy voice, "You're going to look in the phone book for a lawyer to help Albert* with his divorce." He handed her the phone and instructed her to call Albert and find out how his divorce was progressing.

Helen learned from God, through Jerry, that it was not gospel for her to join the military. Jerry said God would remove his protection of her. Helen withdrew her enlistment in the air force. Then came another blow.

"God has a man for you in the church," Jerry told her.

Eventually, Helen was handed a two-hundred-page do-it-yourself divorce packet to fill out, with the understanding that she would be Albert's new wife.

On May 7, 1994, Helen was barely twenty when she married Al and took on his three children. There were plenty of smiles at this wedding, too, but Helen's was because she believed she was being faithful to God, not because she loved a man she hardly knew. Kristel and Helen had been close friends until the year prior, when Jerry forbade them from spending time with each other. Now, in a bizarre turn of events, he'd directed the fifteen-year-old Kristel to be Helen's maid of honor. Her expression at the altar at times betrayed the feelings she struggled to keep buried—confliction and confusion mixed with sadness.

Jerry was awfully busy fielding and sorting messages from God, directives that just happened to give him advantages. He got one holy communication that said he should pastor again at WLCC, simultaneously with one that said it was Pastor Rick's time to go. And with that, Rick was out and Jerry was in. Jerry told followers he knew they were thinking that Rick would grace the pulpit again, and they'd get their power back. "It didn't work." He added as a statement, "Did it."

Pastor Rick went back to being just Rick. Though he and his wife, Margaret*, and their four children continued as loyal attendees, other church members left en masse. In sermons, Jerry publicly trashed them as heretics and infidels.

Members were told the defectors left because they were in sin and going to spend a lifetime suffering on earth, followed by eternal damnation. Fear grabbed hold of the congregants who stayed, acting as a chain that bound them to the church, even as Jerry's behavior got more erratic. From the pulpit, he accused specific individuals of sexual sin, having thoughts of sleeping with his wife, sleeping with wives of other members, and desiring to rape his young daughters. At one point, Jerry stopped allowing people to take Communion because they were in too much sin. His people came to believe they *were* bad, so bad that they couldn't leave, because now they *really* needed help. Instead of preaching God's love, Jerry began preaching God's wrath.

He locked the church doors and installed a gate and security cameras, put up a fence on one side and hedges on the other. Members were required to seek Jerry's permission to speak or socialize with family members outside the church. They were told to let go of their friends, even Christian ones. He was paranoid and thought people were coming after him, former member Scott Aronson* later told police. "It was Jerry's goal to have every member of the church actually living there to protect them."

And the people who remained were much like victims of domestic violence, waiting to realize promises of great spiritual riches and clinging to fond memories and feelings of belonging.

Those of us who stayed believed God called us specifically there, Bruce later said, *a good special church, a pastor with a prophetic anointing, (meaning hearing from God, led by the Spirit.)* And Bruce was learning valuable lessons at WLCC: *forgiveness, being thankful, don't be judgemental, casting praying cares over to God.*

After reappointing himself pastor, Jerry reworked the constitution to make sure it gave him complete authority and could not be changed. He was burned by the congregation's fondness for Rick; boiling inside, really. He would give talks—he called them sermons but would only sometimes get around to reading Bible passages—during which he would quote people in a derisive manner, or make up quotes, contorting his voice to sound like a contemptible hillbilly.

"Hey, praise the Lord, hallelujah," he would say in this exaggerated voice to illustrate any "nasty, rotten, no-good individual" in the church who wasn't living for God, like those who complained about him. "'What's the matter with Jerry?'" he mimicked, to illustrate his belief that people were speaking derisively of him. "What's the matter with Jerry is Jerry knows you're lying through your teeth. That's what's the matter with Jerry. And it bothers Jerry when he knows you're lying through your teeth to me, and you have such a low, disgusting opinion of him that you would treat him with such contempt. Especially when I'm trying to treat you right. And I want you to know, for a long time after I came back, well, I was hurtin' inside. I cried sometimes, because of the rotten way you people here treated me. But, I don't know, just somethin' started happenin', and I started gettin' this determined feeling to win. I'm gonna win."

During a men's Bible study, Jerry quoted Ezra 1:4[1] and told the group it meant they should build the Irwins' living quarters.

Build it, they did. The apartment was luxurious by any standards, with a living room of regal maroon accents and matching mahogany furniture, French doors, a bathroom with a spa tub, an office, a room with a trampoline, and one with a basketball court.

Parishioners were expected to work long hours, often well into the night or the following morning, cleaning and maintaining the Irwin residence and the church. They were tasked with removing large portions of asbestos, including tile flooring. Sometimes the directions from "above" (God's word) would dictate that any broken tiles be stacked in the storage room and left undisturbed. Parishioners regularly walked by these asbestos-laden tiles. They were required to work for at least three hours after each service. They also covered the cost of any materials. It was stingy to expect to be paid back by the people working in God's house.

Bruce was in charge of building grounds and maintenance. Like everyone else assigned jobs—which was everyone over the age of

---

1   And whosoever remaineth in any place where he sojourneth, let the men of his place help him with silver, and with gold, and with goods, and with beasts, beside the freewill offering for the house of God that is in Jerusalem. (Ezra 1:4, King James Version [KJV])

thirteen—Bruce received no pay for his work. Keeping families in poverty was one of the ways Jerry maintained control. He would speak from the pulpit, directing certain members to specific careers or job positions. Bruce would never use his master's degree in plant and soil science. He worked for decades as a landscaper. In 2007, he took a job as a teaching assistant with the Utica City School District, and in 2010, he began working with severely disabled children at Proctor High School in Utica, where he was lauded for his compassion. He would remain in that position until the fall of 2015, after a series of dreadful events that included him being charged with murdering his own son.

From the pulpit, Jerry steered some WLCC members to higher-paying jobs, presumptively because the church relied on tithes. Bruce and Debi couldn't afford their tithes, so they gave their food stamps to the church. Jerry's family was well fed, their state-of-the-art, stainless steel refrigerator stocked with goods. To please the Irwins was to please God.

Dwight Evans* arrived at the church around the time of Jerry's resurgence, at the invitation of his friend Rick Wright. He found Jerry to be friendly, inviting, and enticing. Dwight eventually brought his wife, Patty*, and their children. But several weeks after joining, things changed. He noticed that in a single sermon, Jerry would move swiftly from calm talk to violent ranting. He would quote Scripture and turn it into something dark. He would create his own interpretations suited to accomplish whatever he desired.

"You know, I could be like Jim Jones and make a whole lotta money and deceive a whole lotta people," Jerry once said during a church service. "We could start our own commune. I could have twenty wives. Like I'd want twenty wives. But, um—[laughs]—maybe twenty slaves. How's that?"

During one of the five-hour men's Bible study sessions on the second floor, Jerry kept breaking topic to talk about a room near the boilers downstairs that he'd stocked with weapons. "We would be able to defend the compound really well," Jerry told them.

Dwight never saw any weapons. The door to that room was padlocked.

Jerry informed Dwight that his family was required to attend all church services and needed permission from the pastor if they thought they were going to be late. If someone didn't show for a service, that person could expect a phone call from Jerry, and in some cases, a home visit. If a member wasn't showing up regularly, "Be gone," Jerry told that person. "You're like the plague." He called parishioners frequently. Their time at home was never theirs alone. "How many of you know I call you up, and I say I wanna talk to you, and it's not very nice what I have to say?" In one sermon, Jerry talked about his reasons for doing it. "It's because I began to realize that what you do under my oversight directly affects me, and I'm responsible before God for what you do."

Jerry's level of control went from spiritual counseling to tyranny. Because he spoke to God, his visions were incontrovertible. A parishioner might not remember an instance Jerry was relaying but had to accept it as true.

"If God shows me something," Jerry warned, "I know you're doing something evil and wrong, and I come and ask you a question, and you lie to me, I just make a mental note. I know that you're a liar. You cannot be trusted. You have no credibility. And I will not warm up to you, so to speak, until I know that you have repented and you're practicing truth."

The only way to recover was to admit to the accusation. Scott Aronson, who attended the church as a child with his family, later told police, "He would accuse me and call me a liar, and I had to back up what he said so he wouldn't get mad." He reported that Jerry had accused his brother and father of molesting his cousin, something the girl insisted never happened.

The Evans family was assigned to clean the bathrooms and drinking fountains. Because of his background in computers, Dwight was also put in charge of the computer work, though he was required to pass the finished product to Jerry or Traci for approval. Like the others, Dwight gave 10 percent of his gross income to the church each week, though Jerry and Traci said it would be better if he gave more. This nearly put the Evans in financial ruin. Though they had owned their home, they ran up so much debt paying the church that they were forced to take out a mortgage. After two years, Dwight and his family left. Jerry and Traci told them they were going to hell. They were shunned by church members, their children cut off from their friends. "They burned all of our children's records," Dwight later told police, "and my wife's teaching certificate."

Years after his departure, Dwight would relay to police one incident that never left his thoughts. He'd gone to a birthday party for Joe, the youngest Irwin. Traci brought the adults into the kitchen while the kids were eating cake. Dwight claimed she talked about the disciplinary system and referenced biblical verses from the book of Proverbs. In his report, an officer quoted Dwight's recollection of the verses: *Blows that wound, cleanse away evil; strokes make clean the innermost parts . . . some men must be beaten black and blue, or have very severe correction . . . folly is bound up in the heart of a child but the rod of discipline will drive it far.*

Straight out of the Old Testament, Jerry preached that physical correction was necessary, but he had his own way of driving home that message.

"Sister Joan," he said, in his customary tactic of singling out a member during service. "If your kids do wrong, and you don't spank them, then God says you hate them."

He stood over her. She shrunk in her seat.

"Did you know that? That's the word of God. Is God a liar? Or you?"

To spank their children was to obey God. "You'll call them names. You'll tell 'em they're no good," he said to his flock. "Are you hearin' me? Instead of taking that stick and just spankin' 'em when they need it and obeying the Scriptures that drive the iniquity far from them."

Linda Morey believed in physical correction. She was raised Catholic and graduated from Proctor High School in Utica, where she was popular and once voted homecoming queen. In 1994, she joined WLCC with her husband and two children, Kathleen*, eight, and David, five, though her husband, a parole officer, dropped out after a couple of years. Linda was five years younger than Debi Leonard. She was wiry and, in heels, taller than every woman in the room, despite being just five foot four. Her height was helped by her hair, which was teased and sprayed a good six inches on top. Her jet-black hair was cropped stylishly short with lots of layers, and she wore clunky earrings. Her Lebanese features helped give her a movie-star presence. In later years, she grew dumpy and her features became harsh; eyebrows plucked thin to perfection and tweezed to a comically high arch. In consideration of her character, it made her look not funny but frightening. Linda quickly attached herself to the Irwins, becoming their eyes and ears, tattling on other members. She lived to meet the approval of the Irwins and acted as their enforcer.

Linda was a teaching assistant in the part of the building designated the learning center. At start-up, about twenty-five children were enrolled in the Agape Christian Academy. Their desks were in isolated units that faced the wall, similar to the look of a corporate call center. The desktops were spotless, organized uniformly with a Bible on the left, a box of tissues, hand sanitizer, and two small flags on tiny wooden poles. Students would raise one flag to use the bathroom, another to ask a question. Any student disrupting class, even by fidgeting, would receive a sharp-tongued reprimand from Linda. If the misbehaving continued, she would yank the child up by the arms and deliver whacks with a wooden paddle across the arms, legs, and backside. During recess, the children would line up and go outside to the parking lot, but they were not allowed to speak or interact with one another. Jerry would sit in on lessons, and if he witnessed children not paying attention, he would make them stand for long periods of time. If he perceived any rebellion, he would punish the children by having them write exhaustively, sometimes until one o'clock in the morning. He would yell at the student and their parent, sometimes for hours.

Jerry would tell Helen, who now had three young children of her own with Al (in addition to Al's three children from his previous marriage), that she was sowing the seeds of the devil at home and her kids were going to school with rebellion all over them. Sometimes he criticized her for this in front of the congregation. "You're gonna notice that you've been with the children, they're gonna start acting like you. You can't blame [Al's ex-wife] anymore."

As a result of their perceived rebellion, Helen's children would not be released until midnight or later and went without food the entire time. Helen later recalled, "Typically, they would have to stand for most of that time period because they were accused of being rebellious or they had 'the devil on their head.' So, therefore, they'd have to stand and pray aloud or read the Bible aloud to fight off the devil."

These penalties did not apply to the Irwin children. They were allowed to come and go in the classroom and do as they pleased, and to play with one another at recess.

Grades below eighty were considered failing, and students were tested each Wednesday on their weekly work. Parents would bring their children to the church at three o'clock in the afternoon, and they wouldn't be released until ten o'clock at night. Though testing lasted just a short time, the students were required to fill in the rest of the hours by reading the Bible. They were not allowed food.

During this seven-hour stretch, parents were required to stay on church grounds but were barred from entering the building. They had to sit in their cars in the parking lot, even in the dead of winter. When one mother got up the courage to ask if the children could have food, the Irwins agreed to release them for fifteen minutes to go to the car and eat. There came a time when that mother was allowed to wait inside the church in the hallway, but it was not heated. So she spent the entire time in the women's bathroom with its minimal heat.

Most members never questioned these policies out of fear the leadership would punish them. Punishment was called "church discipline." Some called it "church arrest." Those under church arrest were not allowed to talk to other members. They were ostracized. The criteria for being placed on church discipline were never clear and entirely up to Jerry's discretion. Church discipline could last months, or years.

It was not uncommon for someone to be on discipline, reflected Bruce. *Though not completely shunned, the interaction was limited to necessary communication[.] Since about ½ of us were family it kind of nixed out social family stuff like birthdays[,] getting together. Also the length (time) of discipline was open, under the single direct control/discretion of pastor—hearing from God.*

Kristel was among those educated in the church but not until the start of her sophomore year in high school. It was Traci who dictated that Kristel leave public school. It was also Traci who began drawing Kristel into the family by inviting her to stay in their third-story apartment. During this time, the Irwins vilified Kristel's parents, stepmother, grandmother, and even her best friend from elementary school, causing divides. Soon, Kristel was staying with the Irwins every weekend. Eventually, she was given a bedroom, living at the church and calling the Irwins Mom and Dad.

Jerry prompted Kristel to begin a letter-writing crusade to her real mother in order to save her. The letters were designed to be disparaging and included pages and pages of Irwin teachings: *My ultimate advice and counsel come direct from the Word of God . . . It is truth, and it is sharper than a two-edged sword. It is able to discern thoughts and intents of the heart.*

Her mother, who took her on outings once in a while, commented that Kristel's eyes lost their spark when she talked about what she'd been doing at the church and school. She told her daughter, pleadingly, "Do what makes your eyes sparkle."

Kristel could not let that go unaddressed. The subject became part of her campaign: *I do have sparks in my eyes, Mom. Only they aren't ignited by what tickles my flesh. They glow and grow as I serve God and find out more—more what His will is for my life, and then I do it.*

Having gained Kristel's trust, Traci and Jerry asked for her personal journals, which she handed over freely. *They, in turn, burned my journals with no warning or discussion,* stated Kristel's 2015 New York State Police deposition. Only later did she come to believe this was a way to erase her identity. Looking back, Kristel saw the Irwins' actions of drawing her into the family as making her into a fine-tuned instrument, so they could use her skills for their own gain.

The move-in transition happened over three years, until Kristel's high school graduation in 1997. She was the academy's first graduate. The commencement speaker was Jerry. Kristel was also the school's only graduate that year, but all the students attended, many very young, and some with their parents and baby siblings. They got the genteel Jerry at the podium. In a peaceful, nonchalant tone, he spoke of the school's history. He'd started it "for selfish reasons," because he feared sending his own kids to public school. The school of his childhood was fifteen miles from the nearest city, he said, but catered to children from wealthy suburban families. "When I went to school," he told the children, "there were gangs, there was drugs, there was violence, um . . ." He paused, reached up, and adjusted his glasses. "And there was rape. It was just rampant."

The students clapped for Kristel, who was seated at the cafeteria-style tables with them. Except for a reserved smile at the appropriate moment, she was motionless, her long, golden-brown hair flowing from beneath her graduation cap. Jerry let the students know how lucky they were to keep Kristel at WLCC. "She had many scholarships to many different colleges. Would you believe that God wanted her to stay here?" She would be a teacher in the school.

When Kristel first started spending time at the Irwin apartment, Tiffanie was only about eight years old, a delicate-framed little girl with long, wavy brown hair. Her clothes were simple and her features plain. She had a rounded face full of light freckles, straight teeth, and hooded eyelids that pulled the outer corners of her gray-blue eyes into teardrops. A cowlick on the right side of her head would grow more prominent with age, pushing the hair back and giving the appearance of an oversize forehead. She had a slight cleft chin. Tiffanie would've gone largely unnoticed but for her father's insistence that everyone pay attention to her. To ignore Tiffanie was to invite a stern reprimand.

Despite the age difference, Kristel and Tiffanie played games together, as any kids. They also worked together on Sunday school lessons. When it came time for Kristel to go back to her father's house during the week, Tiffanie would become emotional and weepy.

Tiffanie watched with envy as Linda played dolls with her daughter. She felt her own mother didn't set aside time for her and looked to Kristel to fill that void. But Kristel was unaware. She was just a kid herself, not a mother. And she did not know that Tiffanie was struggling with deeper, more complex feelings, just as Tiffanie didn't understand the craving to lay her head on Kristel's chest.

One day, when the two girls were sitting on the floor, Tiffanie released her inhibitions and let her head fall to Kristel's leg. From across the room, her father asked sternly, "Why do you have your head on her?" He told her to detach herself, something Tiffanie found impossible.

Tiffanie was something of a personal historian, documenting nearly every aspect of her life in diaries, videos, and audio recordings. Almost no memory was left unrecorded in one format or another. In an October 24, 2010, diary entry, she talked of despising Kristel for her *bad evils*, which she described as Kristel's refusal to love her despite all the things Tiffanie did to gain her favor. Tiffanie's perceptions of persecution mirrored that of her father's. She believed that when Kristel left to visit her own family, she was spreading negative gossip about the Irwins.

Through her own fear of rejection, Tiffanie felt bound and controlled by Kristel. She wrote of making sacrifices to keep Kristel happy, like giving her *goodies* whenever she could. But she felt Kristel did not return her favors with gratitude and so began to detest her. Still, Tiffanie was unable to break her emotional attachment, feeling that if Kristel left, she couldn't possibly survive. She believed Kristel was intentionally showing love and affection to everyone but Tiffanie, in order to keep Tiffanie *exclusively jealous* for her attention.

Tiffanie would be twenty years old before reading a book called *101 Frequently Asked Questions About Homosexuality* and acknowledging the feelings she had for Kristel were of romantic love—albeit unrequited. These repressed feelings caused bitterness and anger toward Kristel that eroded Tiffanie's mental well-being like battery acid. She saw Kristel as willfully committing a shakeup, displacing her as the oldest sibling, *taking advantage of* her. Year after year, in page after page of venomous diary entries, Tiffanie blamed Kristel for everything from causing Tiffanie's friends to loathe her, to ruining Tiffanie's relationships with each of her family members. She wrote of hating Kristel for pushing her to the point of suicidal ideation. In a journal entry on September 25, 2011, a twenty-five-year-old Tiffanie recalled the feelings of rejection from Kristel with such despondence, it was as if the pain was fresh. She noted God promised it would never happen again and spoke to her a Bible verse: Malachi 4:1, 3 (1 KJV).

For, behold, the day cometh, that shall burn as an oven; and all the proud, yea, and all that do wickedly, shall be stubble: and the day that cometh shall burn them up . . . And ye shall tread down the wicked; for they shall be ashes under the soles of your feet in the day that I shall do this, saith the Lord of hosts.

I'm sure nobody in here does, but when you were in the world, you did. You let your children turn on these television shows where you've got these demons. . . . We let our kids watch these ninja mutants, or whatever. How many of you know what the ninja were? They were paid assassins, you know. They would ruthlessly and coldheartedly murder people. But now they're our heroes. A ninja was nothing more than an assassin. A paid killer. And there's so many other things. I'm sure there's a multitude of new programs on that teach you demonology and witchcraft and, and all those evils. . . . And then [kids] come to church and they have this stupid look on their face. "This is boring. This is boring." Well, I tell you what. You just keep it up for a few more years, and you get into hell, and you won't be bored for one second. They'll keep you on your toes. The very ones that taught you all those things through the cartoons will be there to teach you some more.

—Pastor Jerry Irwin
to the congregation on October 6, 1996

CHILDREN OF THE FLOCK

The school halls were as long as the days, the building a maze of adventure—and later, imprisonment—with its cold plaster walls, linoleum floors that squeaked when scuffed by rubber soles, and desolate stairwells with peeling lead paint. The Irwin kids rode their bikes through the corridors, passing whatever time was left after Bible study and worship. Any activity made it difficult to take in a clean breath, as mold overtook the building. Traci used odor-masking spray and ozone generators that she'd built, but the mold spores prevailed.

The Irwin children played outside sometimes. But the neighborhood kids could be cruel, often whipping eggs at the building. Someone smashed one on top of Jerry's car. Delinquents broke past the gate and snuck into the parking lot one winter, and when parishioners jumped in their vehicles to chase them away, one car slid on the ice and almost hit a boy. That troublemaker didn't return for a while.

Linda's son, Dave, was the Irwin boys' playmate. Though he was two years older than Dan and four years older than Joe, he acted as their lackey. But Dave's friendship with the Irwin boys gave him confidence—or conceit. He became part of their inner circle. Dave was at the church every day. It was his life. Like most of the children of the flock, his family didn't go on vacations, though sometimes he or his mom would go along with the Irwins on theirs. He didn't roam the community. He would never have a driver's license, a car, or a girlfriend.

Dave was black-haired with deep-set eyes, hooded eyelids with a purple tint, and the bushiest brows. He'd inherited his mother's Lebanese features, but his personality could not have been more different. He was introverted and submissive. Jerry once angrily accused Linda of believing his sons existed solely for Dave's entertainment, but it was the other way around. Away from the Irwins, Dave was a good kid. But he was rarely away from the Irwins. Without them, he seemed lost and incapable of making decisions.

He would grow spindly and tall, peaking at six foot two. Dan would hit six foot three, and Joe, six foot four. The brothers Irwin, as adults, would have fifty-five to eighty pounds on Dave, with Dan topping out at three hundred pounds. Dan had a pleasant personality. Growing up, he was fun but often too wild. However, he did as he was told. Joe, the youngest, was his father's son—completely out of control and a tyrant. Naomi showed the most kindness.

Though children of the flock were required to attend worship services and pay attention for hours, the Irwin kids were the exception. They often didn't go to services, and when they did, they walked around aimlessly, even slept on the floor. Sometimes, they'd wander into the nursery, where Joe would roughhouse with the younger kids, throwing fake punches and wrestling them to the ground. The other kids ate up the action—they loved it—but didn't dare get caught showing that kind of physical contact.

In the Word of Life Christian Church, horseplay could be seen as molestation. So could a child sitting on another's lap, or tapping another on the shoulder. Sometimes just looking at someone a certain way would end in accusations of molestation. There was an inordinate focus on sexual perversion. It was considered a sin to have a dream about sexual contact. Grace Leonard once dreamed she'd molested her sister Sarah's baby and was sure to keep that from her sister. To dream it was equivalent to being guilty of it. Adolescent boys checking out girls their age was sinful. Prepubescent children holding hands could lead them to temptation.

One child, Dylan Aronson*, was eleven or twelve years old and doing well in school, so he was allowed to play with the Irwin children on the third floor. He later told police that Naomi ran up behind him and grabbed his hand while they were running down the hallway, and Jerry saw it. In their report, police wrote: *[Dylan] stated that he went to see Jerry Irwin as directed and he was taken into a stairway* [and] *yelled at for holding [Naomi]'s hand, which Jerry Irwin advised was inappropriate behavior.* Dylan's father then told him not to play but to read the Bible to Jerry while upstairs. But Dylan refused. He was coming to realizing things weren't right. *Jerry wanted us to report when we went anywhere, and even when we spoke to anyone. The church was turning me against my family, and my family against me.* The church, he told police, was brainwashing everyone. When Dylan was fourteen, Jerry accused him of feeling lust for a woman, simply because the boy had remarked that he thought she was pregnant.

As a young child, Tiffanie spent time in play, but most of it was Jesus related. By age seven, she was leading her family in prayer each morning and reading the Bible fluently to her parents. At the breakfast table, even baby Joe would speak in tongues. Little Naomi would lift up her voice in hymns. But Tiffanie's dedication to God continued well beyond breakfast. By age eleven, she was reading the Bible to her father for two hours a day as he tinkered with computers. On top of that, she'd spend hours alone in her room studying the Bible and praying. Every day from the age of nine, Tiffanie read twenty-five chapters in the Bible and refused to do anything else until it was done. From a very early age, she wholeheartedly believed God was speaking to her, that she had the gift of prophecy and the power to heal and to raise the dead.

She was passionate about performing, and in first grade started a program where she would sing along with a tape of Scripture music and make up dances to it. It was a tool to witness to people in the church—to draw their attention to God's words through dance. Tiffanie's heart was in acting, and in the end, she would star in a one-woman show—sadly, her audience more captive than captivated.

Tiffanie loved to sing and had a natural voice, the kind that lands the lead in every high school play. Untrained, it was shaky, too soft, and stretched thin on a handful of measures. But it was easy to miss the spots where it wasn't strong because it was a pretty voice, high-pitched and lyrically smooth and soothing. She learned to play the keyboard; her brothers learned guitar and drums. They were sometimes her backup singers.

The Irwin children, and other children of the flock, ventured outdoors and to stores, or for a quick walk down the block, but mainly stayed confined in their homes, or in the old brick schoolhouse with its rooms of painted cinderblock. They didn't celebrate holidays, never had a Christmas stocking, never walked a trick-or-treat trail. Instead, on Halloween, they hid in the bushes or conducted foot patrols to make sure no one went to the door asking for candy. They never went to a baseball game.

It was a lonely life, after a time.

Years later, Tiffanie would see her youngest brother, Joe, in a slump and push him to tell her what was wrong. No one listened to him, and no one cared anything about him, he told her. Everyone took jabs at him, even Dan and Naomi, who were jealous of him and wouldn't play with him. He was intensely spoiled, and it was the one thing he wished he could go back and change. It was for her, too, Tiffanie told him. At one point, Joe considered killing himself. Instead, he simply resolved not to care anymore. He wanted to get a job, meet new people. He *had* to get away. It upset him when he asked his father about getting a job and was told he needed to have a relationship with Jesus first.

The children of the flock were not allowed to follow their hearts. But they would be rewarded in the end. Jerry preached, "When you're like the oak of righteousness, when you're like the tree that is planted by the rivers of water, I tell you, when the winds blow and the storms come, you might move a little bit, but you're not gonna be taken out of your place. That's the biggest sin that Christians commit in the church today, is not being in the place that God wants them to be in."

If a member had a goal or desire, they kept it to themselves and waited for Jerry to get word from God that they could pursue it. Most times, word never came. Getting what they wanted was selfish, selfishness was a sin, and sinners went to hell. The very reason Kristel never went to college is because she so desperately wanted it.

After graduating high school, Kristel continued living with the Irwins, and they kept working on her. Traci eroded her confidence by condemning it as pride and arrogance—sins. Traci helped her develop more "feminine" traits, taught her to pluck and wax her eyebrows and shorten her stride.

"Your hips are wide because God made you a baby factory," she told Kristel.

Even Debi, despite nearing the end of her childbearing years, was told to have children because Jerry wanted a church full of them.

The Irwins, Kristel later said, brought the wild girl inside. "I became a mushroom."

Kristel was now heavily involved with the church, and her role was strengthening. She was part of the worship team, a group of members tasked with enthusiastically leading the congregation in a series of pre-selected songs. Their goal was to manifest the presence of God so the congregation could receive the holy message that Jerry was about to deliver. She played piano during Jerry's prayer sessions and sometimes throughout the sermon.

The Irwins also gave Kristel more responsibility in the school, having her write curricula for music theory, literature, penmanship, and history. At the same time, Tiffanie was placed in a supervisor position. She was only twelve years old but charged with overseeing children her own age and younger. Tiffanie was said to be a cruel, unforgiving monitor, forcing children to keep their arms and flags raised for long periods of time without calling on them. This was when Tiffanie's behavior toward Kristel became openly hostile.

When Kristel turned twenty, Traci informed her that she would be going on a date with another parishioner and gave her a crash course on cooking. That, said Traci, was Kristel's duty. Two months later, Kristel was told to marry the man and to "rein in his loyalties to us." Kristel and her husband-to-be did not love each other. They weren't so much as friends.

Jerry's early sermons, from the 1980s, had contained vague "prophecies" suggesting to Bruce and Debi that they should cut loose their spouses and wed each other. It was not the level of Kristel's and Helen's dictates, but it was tampering nonetheless.

During the time Kristel was staying with the Irwins, contact with her family was severely restricted because of Pastor Jerry's edict that socializing was not acceptable. "I have felt that the Irwins' ultimate goal was to create lines of loyalty from each individual directly to them without any loyalties to family or friends standing in the way," Kristel later said. "The natural loyalty between spouses, parents and children, siblings—these were deliberately erased, and because it is human nature to be connected, the only remaining option was to be connected to the spiritual leadership."

Fiercely loyal to her father, Tiffanie enforced the lockdown on chit-chat. It was one day in May 2003 that Jerry was wrapping up the worship service with a warning: "Some of you, the devil just dropped on you about what you're going to talk about. Just stay in peace."

As worshippers left the sanctuary, it became evident someone left behind a prayer reader. Traci approached a few of the women, trying to track down the owner. Seventeen-year-old Tiffanie was appalled to find her mother surrounded by three or more women. She saw it as socializing "getting out of hand." Tiffanie joined the group, and, in a phony happy tone, said, "After Daddy said not to talk, we're standing here talking."

No sooner did the words pass her lips than she was hit with a dark feeling, an oppression that caused her physical pain. Tiffanie went to shut off her keyboard but couldn't keep her cool. Convinced the women had ignored her reminder, she returned, only to find her mother talking to yet another woman, Anne*. It was about a school document that Anne, a WLCC teacher, needed to find by the next day. Tiffanie stormed over and reproached them, shaking with anger. "After what I just said?"

Neither responded, and Tiffanie believed Anne was ignoring her intentionally and refusing to make eye contact out of disrespect. The teenager repeated herself, and Anne walked away.

Tiffanie chided her mother. "After what I just said, you let her sit there and talk anyway?"

"I don't think that was a problem. It was something pressing. School related."

Jerry would have to settle it. They went to see him, only to learn that Traci was very wrong. He instructed his wife to seek out Anne and tell her that she'd defiantly initiated conversation with Traci just because Jerry told them not to and that Anne thought she could get one over on Traci. Traci was also to tell Anne that she would no longer put up with people patronizing their daughter.

"I'm really sorry," Anne said in response to Traci's admonishments. "I'm so stupid. Stupid me."

Parishioners were told that if they were chatting with one another for no explicit Christian purpose, such as getting together for a Bible study, they were wasting time and being led by the devil. Members of each household were to keep to themselves. If Kristel went to her father's house and Debi was there, she was not allowed to talk to Debi because she wasn't Kristel's biological mother. When Kristel and her husband moved into a home of their own, Debi was not allowed to visit. If anyone went, it was just Bruce and the kids.

Forbidding conversation among church members was not enough. Pastor Jerry was militant when it came to members socializing in the community. That was cause for church arrest. As a result, when they weren't at the church, children of the flock kept to their homes and avoided social interactions. It was also sinful to watch television, because most programs were evil influences. Children had to ask their fathers' permission to watch a particular program or movie. When students in the Agape school weren't studying, though, Jerry would entertain them with government conspiracy movies.

Naomi was always skirting the rules. She dared to watch what she wanted, like *The Bachelorette*, considered highly inappropriate by the rest of her family.

Dating didn't happen with children of the flock unless they were instructed to go out with an assigned person connected to the church, and that word would come from God (via Jerry). And while chastity is not uncommon in Christianity, at WLCC, it was an obsession. So was refraining from masturbation. Not only was masturbation seen as sinful at WLCC, but it meant the devil had taken control.

According to Jerry, Satan wasn't the only one taking over WLCC members' bodies and minds. Jerry repeatedly accused parishioners of controlling other members through witchcraft. Tiffanie was convinced of its prevalence, and it became a fear and an obsession. She believed a demon emanated from Rick's wife, Margaret, and attacked Tiffanie when she played the keyboard. It caused sheer panic. Unrelenting what-ifs whipped around Tiffanie's brain: What if the witchcraft caused her to mess up the chords? What if it wasn't God's will for her to play that part of the song? What if she brought Satan into the room by playing a part of a song or shouting when it wasn't God's will? What if she gave into Margaret's witchcraft right there in front of her? Tiffanie wrote of these panic attacks in a diary entry on June 14, 2003, when she was seventeen. She would calm herself by silently praying, but it would relieve the tension for only a few seconds, before it came creeping up again, leaving her feeling defeated and disgusted and fighting depression.

The pastor's kids enjoyed more freedoms than the rest. On the church dime, Jerry would treat his family to religious conferences around the country—Indiana, Florida, Arizona, Missouri—and the world (Italy). They stayed at lavish resorts and bought time-shares in Arizona and Indiana. They would easily drop more than a hundred dollars on a dinner out, as though there was an endless supply of church funds to cover it.

Jerry had a prophecy about the climbing expenses. "I know that God's going to multiply the money back to us," he told his family after a prophetic night session at a ministry in Sedona, Arizona. "We're going to pay off this thing right away. Pay off this thing. And God's going to multiply the money back to us. We're going to have plenty of money to fly places and drive places and go places."

Jerry would make sure that prophecy was realized. His minister's income was only $12,000 a year, so funding the lifestyle depended on tithes and offerings. He continued to invest in retaining followers—a complicated strategy, since he also feared new people would try to take over the church.

A single mother of a three-year-old girl, Leslie Howard* was pursued for membership by the Irwins for about eight months. Leslie was awaiting a $20,000 settlement for a back injury and had made the Irwins aware of it. As the time neared for receiving her settlement, Traci and Jerry wooed her with dinner and a tour of their apartment while impressing upon her the importance of giving money to the church.

"What you sow, you shall reap," Jerry told her tenderly.

"I fell for it," she later said. When the check arrived, Leslie gave the church $2,000 and Jerry and Traci turned mean, beginning to accuse her of despicable acts. Just two weeks later, Traci and Linda Morey escorted her out the door.

Leslie told police years later that as soon as she left the church, a member began calling her ex-husband, who was a police officer, and accusing her then-husband of molesting their daughter. "I think they wanted our marriage to end, which it did, nine months later."

The Irwins got additional revenue from selling exotic birds: Amazon parrots, African gray parrots, umbrella cockatoos, breeder macaws, Quaker parrots, and cockatiels. Traci added a dog-breeding business, spending hundreds of thousands of dollars on dogs, pet food, and supplies. Traci enlisted the church kids to care for the animals, including the Irwins' pet rabbits and prairie dog. Loyal Linda Morey was known to spend up to eight hours a day on her hands and knees cleaning dog excrement.

Every canceled membership drained money in the coffers. And there was the potential for a chain reaction: the defector could persuade others to leave. From even before his deliverance ministry days, Jerry had taught his disciples that if they sinned, it meant a demon was inside of them causing them to do it. He now warned members that backsliders who left were contagious. Their demons could infect his precious flock. *We were discouraged from having contact with former members, and if we did we should let the pastor know what happened,* Bruce recalled. Those who left the church were to be shunned. (A notable exception was Linda's husband. It is believed that because he was with law enforcement, the Irwins left him alone.)

Quite a few people came and left, Bruce recalled. *The usual explanation being that they had their own agenda, wanted personal control (rather than led by God) and pastor wasn't going to allow that. Our church was to be led by the Spirit rather than be a social club under the influence of who [gave] the most money or had a dominating personality. When those people didn't get their way, they left. Other people got confronted, challenged about sins . . . They refused to repent or didn't want to be exposed and left. This, in general, was the explanation given for when people left.*

Although the Irwins had control of their followers, they had none over those who walked, and the smear campaigns they feared came to pass. Tiffanie discounted it as the result of malign influence and vented about it years later in a letter addressed *Dear Someone*.

People, she wrote, stubborn ones who refused to repent, left the church and spread rumors that WLCC taught things that were not in the Scripture, and that the church was anti-Semitic, antisocial, and a cult.

I'm supposed to stop everything I'm doing, sympathize with you even though I know that you rebel continuous and the reason you're in this situation is because your sin and your rebellion. I'm supposed to stop and act like—oh, you poor thing. Isn't that terrible what's happened to you? And God forbid the leader say to you—well, you've been told over and over not to do it. You know—why are you acting the way you are?

—PASTOR JERRY IRWIN
TO THE CONGREGATION ON OCTOBER 27, 1996

DEMON STRONGHOLDS

Debi broke the rules.

Jerry believed her to be a "host of evil spirits" and Bruce her accomplice, and that's why she was always so bubbly and drawing others into socializing. That was sin. And when she drew others into her sin, he warned, they would reap judgment, too. God sent Jerry word that church discipline needed to stop being treated like a joke.

Debi allowed her children to go outside and have fun, knowing it would get her in trouble. The Irwins considered children engaged in normal outdoor play to be "roaming the streets." Debi was constantly rebuked for this. She also sometimes allowed her kids to join in community activities, hoping to stay under the radar, but mostly, she got caught. When she did, the pastor would shame her in front of the congregation during worship service, and then, she would be placed on church discipline. That didn't stop her. She was placed on church discipline again and again. There seemed to be no end to it.

"The spirit of sickness attacks this church because, either the devil uses the filth of your house to make your kids sick, or else he moves on them to go to someone else's house in the neighborhood who is sick," Jerry publicly chastised Debi during a sermon in 2009. "Then, he'll move on to Kristel's house or [another female parishioner]'s house and it spreads around—a vicious cycle of sickness. I don't know why you have hatred in your heart, but your hatred, your rebellion against me, your burning desire for revenge is not going to help anyone. It's only going to hurt them."

Jerry said a lie that Debi told is what caused her father to die. He mimicked her: "'I don't let my children roam the streets.'" That lie, he said, manifested sickness and death in her father's house. "You're making the children that you have now twice the children of hell as Sarah and Jayden. I'd warned you long ago that I had a vision, that an eyewitness later confirmed—they were roaming the streets with three teenagers."

Sarah and Jayden were at the post office, he said, and those teens with them were a bad influence. Now Luke was in jeopardy because Debi allowed him to spend time unsupervised. "If you would spend more time with the kids, and help them with their schoolwork, then they would actually do well in school and feel good about themselves." He continued solemnly, "They haven't been doing so well in school. Luke was doing well, but I don't know what happened—what influence got over him—but he started doing poorly."

In front of the congregation, he talked openly of Debi telling her husband she's "not in the mood," and warned her, "The devil won't make you have lust for your husband. Only for other men."

Debi was crying. Pastor Jerry had everyone lay hands on her. One member prayed aloud that God would heal her broken heart, another that God would give her encouragement and strength. There was one final blow that made Debi sob uncontrollably.

"People wonder," said Jerry, "'Why me on church discipline? Why not him or her?' The answer is that I don't know why. I hope it's not the thought that keeps coming to me—that God isn't even going to bother with them."

The church began placing more laborious, time-consuming demands on members, committing them to obscene blocks of time at the church. If they were home doing housework, the Irwins made them feel guilty for not using that time to read the Bible or pray. The Leonards couldn't keep up. And they couldn't tell Jerry or Traci, because it would be an acknowledgment they were listening to the devil or doing something wrong.

On June 24, 2009, Tiffanie, who was now the school administrator, sent Bruce a letter that his children were behind in their schoolwork by as many as two grade levels. He was to send her a schedule of his plan for improvement. She notified Bruce that his children would be required to spend summer vacation in school.

Not long after that letter, Pastor Jerry approached Bruce in the church hallway. "The stress from working with your family is causing Tiffanie physical illness."

Bruce began disjointedly, "Yeah . . . on our end—"

"There is no 'on our end,'" Jerry snapped.

Concerns with schoolwork came to a head six months later, in January the following year, when Bruce left a message on Tiffanie's answering machine asking that his children be excused from testing. They'd been sick and didn't finish their work, so he didn't think they would test well. "And I'm also quite sure that God showed me this morning that our real issue is—we just plain haven't put him first," he said on the answering machine. "What we've been doing is just to stay out of trouble instead of trying to do good. So, try to repent, and I intend to see to it that my family does, too."

Tiffanie returned Bruce's phone call. "What do you mean by 'issue'?"

"Um, sickness," said Bruce. "Same pattern as has happened before. Probably got sick because the house isn't clean."

When pressed—and Tiffanie always pressed—Bruce admitted sickness wasn't the only issue. Ezekiel was taking too long to do his work.

"You saw this, or did Debi tell you?" she asked.

"Yes. I actually sat down and worked with him."

"Where was Debi?"

"Working on other stuff."

"What stuff?"

"I sat down to do a sheet or two with him, said, 'Write.'"

"What was Debi doing?" Tiffanie asked firmly. "Why, if she's working with him as she's supposed to, has he not overcome this?"

Bruce dodged answering directly, instead describing Ezekiel's educational challenges. But Tiffanie brought it back to Debi and said God showed her Debi wasn't working with her son. "Does she sit with him when you're there?"

"Well, part of it. She's trying to keep him doing it when she's doing other things."

"So the answer is no? What is she doing when she leaves the room?"

"She doesn't leave the room."

"What's she doing?" she demanded. But silence followed. Tiffanie had turned twenty-four just five days earlier. Bruce was about to turn sixty.

"Are you covering for her or don't you know?" she battered.

"I guess . . . doing things . . . around . . . the kitchen," Bruce eventually answered.

"If she was doing things around the kitchen, it wouldn't be messy. You have to tell me what you see, and what she says, because she's not been an honest person."

Bruce said, "All right," in a much stronger voice but then went silent as Tiffanie continued to demand an answer. Finally, he said, "We are being beat on by the devil." Because they had tried to make school their priority, there was no time for housekeeping. "We are living in a pigpen."

"About Debi being in the kitchen," she said. "I have to assume you're lying or you're covering for her. I have to assume she's online." Debi wasn't cleaning the kitchen, or it wouldn't be messy.

"I guess that's true. I don't know what she was doing."

"Why wasn't she working with Ezekiel?"

"I thought I could get him to do it faster. So . . . I told her to do something else."

"Was she complaining?" Tiffanie asked.

"No, I don't think so at that po—"

"You can tell me she doesn't complain, but I don't think you will, because I know she does."

Bruce needed to keep his family in line, Tiffanie lectured, particularly his wife. That they couldn't maintain a clean house because the kids had too much schoolwork was just an excuse.

Bruce acknowledged, "This is something I pointed out to Debi as essentially proof that we don't have it right. Because if we're doing it right for God, then we should have everything. It should be improved. We should not be getting less done. We seem to be having this incredible stress over school, but we've been having— I told Debi she's going to have to be more physical with the kids, because she yells at them in terms of 'Let's get going.' Stop with the yelling and do something physically. Spank. Lot of energy lost in terms of yelling to fix something. It seems to me like a lot of energy gets lost there."

"Why are you blaming the kids when it's Debi's fault? She's the one who's not making sure the house gets clean. She's the one that's not working with the kids."

"I don't know."

"Are you afraid to go against her, or do you really believe what she's saying?"

A little bit of both, said Bruce. "I don't know how to enforce things or change things." He said Debi got anxious about staying out of trouble.

Anxious about what? Tiffanie wanted to know.

After going around in circles with this question repeated a few times, Bruce answered, "With people she considers being in authority over her, Pastor. That would be with you. Hard admission."

"If she was really anxious about getting into trouble, she would be changing what she's doing, instead of doing the same thing."

"Seems on different occasions we make a real effort to change. Fall off the wagon."

Change begins with truth, said Tiffanie. "That's the reason I keep asking all these questions." She took a long pause, and then made a grammatically incorrect statement just for effect: "Debi don't make sense."

Bruce agreed.

"She's not stupid," said Tiffanie, and told him Debi manipulated him into working with Ezekiel. "I guess I just don't understand why she's smart and on the ball with everyone but you."

Bruce's words came slowly. "I don't think she is."

"You won't like this, but I thought she was duping you, pretending that she wasn't smart, to get you to do things for her. She's smart, has sharp eyes, pretends to not know stuff around you."

"How do I change my wife?" asked Bruce, his voice quivering. "You've brought me to an issue I've had on different occasions with Pastor. I've almost come to this same place. How do I train my wife?"

"Did he tell you what to do?" asked Tiffanie.

"Years ago, I had a word to be the head of household. I'm remembering that again, even with part of what I proclaimed today, that phrasing came back: be the head of household that God has called you to be. And I feel like I need something firm to work with, and I've got much to work with. Make sense?"

"Not really."

"Well . . ." Bruce began to cry.

"As long as you don't see Debi for who she really is, you can't begin to change things. You'll keep skirting around the issue instead of facing it head-on and changing it."

He would keep on himself, he said, and Debi would have to stay out of trouble or they weren't going to make it. "Fears—kicked out of school, kicked out of church. We don't have any place else to go. We really don't. We have not shopped around churches. This is where we are. As poor as we're doing, this is where we are." Bruce continued to cry. When Tiffanie pushed him to acknowledge Debi's role, he said, "It's hard for me to believe I'm married to a wicked, mean person."

"You're head of household, not servant who does things when others won't. You point things out, and they fix it. Debi should have fixed that problem herself when you pointed it out. You shouldn't have done it for her." He would need to take a stand, she said. "They'll only think you're stupid if you back off."

Just three weeks after that conversation, Tiffanie threw the Leonard children out of school. She wrote in her journal of a great weight of oppression lifted, like a raging storm quelled. The *demonic stronghold* in the classroom, she wrote, was broken. Tiffanie openly addressed the remaining students about the sudden peace she felt in the absence of the Leonard children.

Her father, there in the classroom when she said this, was less optimistic. "I know it's peaceful now, but the devil's going to try to punish you for this," he prophesized. "I just saw something like a great ball of fire rolling toward you."

It was no coincidence, she told her father, that in the latest Bible study they'd read from Psalm 31:13, 15, 17.

Fear was on every side: while they took counsel together against me, they devised to take away my life. . . . [D]eliver me from the hand of mine enemies, and from them that persecute me. . . . [L]et the wicked be ashamed, and let them be silent in the grave (KJV).

Debi began homeschooling, and Bruce requested school records from Tiffanie. What a farce, Tiffanie scoffed—the Leonards schooling their children. Suspicious of Bruce's request, she prayed not to be trapped by their scheming.

In this year, Tiffanie took on the role of assistant pastor. She put together special series, including one about merging Gospel stories with signs of the zodiac. It was a novel approach the congregation found refreshing. Her gift for performance made it engrossing.

At twenty-five, Tiffanie became a self-ordained minister. The length of worship service doubled from two hours to four. Tiffanie's daily log of activity indicated she was immersed in Bible study and prayer for as long as four hours a day and included notes about having to work on pride. She knew more than everyone else, she wrote.

Joe turned insufferably despotic. Like his father, he would sometimes sit in on classes, leering at students as they did their work. When
he entered a room, his presence squeezed the oxygen out of the air. At
worship services, he and Dan were the church muscle. Giant men, they
stood at the doors with their arms crossed and glared down families
as they entered the sanctuary. Joe was said to come to each service
with a bowie knife strapped to his leg. He developed a fascination
with weapons—guns in particular, especially semiautomatic rifles.
The Irwin brothers binged war movies and spent thousands of dollars
on tactical gear. They were consumed with playing war games online,
through consoles, and on tables, shelling out more than a thousand
dollars on tabletop war game miniatures and accessories. They filled a
tabletop battlefield with tanks, terrain, and World War II soldiers that
they painstakingly painted by hand. Joe got to command his own fleet
into pretend deadly battles against his brother and a couple of other
young men in the church: Dave and Seth*, Rick Wright's oldest son.

Joe would practice on drums in his bedroom and become so angry
that, as members cleaned the family's quarters, they could hear the
cracks of drumsticks snapping in half. During one service, Joe got so
mad that he bashed in a drumhead, leaving a hole through the mem-
brane.

Around the same time, Linda Morey's role as underling became
more prominent. She was the female version of Joe, carrying out Tiffanie's will in brutal fashion. It was a climate of festering abuse.

Naomi wouldn't step in line. Church services began with Christian
rock music blaring through the speakers, or from Joe and Dan playing
guitar riffs. While followers swayed with their heads lowered or arms
raised, Naomi danced sensually. She remained devoted to Jesus, but
began questioning the operations of her family's church, and considering that it might actually be a cult. Tension grew as Naomi watched
her sister rise to power and other family members dutifully submit to
her sister's orders.

As time went on, Tiffanie saw just about everyone as an enemy trying to persecute her. She saw demons inside of people glaring at her through their eyes. People were trying to hide things from her, attack her. According to her writings, when someone was thinking critically about things other than God, she believed that meant the person had a demon inside of him, and the demon would keep Tiffanie from receiving God and achieving what God had planned for her. Nearly everyone, in her mind, found her objectionable—they were mean to her, had bad opinions of her singing, and only put up with her because she was the pastor's daughter. All they could do, based on the conclusion of her ruminating, was sit and stare at her with mean, dead looks, as if she were in the way. She believed that parishioners had become crafty at hiding their utter disdain for her and had found secret ways to communicate to her that she was a nobody who deserved nothing. Tiffanie's own mother didn't give her attention, and her father felt contempt for her. When her siblings showed love, she was unable to receive it. Those were her views. She was constantly in anguish. She felt empty.

She would confide in God that she was tired and couldn't take it anymore, wishing her journey on earth would end so she could go to heaven and be with him. Her life, according to her writings, was going nowhere. At twenty-five, she'd never left her father's house and awaited God's choice of job for her outside the church. She was hoping it would be in acting, architecture, or interior design. She loved arranging rooms. Floral design could be a side job, she thought, or modest evening gown modeling and designing. At five foot four, Tiffanie didn't have the height for modeling. She was a wisp of a thing, the size of a child and so thin she looked breakable. Her flat chest would fall short of filling out the top of a gown. But in her mind, modeling was more than just a fanciful notion. She categorized her profession choices according to her level of interest and competency. She listed being a disc jockey as merely an "option."

Dancing was given more weight but only as a supplement to a performing career.

But God hadn't chosen anything. He hadn't chosen any*one*, either. In her diary, Tiffanie expressed a nagging, painful loneliness and desire for human connection and lamented that she had no children, no husband. Each Valentine's Day, she would get the notion that her future husband was fervently praying that God would bring them together. She wrote about normal crushes and store clerks who made her insides flutter, but never knew how to approach those guys, waiting for direction from God that never came.

Her diary, for years, reflected utter hopelessness and despair over not finding love in a man. She believed that God kept her from those things she wanted because he had something better planned. She continued to blame Kristel for everything wrong in her life, including what she presumed would be the failure of any future marriage. There were things she needed to address, she wrote, before getting married, the first being Kristel—she was never supposed to happen. Tiffanie also resented the view of marriage that had a man telling a woman what to do. She did not want to be weak. While spending years praying for a husband, Tiffanie also prayed that God would remove her fear of men. She believed men existed to take advantage of her, that every single male who came into contact with her was entertaining bad thoughts. The messages were coming from Satan. She heard voices—loud, raspy whispers—that she assumed were men having immoral thoughts about her.

She often heard voices.

Tiffanie lived in constant fear of being raped or kidnapped, of men with designs to overpower and hurt her. When she was twenty, she wrote of a vision in which God came to her and addressed these fears, telling her, "No one will in any way hurt you." Still, she had nightmares of being raped by a man in church. She loathed men for watching porn and believed them to be sexual predators and child molesters. One diary entry talked of being as young as seven years old and having men covet her like a piece of property to steal. The entry went on to name several adult males in the church and accuse them of sexual thoughts for having offered their laps to her as a young child. In another entry written when she was nineteen, Tiffanie said her fear of being sexually assaulted developed when she was a young girl, after a church member played a film about slavery that included a scene of a little girl being molested.

It was approaching the spring of 2012 when Tiffanie experienced delusions of Luke as demon-possessed, trying to infiltrate her dreams with sexual deviance in a playground of witchery. He was sixteen; she was twenty-six. After a long night in which she believed she had brought a dead newborn puppy back to life, Tiffanie laid down to sleep and had visions of Luke with a whip and a desire to hurt someone. In her diary, she recalled pleasant, lustful thoughts of the boy permeating her half-awake state and causing a cramping pain and discharge, indicating an orgasm or wet dream. The temptation crept up over and over again, and she fought it. Tiffanie apologized to Jesus in case she'd given in (she wasn't sure) and promised that she would never sleep again rather than sin. She blamed the occurrences on Luke's sorcery.

Jerry had not been well that year. He'd broken his feet a few times because he had no feeling in his feet from diabetes. His eyes were puffy, his complexion pasty, and his face swollen. His blood pressure was off the charts, and it burst a blood vessel in his eye. His eroding physical health wore down his mental health even more. Though parishioners saw Jerry as fiercely protective of Tiffanie, she did not escape the impact of his bad days.

The first week in May, after he'd had a run-in with a church member, Jerry approached Tiffanie, snarling, "You need to stop acting like a witch. You need to start saying what you're really thinking."

But anytime she was candid with her thoughts, it would send her father into a tirade. Jerry dictated to everyone in the church, including his wife and children, how they were to behave, right down to specific actions and words they were to use when carrying out his commands to confront others, and not even his children escaped his biting words and meanness.

Within days of calling her a witch, diminutive Tiffanie stepped gingerly to her brute of a father, who was sitting in a living room chair, and sat beside him. "Dad." She spoke barely above a whisper, careful not to arouse his rage. "Why do you seem depressed all the time?"

"I feel anger when things aren't done," he grumbled.

"I love you more than anything, Dad," she replied softly, "even when I forget to take my dishes out sometimes."

"You," he said in a subdued tone that still rattled her, "you are high-minded and arrogant."

Tiffanie quickly diverted her watering eyes. And it was only a passing breath before he threw in, "You're self-righteous."

It was all true, she thought. She let those words cook in her brain too long before praying about it and reminding herself that Jesus loved her, faults and all.

It was May 9, 2012—a Wednesday—about 8:50 P.M., and Tiffanie was in the learning center with at least an hour of student testing left. Her father bolted down the stairwell, threw up a hand, and said, "Hello," as he passed. Jerry's neurotic surveillance had captured two people walking down the road. He was headed to the ground level to make sure they went on their way.

Tiffanie claimed it was God who told her, about ten minutes later, "Go upstairs and have your break now, and finish work afterwards."

She phoned her father, something they commonly did, since the old school was so vast. But there was no answer. Tiffanie coolly declared to the students, "You may take a break."

She went upstairs. There was not a sound. She peeked around the corner and stepped into the living room. There, she saw the butcher block smashed into pieces across the floor, the glass decorations once displayed on it now a torturous bed on which her father lay, his face ashen. He tried to roll over, tried to get up, but his leg was limp. Tiffanie put all her strength behind pushing her father to help him move, but her palms made only fleeting dents in his skin. All she could do was make him comfortable. Tiffanie phoned her mother, but she didn't pick up. As she awaited her family's return from the store, she tried getting her father to talk. Jerry had suffered a stroke.

"Is anything broken, Dad?"

He didn't answer.

"Where do you hurt?"

He pointed to his right arm once, twice, three times. He couldn't move it.

Tiffanie laid hands on her father and prayed fervently, repeating over and over, "Thank you, God, for who you are, and the promises you have spoken to my father." The fear was as powerful as her prayer. "God, if there is anyone that you want to be praying with me right now, please move on them to do so."

Jerry seemed to be looking at her, but not seeing her, his eyes unfocused. He was yawning. Tiffanie called her mother again and left a message. Her phone log showed a third call that she didn't remember placing. Seconds dragged. At 9:11 P.M., she called church member Brooke Bowden* and told her to get Linda's daughter, Kathy, and pray. She wouldn't say why. The Irwins had always told their followers that if they became ill, it was because of their own sin.

Jerry's eyes were opening and closing, but mostly closing. He became increasingly lethargic. Tiffanie prayed, "Please, God, give us wisdom. Should I call 911?" She didn't dare make that call without direction from above. And because she believed God spoke through her father, she asked him, "Dad, do you want me to call an ambulance?"

Unable to speak, he glared at her. She did not receive indication from God to call for an ambulance and felt shame for even asking. Her father had made a comment years earlier that he didn't want to go to a hospital, even if he were dying. In his eyes, doctors were godless people who believed themselves to be God.

When Traci arrived, she took over. Tiffanie met her siblings at the bottom of the stairs and made sure they didn't let anyone else upstairs.

The boys carried their father to bed. All four siblings went into the hallway and joined together in prayer.

"I saw a spirit standing right where Dad fell," said Dan. "He was pushed. That evil spirit pushed him to the floor." He was insistent. "Dad kept pointing in the direction of the spirit when he was lying on the floor."

Naomi joined in, sobbing. "God told me to tell the boys not to watch that supernatural show on TV, but I didn't do it. I"—she sniffed—"I didn't tell them. I am so, so sorry." That was how the demon got in. She was certain.

"A few weeks ago," Dan said, after some thought, "I saw the spirit of death in the nursery."

Each of them reaffirmed their hunch that a particular member had been praying their dad would get sick.

Naomi left and came back with a small vial of olive oil. She pried off the cork, wet her right thumb with the oil, and rubbed it on Tiffanie's forehead in the shape of a cross. She and Dan prayed for Tiffanie, that she would be sent to minister in hospitals and clear out the sick. While they were praying, Dan placed his hand on Tiffanie's head, and then spontaneously jerked it away. "I feel something shooting off the top of your head."

"I feel it," said Tiffanie, nodding. "It's like . . . a beam of light shot from the top of my head up to the ceiling."

There were prayers and prophecies all around, except Joe—he was holding something back.

Tiffanie asked, "What is God speaking to you?"

"You're not going to like it," he warned, "but on Sunday, Dad is going to be standing up beside me. God's going to have me say to the people, 'Either stand with us, or get the fuck out.'"

"Don't use that language," his mom cautioned.

"God might tell me to say it that way, Mom. And we couldn't be mad at him if he did."

Still fixated on the reasons for her father's attack, Tiffanie murmured, "Dad was right. There were demon strongholds in the house."

I was seeing a person that was, in my opinion, very dangerous; that she does not know how to control her temper. She does not care what kinds of injuries she inflicts on people.

—Oneida County district attorney
Scott McNamara on Sarah Ferguson

Bruce Leonard was "Dad" to Sarah. When Debi's daughter came into Bruce's life as a preteen, he spoiled and loved her as his own. Neighbors recalled a pleasant Sarah with a sweet disposition. Others, like her ex-husband, remembered her erratic behavior and eccentricities.

Sarah had a bohemian fashion sense and used words like "really" every other sentence, and "beautiful," "super awesome," and "coolest ever." She was a free spirit who got wrapped up in the church vibe, swaying to the Christian pop music, spreading her arms overhead in praise to the Maker. A solid backer of the Irwins' teachings, she found their services liberating and enlightening. At twenty-one, she left home and the WLCC, but unlike others who were shunned, Sarah was always welcomed back. That's because she still submitted to the Irwins' rule. She was a devoted disciple, and at times when she returned, she moved in with the Irwins at the Word of Life Building.

Sarah's first job was a flight attendant at the age of nineteen. That lasted about a year before a drinking problem forced her out of the job. She subsequently held a variety of jobs from retail to landscaping to student loan processing. Over a decade, she moved all over the country: Ohio, Texas, Florida, and a variety of locations across New York. She even spent time in New Jersey living with her biological father. Sarah returned to her Clayville home three or four times that decade, first in 2005. She got a job at a major retail distribution center in Sharon Springs and a year later met Andrew Ferguson*, a coworker who was in the process of moving to Florida.

Andrew was drawn to Sarah, a strong woman with a sunny disposition, full of life, and so pretty. The two began dating, and things were going so well that inside of a month, Andrew invited her to move with him to Palm Springs.

Something unusual happened en route. Sarah wanted to stay with a friend and have Andrew continue to Florida to look for an apartment. Once he found a place, he could go back and get her. Andrew agreed to it, but he soon learned that apartments in Palm Springs weren't cheap. Finding one took longer than expected. The arrangement added distance to the relationship physically, but emotionally they were closer than ever. That was what Andrew thought. They were in constant communication.

Once he got settled and returned to pick up Sarah, he got a sobering splash of reality: she was involved with another man. Andrew left, shutting her out completely.

A year went by. Somehow, the two reconnected by phone. They still had feelings for each other. Sarah was living at the Word of Life Building, and Andrew wanted to move back to New York. They saw each other to talk things over and decided to give their relationship another try. But discussion apparently wasn't all that had happened at the rendezvous. When Sarah flew to Florida to help Andrew pack, he was in for a shocker: Sarah was pregnant with his child. The couple migrated north and settled into an apartment in Schenectady, New York. And in 2007, they got married.

It was a small ceremony at his parents' house, and Pastor Jerry Irwin was among the guests. It was so odd, Andrew told investigators in 2015. Sarah had the strangest attachment to her pastor. There was Andrew, grinning like a luckiest man as he danced cheek to cheek with his new bride; yet, in the middle of their wedding dance, she stopped midstep and left the dance floor. She pushed her way through the crowd that had circled around them and glided over to Jerry like a magnet. The music continued without her, and Andrew was left standing alone.

Sarah spent her wedding day talking to Jerry, and when Andrew walked over, Jerry reproached him. "You should've invited me to perform the ceremony."

Sarah's strange behavior on their wedding day continued, and Andrew was certainly upset. More so, he was bewildered. But he resolved not to let it ruin his day.

It was two years later that Sarah gave birth to their daughter, Ada*. Their first baby had been a boy, Gabriel*. Sarah's religious zeal at this time became alarming. She would stay up through the night writing Bible verses and talk to Andrew of things she'd done in the past that she considered sins. She confessed to kissing another man while married to Andrew.

To keep her happy, Andrew attended Sarah's church from time to time but increasingly found the services unsettling. Jerry would start off quoting Scripture and then go on for hours about subjects that included politics and church members needing to protect one another against external influences. With an "amen!" and a "hallelujah!" he told his disciples they were special and that the community had it out for them, inspired by the devil to victimize them.

A big antigovernment guy, Jerry refused to let town officials or emergency responders into the building. On one occasion, Traci started a dryer fire that set off smoke alarms. When the fire trucks arrived, the Irwins locked down the building. As the Irwins laughed it off upstairs, complaining the firefighters just wanted to get in and poke around, firefighters broke down the door.

Andrew was privileged to be allowed inside and to participate in the services, but when he did, he found himself heavily guarded and felt unable to walk freely. He would later tell police that Jerry's boys were always "standing guard in the church so that no one could get in or out."

At each service, the Irwins passed around the collection plate as many as three times. And Jerry concluded each service by reminding members they were required to help with maintenance and restoration of the building. Andrew sat out the labor that went on for hours around him, refusing to participate. But Sarah would not leave until she was finished. Once, while waiting, Andrew used the bathroom in the Irwins' upstairs apartment and was appalled to see the whirlpool tub. He would later tell police, "If they were asking for money, they should only use it for the church or for necessities."

One service in 2009 was almost the last for Andrew. He watched in disgust as Jerry performed a public shaming of Bruce and Debi. In front of the congregation, he hollered at them for a half hour for not keeping their house clean or helping their children with schoolwork. He pointed to Luke and Chris as examples of how they had not performed adequately in education. Sarah's brother Jayden was visibly upset.

Andrew told Sarah he disagreed with what he'd just witnessed, but Sarah told him Jerry was right to do what he did and that her parents were wrong. Andrew went to one more service before putting his foot down—he would no longer attend. It was, he later told police, "just too crazy."

Sarah continued at WLCC, and the year after Andrew stopped going, she gave him an ultimatum: pay 10 percent of his gross earnings to the church or she would divorce him. Andrew could not afford it. Sarah took their two children and left.

She returned to Clayville in 2012 and rented a home on Main Street. Still married to Andrew, she got pregnant with another man's child. Sarah wanted to attend college and, despite the pregnancy and having two kids at home, enrolled in Mohawk Valley Community College in Utica. Noah* was born ten days before the semester started. Caring for a newborn, two other children, and going to school became too much. She dropped out of college. Then she got pregnant with a third man's child.

Threatened with eviction, thirty-one-year-old Sarah asked her step-father if she could move into his home temporarily. It was October 2013, and Sarah's oldest child, Gabriel, was six; Ada, three; and Noah, one. Her youngest, Ivy*, was two months old.

We need to fight, and we need to war, and we need to enter into his kingdom with violence. It's not something we can just, you know, be a pansy about. We can't.

—Pastor Tiffanie Irwin
to the congregation on November 9, 2014

RESURRECTION

In May 2012, Jerry stopped showing up for services. Members didn't know why. They didn't ask, because they were conditioned to not question the leadership. Tiffanie seamlessly replaced him at the pulpit.

Traci kept Jerry in the third-floor apartment and provided in-home care, never taking him to a doctor. She tried natural remedies to help him recover from the stroke, like feeding him foods with cayenne pepper. She also reportedly paid an international vendor about $30,000 for a hyperbaric chamber. Hyperbaric oxygen therapy involves breathing oxygen in a pressurized chamber. It operates on the principle that increased oxygen helps heal injured tissue. In a hospital setting, hyperbaric chambers are used for treating a number of medical conditions, including decompression sickness, a hazard of diving.

Traci's hyperbaric chamber was not the type of hard-shell medical device used in hospitals. It was a "mild" or "soft" hyperbaric chamber, FDA approved in the United States only to treat altitude sickness in mountain climbers but marketed as an alternative medicine. Buying one from a US vendor requires a medical prescription. The soft chambers are drastically different than the hard chambers, delivering substantially lower pressure, and they use ambient air delivered through an air compressor, instead of pure oxygen from tanks. The soft chambers come with an FDA warning: they are not approved for treating stroke, as the safety and effectiveness has not been established.

One outsider saw firsthand the medical care that Traci was providing. Beverly Visser*, of Mishawaka, Indiana, had connected with Traci through their mutual interest in dogs. Beverly had raised and shown dogs for thirty years, and Traci was also in the dog-breeding business, having taken over a website from a well-known Yorkshire breeder who was retiring. Traci was buying and selling dogs all over the United States. They were a cash crop for her. Now, she had her sights on Beverly's high-quality chocolate Yorkshire terriers. Traci was in the market for older dogs, six to eight months, a little pricier because the dog's personality is established. She bought twenty-five of Beverly's dogs over a six-month period and made a down payment of $7,000 in cash.

Beverly drove with her adult daughter to Chadwicks to deliver the first batch, somewhere in the range of ten dogs. They arrived at night, and it was eerie. They got the weirdest feeling about the place. Beverly had to let Traci know when they were arriving so someone could unlock the gate. But the bigger surprise was when they walked into the building. The sound of Tiffanie preaching blared through loudspeakers in every room, as it did all day and all night. The sermon would play on a continuous loop until Tiffanie's next sermon was recorded. When the visitors got to the second floor, they saw rooms filled with dozens of dogs, possibly more than a hundred. There were animal pens, like in a barn, made of plastic fencing and PVC pipes, and fish tanks acting as incubators. On the third floor, the Irwins had put in a sliding glass door and built an upper deck. They would let some of the dogs out there. They'd installed waist-high fencing around the platform and blocked the dogs from public view by tying bedsheets to standing planks of wood. This whole contraption was painted in solid red-barn paint.

Traci offered to put up the women for the night, but they declined. "We gave them the dogs, and we went to our hotel. And my daughter said, 'Mom, I will never, ever let you go to that place alone,'" Beverly later recalled.

In email discussions leading up to their visit, Beverly had told Traci she was a retired nurse. She also came from a strong Christian background. Her grandfather was a pastor and one of the founding fathers of the Assemblies of God, a group of Pentecostal churches known for fire-and-brimstone preachers and belief in faith healing and speaking in tongues. Beverly found Traci interesting because she was extremely intelligent. She was a penny stock trader. She was handy around the house and had even built their air purifier. Traci had worked a few years as a nurse's aide and was trained in CPR.

Traci had previously confided in Beverly that her husband was ill. When Beverly visited the church the day after dropping off the dogs, Traci brought out Jerry. Beverly talked to them about church politics and legalities.

"They were very worried about that," she later said. "They wanted to see the kingdom passed from Jerry to Tiffanie smoothly, and I gave them a little bit of advice on how to do that. It was more moral advice."

Jerry couldn't speak, but he could understand and nod his head. He had little control of his bodily functions. On his foot was a decubitus ulcer—commonly called a bedsore—that had eaten through several layers of skin and tissue. Traci had been debriding it, having taught herself medical procedures by reading books and internet sites. She'd also been ordering medications from Europe. Beverly was impressed that Traci had been correctly using the medications and doing the procedures without formal training, but she cautioned her against it. Traci told her they couldn't get physician coverage and didn't believe in taking Jerry to a doctor. They believed in faith healing. Well known in the Mishawaka medical community, Beverly convinced Traci she could connect her to a doctor who would at least steer her in the right direction and order the medications.

Beverly stayed in town again that night and took up Traci's offer to speak at Sunday's service. "And that church. Wow," Beverly later reflected, a slight Southern twang giving flavor to the shock in her words. "Was that interesting. It was odd. It was odd in that the people seemed pretty normal. And they seemed sad. And they seemed . . . um . . . bound. They were suppressed."

Beverly told the congregation the biblical story of Rizpah, whose two sons had been murdered to atone for the sins of their father. The story illustrates the undying spirit of a mother's love, Rizpah having protected her sons' bodies from prey until they could be properly buried.

"And when I stood in that pulpit, and I gave that message, people sat in their seats, and they wept. And one woman in particular—well, several of them—they just cried and cried and cried and cried. And I knew something was wrong, but I didn't know what it was." Beverly wouldn't know until 2015, after news reports of the church broke internationally. "And I realized it was the first simple gospel message they'd heard in years."

At the end, she gave an altar call, an opportunity for people to come forward for personal prayer or to give their lives to Jesus. During a typical service back home, Beverly would see a handful of worshippers at the altar, but when she gave the call at WLCC, every single person in the church went forward. Beverly started at one end of the altar and went down the line, praying for each individual. The women were weeping. "I just knew that they were wanting something from me, and I didn't know what to give."

Following the service, the Irwins offered Beverly gas money, and she drove home.

It wasn't until August that the Irwin faithful learned of Jerry's stroke. Tiffanie informed them at the pulpit. Traci then relayed a story to the flock, telling them the night he had taken ill, she and her family had been shopping when they got a message from God that they should return home immediately. They rushed back to find Pastor Jerry unconscious on the floor, she told them, omitting the part about Tiffanie calling to tell her to hurry home.

October was when the congregation got its first glimpse of Jerry in months, and he looked awful. His six-foot-one frame had shrunk to 175 pounds. Parishioners pulled together in support. Kristel and her husband funded a motorized wheelchair and new medical technology from Israel to stimulate his muscles. Bruce and his boys helped build an impressive system of ramps so Jerry could get from the third floor of the building to the garage, for access to transportation.

In November, Traci bought a van and followed Beverly's advice to travel to Indiana for medical care. Naomi stayed home.

In the six months since their father had taken ill, the relationship between Naomi and her sister had become fractured. Their brief interactions were hurtful outbursts that usually ended in Naomi running out of the room. She called Tiffanie a "Bible thumper," told her to take a course on how to treat people, labeled her patronizing and arrogant, and lambasted her for being controlling and disrespectful to their mother.

Before the trip to Indiana, Tiffanie informed her sister, "Until you get a handle on this, I don't want you speaking anymore."

Naomi asked if she meant preaching.

"All speaking," answered Tiffanie.

Tiffanie and her brothers went to Indiana with their mother and brought Dave Morey. They got a room at Varsity Clubs of America in South Bend, a resort with an indoor heated pool, hot tub, mini golf, billiards, bocce ball court, pool table, and other luxuries. Beverly visited them once or twice a week over the next six weeks or so. She took the boys to a gun store in Mishawaka that was known all over the world. It was part of the Irwins' fascination with going to Indiana. Beverly recalled Traci telling her that her sons were shooting AR15s indoors and would defend the church if necessary.

Traci freely discussed most subjects with Beverly. "With Traci, there was always a sexual angle to everything," she later said. "Traci was convinced the men in the church were after her. They wanted her body."

Beverly arranged to have Jerry seen by two doctors: a family physician and a podiatrist. The foot doctor did a lot of work, including straightening Jerry's toes, because Traci was convinced he was going to walk again. Traci paid cash—about $8,000.

On December 8, Beverly went to Traci's hotel room and knocked on the door. They'd planned to have breakfast together. There was no car in the parking spot, but sometimes the boys would take the car and leave Traci at the room, so Beverly waited. She knocked again, several times, and also called her. Not wanting Traci to think she'd stood her up, Beverly stayed for about a half hour. Even after she left, she continued for several hours to try to reach Traci by phone.

—

That same day, back in Chadwicks, Naomi called WLCC members in the morning and asked them to get to the church to pray. Her father had died in the middle of the night, and they would have to resurrect him.

At this time, approximately thirty-five people attended the church, including the Irwins. Families began arriving early in the morning and trickled in throughout the day as they got off work. They gathered in the main sanctuary, the old school gymnasium, a room so big they could never fill it. The back two-thirds were empty. A blue-gray carpet was on the floor and strips of red carpet ran up the riser that supported the podium. There was a tower speaker on each side, from which Naomi occasionally blared high-energy Christian rock music, but more often did not, as this was a solemn occasion.

The worshippers did not speak or greet one another, as was ingrained in them, but some made accidental eye contact before correcting their gaze. They stayed in their assigned seats, black vinyl stackable banquet chairs set out in rows. As they prayed, the congregation was told that Traci was driving Jerry's dead body across state lines, from northern Indiana to a Christian ministry in Missouri, so that TV minister Mel Bond, who claimed to heal and perform miracles, could lay hands on Jerry's body and bring him back to life.

Naomi went to the store to buy bread so that when the TV minister was resurrecting Jerry, coordinated by phone, she could give the disciples Communion.

———

Because Beverly didn't end up having breakfast with Traci, she decided to meet her daughter for lunch. That's when she got the call from Traci: "Jerry died."

Beverly screamed, so loudly that her daughter put her arms around her and got her to walk to her car to sit down.

"He died, and I'm taking him to see the faith healer Mel Bond," said Traci.

"That's against the law, Traci! You can't do that!" Beverly was screaming louder, but not out of grief—this was nuts. Her daughter was trying to get her into the car so she wouldn't make a scene.

"We're going to raise him from the dead," said Traci.

"You *must* bring him back."

"No, I'm not gonna do it. I'm thirty minutes away from Mel Bond right now."

———

At WLCC, the mood was hopeful, intense. It was desperate. A few of the men paced along the sides of the sanctuary. People stood alone, praying silently; others led prayer aloud. This went on for more than twelve hours.

At about 9:30 P.M., Traci reported to followers that it appeared Jerry had come back to life; his heart was beating weakly, and he was taking shallow breaths. There was an atmosphere of immediate relief. Moods lifted. But there was still an air of confusion. Some members silently questioned how—and why—this had happened at all.

With word that their exhaustive efforts had paid off, the women and children were dismissed to go home. It had been physically draining, especially for the very young. They had been at the church with no food or rest. The men were invited to stay and continue to pray. But morning would bring different— and shocking—news.

———

Beverly and Traci continued to communicate sporadically throughout the evening, the retired nurse trying to reason with the new widow. Traci swore she saw a tear come out of Jerry's eye. Beverly told her it was a sign the body was decomposing.

"I'm a committed, strong Christian," Beverly later said. "And I believe that God is almighty and can do anything. And sometimes he does. I believe he does unusual things sometimes. But, girl, I'm telling you—that raised-from-the-dead thing—that was beyond me. Not that I didn't think God *could*; I just felt like he wasn't going to." She laughed.

As Beverly nervously awaited word from her friend, Traci and her kids—and Jerry's corpse—showed up at Mel Bond's ministry and were promptly waved away.

The hands on the clock ticked. Beverly called, asking, "Where is he, Traci?"

He was on the floor, wrapped in a blanket between the kids. The Irwins were heading back to South Bend. Total round-trip drive time: about twelve hours.

"Do you understand what you're doing to your children?" asked Beverly in disbelief. Joe was just nineteen. "Your children have their father dead at their feet! They're traveling across country! I cannot help you. When you get here, you have to call the police."

But that wasn't on Traci's agenda. Back at the hotel, in the wee hours of the morning, Traci called Bubb Funeral Chapel to pick up the body. But it wasn't supposed to work that way. The funeral home staff told her they couldn't simply collect a dead body and directed her to call the police. By the time she got around to doing that, police found reason to be suspicious.

On December 9, at 3:43 A.M., a Mishawaka police officer was dispatched to room 402 of the resort for a report of a male not breathing since 9:00 A.M. the previous day. The officer arrived to find a stiffened body in the bed. The Mishawaka Fire Department was on scene and pronounced Jerry dead on arrival. The officer questioned the family for three hours. His report detailed that the Irwins were in town for Jerry's foot surgery. *Traci stated that Jerry was awake and well the last time she saw him.* That was midnight Friday, December 7, into the early hours of December 8. She awoke at 9:00 A.M. *She found Jerry and he was very stiff. She stated that she knew it was too late for medics to bring him back, but she believed in her religion that with prayer the dead could be raised.* The officer noted that Traci claimed she and her children prayed until December 9, 3:43 A.M.

Under "offense detail," the officer designated the code for an unattended death.

—

Irwin followers awoke the next morning to devastating news. Traci had reportedly passed along that Jerry spoke to her in a vision and said his quality of life after resurrection might be severely diminished and unsatisfying. He would struggle with a long and difficult recovery. Traci had decided to let him go. He was fifty-five.

The Indiana State Department of Health recorded Jerry Irwin's death as 4:00 A.M. on December 8, 2012.

Traci wanted the body cremated and used a crematory in Elkhart, Indiana. She stayed in South Bend for about two more weeks, and then went to Beverly's house to say goodbye, but it was not the end— far from it. Dogged police work many states away would one day unearth this outlandish story, and a critical piece of it would send one investigator chasing down answers.

We are gentle towards all. That's what we must be. And so even when we're fighting, we're gentle towards all. To give you an example, even when Jesus was fighting for everything on the cross, he spoke in gentleness to the ones that cursed him.

—Pastor Tiffanie Irwin
to the congregation on November 9, 2014

THE NEW SENIOR PASTOR

When Tiffanie became senior pastor at the start of 2013, she was twenty-seven years old but looked like a teenager. She wore her round face makeup-free and her mousy brown hair in a loose bun, exposing her large forehead. She wasn't homely, but rather plain, with a droopy left eye and jutting chin.

During Jerry's illness, and right after he died, Tiffanie had relaxed some of the stricter rules he'd imposed, such as mandating that parishioners seek permission to speak with their own family members. She preached forgiveness, love, and grace. Irwin followers were hopeful that with Tiffanie at the pulpit, things were going to be better. And they were. But not for long.

Tiffanie slid into full-time preaching with ease, having had plenty of warm-ups and a lifetime desire to be onstage. Like any performer, she knew the value of strategically amplifying her voice when the message called for emphasis. She had good timing and, though her grammar was impeccable, knew when to break character and say things like "ain't" and "it don't" for effect. She inserted comic relief in the form of ridicule, funny only to the WLCC audience, who burst out laughing on cue because they were conditioned to do so. Tiffanie enunciated each syllable, almost like an actress. But her diction was too deliberate, sounding self-trained. Nearly every word was pronounced staccato style in a deep voice incongruent with her delicate frame.

Tiffanie's expressive delivery was the result of years cloistered in a brick building with virtually the only entertainment watching her father command an audience. She copied his style of smooth flowing words that mesmerized and warmed hearts until they landed a sock in the face. Tiffanie maintained her even tone while serving up her wicked comments on a cake platter, the sweetness betrayed by her caustic words and dead eyes. Like her father, she called out individual worshippers for public shame.

"If you guys think it's funny when I speak to somebody, then I'll just point you all out and tell everybody what you're all thinking, and what you're doing, and what you're dealing with—not what you shared with me, don't worry—what the Holy Spirit tells me at this moment that you're stubborn and rebelling in. Okay?" The *okay* was said with rising intonation; a firm scolding with a tight jaw. "So just mind your own selves, please. Because everybody in this room needs help."

Ian Kercher*, who was with the church till the bitter end, later told police in a deposition that he'd always tried to stay under the radar. *You never knew when you would be called to the mat and what would be said. There was always that fear of embarrassment. You had the liberty to disagree but the repercussions of that were not comfortable.*

Tiffanie's sermons repeated her father's themes of rebellion, witchcraft, sexual perversion, and church finances.

When Traci complained privately that Jerry's care put the Irwins in debt $110,000, Tiffanie took up the torch at the worship service to encourage donations. "Anybody you give to, you're connected to spiritually."

She faced members in a smaller sanctuary adjacent to the big one. One had only to walk through a door to get from one sanctuary to the other. They used the smaller room in the colder months to save money on heating. "Mom and Dad broke through the spiritual warfare when it came to finances." She picked up her metallic green tumbler filled with water and took one sip of what would become many.

Ezekiel, in the second row, let his head fall to his father's shoulder and drew up his legs onto the chair as the sermon droned on. Everybody moved, shifting in their seats, some more than others. Fast-forward video of the sermon and you would see people in motion—scratching heads, crossing legs, folding arms, swinging feet—except Luke. He was like a freeze-frame inserted in the footage; an inanimate object. He would rise when everyone rose, but upon standing would make no movement. When seated, he did not so much as a twitch, his face to the floor the entire time.

"When I was just a little girl, they could not buy me clothes," continued Tiffanie.

The small sanctuary used to be a classroom, but they'd dressed it up. They used the same banquet chairs as in the big sanctuary, set in five rows of five, with a lot of empty seats. Tiffanie's pulpit was a desk draped in fire-engine red cloth with gold tassels at the bottom. Facing the pulpit, to the right was a keyboard where the preacher sat and fulfilled her dreams of being a singer. She would sing songs back-to-back at the keyboard, like a concert, the headliner to an audience of her biggest fans. To the left were music stands, electric guitars, and a drum set where Joe and Dan played for long stretches. Sometimes Dave and Seth Wright played along with them. At this service, there were only about fifteen people. All sat with their heads bowed. Children younger than Ezekiel were in the nursery. They would be brought in and out during services. Sarah was in the farthest row, beyond where Seth's camera was recording on a tripod. Most of the recordings were interspersed with Ivy's baby babble, whining, or crying, and Sarah's other children squabbling. Grace sat on the end seat behind her parents, in a row all her own. From the back, you'd see her lightly shake her head, and from the front, you'd see her lips move without sound. She would pray virtually the entire time and sometimes would stand after service, praying long after everyone else had left. Members took copious notes in spiral notebooks as Tiffanie preached that God offered blessings and protection from illness and death to those who gave money to the church, and how tithing showed obedience to the spirit of God.

"Dad would be so careful," she said. "He would never spend money on himself. And we finally put our foot down. The church would give him a thousand dollars, and he would immediately give five hundred away to other ministries. And it would take us a while to save up—" In dramatic fashion, she cut her own thought, interrupting herself. "Actually, it was more than five hundred." She looked to where her mother was sitting.

"Yeah," Traci jumped in, "it was . . . two-thirds . . . it . . ."

"I don't remember. It was over five hundred."

"Yeah, it was well over that," Traci chimed in, like a rehearsed skit.

Tiffanie told of her father's generosity and how it would take years for the Irwins to save because he was just that giving and unselfish. "The funny thing is, I would watch people who didn't know how to live in blessing walk through this building, and I would discern that demons would talk to them and say, 'They bought that with church money. They shouldn't have that. They're wasting church funds.'" Her voice picked up pace, and she raised and lowered her arms and flicked her hands. "And I would shake my head, because I am telling you"—she dropped her voice to baritone—"we didn't have hidden financial things going on."

The beauty of the round-the-clock rebroadcasts of Tiffanie's services was that members would get the fund-driven messages drilled into their heads over and over again, along with messages striking fear in every one of them, such as: "If someone, as a rule, does not submit to authority, they are considered insubordinate. That's sometimes the attitude people have. 'That's just not me. Nah. I don't submit. That's just not who I am.'" Pause for zinger. "Okay. That's why you're going to hell."

And there were repeated messages of a vindictive God: "The enemy wants us to lie. . . . He'll try to make us lie. He'll try whenever he can. . . . But there are consequences. And if a person doesn't catch you, there are still consequences. Because God's gonna have to punish you for it."

The audio replay lost the effect of Tiffanie in the big sanctuary, wearing a pink zippered jogging top paired with neon blue sneakers.

"Just because nobody ever finds out—God knows. And just because he doesn't come down and be, like, smack you right there, turn into a person and smack you and say, 'Don't you ever do that again,' doesn't mean you get away with it."

The big sanctuary had a rock-concert feel when the boys played their drums and guitars. A thin woman in a tie-dyed T-shirt whipped around a large, brightly colored flag like the color guard in a marching band while Linda twirled in front of the stage. Others stayed near their seats but jumped straight up and down, accelerating as the beat kicked up, like punk rock fans in a mosh pit, minus the personalities. Some awkwardly stepped side to side, hands in the air.

Tiffanie took off her running shoes and lay on her back on the floor, right there on the stage, with arms stretched upward, offering praise. At her desk, a pottery mug of steaming tea awaited, and a box of tissues.

The services were not one long sermon. They started and ended with music, and in between, had blocks of about an hour when worshippers would do nothing but pray. The service might start with a youth meeting in which Tiffanie would give a boiled-down sermon directed at the children, after she spent time arranging where each would sit.

"Now, one thing there will not be is—there will be no hands or touching. No boys versus girls. Do you understand?" She said this like any gentle woman to a child, encouraging and soft-hearted. "I don't wanna see that at all. Okay? We're not gonna give the devil a place to try anything. Okay? So if it's your brother or sister, even them, what's the point? We're gonna make a rule: no touching." She related well to the kids, wearing a friendly smile. It was her words that were unsuited. "I don't want you holding hands with each other. Do you understand that? If I see anything, I'm telling you—you're gonna be in trouble."

All the younger members of the church were lustful, Tiffanie believed, even if they hadn't hit puberty and didn't know what lust felt like, and most of the adults came to church because they were child molesters and viewed Christians as good targets.

"Thank you, God," she prayed, "for all the demons you send to the church, and all those bound by the devil, so that they may listen to your word."

She told her devotees that she was tired of having the same sin-related discussions each week, but they wouldn't stop sinning.

In a snap, Tiffanie could become enraged while giving a sermon and verbally disembowel her followers. During one episode, she told disciples they were not normal but needed to be when entering the building. They could not cut her off, either, she cautioned, because God told people things through her, and if they cut her off, she could not be that mouthpiece.

Her suspicion that Irwin followers were engaged in witchcraft wasn't going away, either.

"What's glorified on television is, like, every demon in hell uses you. Not just a few, like"—she opened her arms wide—"every one of them."

Parishioners stared numbly.

"Can I have some acknowledgment, please? You'd think some of *you* were into witchcraft on purpose by the way you're acting." She looked around the room. "Hmm . . . hmm . . . okay." Then she rested her gaze on one member after another. "Well, that's funny. Believe me, if any—" She interrupted herself and shot up two fingers, paused, squeezed her eyes, and then talked to no one. "Oh, okay. I see." She nodded with her eyes closed, a conversation in her head. "I see." Then she rejoined the sermon. "You know, God knows. You know," she continued in a singsong voice, "he's not stoo-pid."

Once Tiffanie took control, the Irwins' religious fanaticism grew until there was little room in their lives for anything else. They started a prayer room for their family exclusively, in which to pray, read the Bible, and share holy visions for three hours each morning and three hours each night. In between, they added a worship set, a series of hymns and songs focusing on a different theme each session. Then they added up to six hours more of prayer each day. Sometimes they would hear God speak Scripture to them fifteen minutes before the end of the morning session, and then would spend so much time reading and discussing the piece that they would be holed up in the prayer room until five o'clock at night, with no one having eaten and minimal bathroom breaks. Before they knew it, they would have to be back to the prayer room for the evening session.

The Irwins encouraged members to keep pace with their level of devotion. Rick Wright's youngest son, Cal*, was already reading the Bible eight hours a day, but Joe felt Cal should be praying each day for at least two hours, so Cal upped his goal to ten hours of worship each day.

The Irwins kept the congregation overnight on occasion, claiming that God was waiting to hear from individual parishioners and it would be dangerous for them to leave. The all-nighter would follow a five-hour service. Tiffanie gradually increased the length of services, explaining that she wanted to spend as much time with God on Sunday as she did every day. She claimed her fervor was decried by "hellacious sewage," a label she gave those she considered rebellious—essentially everyone in the church.

"If your service goes on too long, you are a weirdo. You're, like, a cult. You're, like—out there," she preached from the pulpit. "You know what I think? If your service doesn't go on long enough, you're like— out there. . . . It's ridiculous. If you don't wanna be in a long service, go someplace where there's a short one. Keep your stupid mouth shut."

Tiffanie did not hide her intense dislike of certain members, particularly the Leonards. This made it likely that Linda Morey, who lived to please Tiffanie, would hate the Leonards with equal intensity. To win Tiffanie's favor, Linda would record herself ambushing her own daughter on perceived rebellion so she could play the audio for Tiffanie.

On one such occasion, Linda had the recorder rolling in the car when she went to pick up Kathleen, who was twenty-eight years old at the time. Linda's footsteps crunched across the grass. The women got into the car and made small talk. Linda interjected a few phony polite uh-huhs before delivering a wallop to the tune of a turn blinker.

"Do you know that every time you play with yourself, masturbate, whatever you're doing, or you're thinking about it, whatever, do you know what you're doing?" asked Linda. "You're having sex with the devil." Her voice was fiendish. "With a demon." She sounded possessed herself. "Do you understand that? You're givin' yourself to a demon."

"I . . . I . . . I haven't . . . I haven't been doing that . . . though."

"Listen to me." Linda's tone was harsh. "But when you were, you were givin' yourself to a demon. It's like you were havin' sex with a demon. Do you understand that?" After a long silence, she continued. "Do you remember Pastor Tiffanie said to you, 'Kathy, if you don't stop that, you're gonna become demon-possessed'?"

Linda continued, sounding rabid. "Mrs. Irwin told me she's read this book on devil worshippers, and they do that as a practice. They have sex"—she paused—"with the devil. And the devil ends up taking blood from you. And he spews it out in the earth. And tries to destroy lives. And people. Do you know how serious that is? Do you know how disgusting?"

"Taking bl—?"

"Blood!"

On and on Linda jeered, her daughter hesitant to speak. And when she did, it was barely audible denials. "I'm not . . . I'm not doing that."

"So what are you doing?" Linda hammered. "You're not doing that, but what are you doing?"

"Controlling—"

"I can't hear you," barked Linda.

"Controlling it."

"Talk louder!"

"I'm controlling it." Kathy's voice shook as she tried to talk her way out of her mother's wrath, trapped in the front seat of the car.

"Wait a minute, wait a minute, wait a minute. You're squirellin' on me right now." Linda's behavior was as terrifying as her message. "You're not stickin' to what I've been sayin'. I wanna get back to this . . . uh . . . havin' sex with a demon . . ."

Kathy tried to interject, but Linda screamed over her. "I wanna know what you're doin' . . . to make it . . . I wanna know! So you've told me you were up all Sunday night. So what are you doin'? I wanna know! And how long have you been doin' this? And don't lie to me, because you know what? God's gonna tell me."

In broken sentences, Kathy managed to say that once in a while, she'd think of having a husband one day.

"So you're courting demons. You're courting demons. With committing set fornication. And you willfully did it. You know it's wrong. And you just—you just went with it. This is nothing to take lightly." She likened sex to an alcoholic and, in a cartoonish voice, mocked, "Oh, my life's so bad I'll have a drink. I'll have another drink. I feel so good. And then, before you know it, the devil has you so trapped where you can't get out of alcoholism. And that's how sex is. Devil comes to steal, lie, and destroy. He's a deceiver," she said, the "e" in the second syllable sounding as long as the day.

They reached their destination, but Linda wouldn't get out of the car. "Are you going on websites and looking at puke?" She spat the last word.

Kathy admitted she'd seen some inappropriate pop-up ads on a website and began to cry.

"Sex does not feel that way," warned Linda. "I'm telling you right now, Satan is lying to you. That door has to be completely closed. You cannot let your mind go an inch. You have to fight. You have to speak the word of God. Fornication. Uncleanness. Ludeness."

Linda pushed; Kathy erupted. "It was in my head," she sobbed. "Months ago, maybe a year ago, I would lay in bed and think about having a husband . . ."

"Oh, brother!"

"I stopped—"

"Kathleen, come on!"

"I stopped," she wailed plaintively.

"That's disgusting!"

Linda assigned her daughter a night of writing proverbs and told her she would no longer be allowed to access the internet.

Another of Linda's recordings had Linda confronting Kathy about lying. "Pastor Tiffanie told you she wanted you to tell me *everything*. You made a joke outa me." In a diabolical voice, Linda told Kathy that if she was going to act like a child, she would be treated like one. "You know what you do with stubborn little rebellious two-year-olds? You beat the *crap* out of 'em." She told Kathy to shut her mouth or she'd take a punch to it.

"You don't have to beat—you don't have to beat me, I'm gonna—" Kathy cried.

Linda had added muscle to the interrogation tips she got from Tiffanie. Tiffanie was a master of evisceration by words. Members would go to the young pastor for counseling and end up with a mental assault, earning labels like "worthless," "pig," "twit," "moron," and "pervert."

Sometimes Dan and Joe counseled members, usually by text. They called themselves "spiritual guiders." Joe was Luke's guide. A year or two before Luke's death, Joe warned him that if he walked away from God, the devil would take his life. He prophesized Luke would die before he was twenty or twenty-one. But that didn't get Luke's attention. He was slipping from the Irwins' grip. He told Joe that he wanted to repent "five minutes" before he died. And when Luke's comment got passed along to Tiffanie, her smug retort was that God was so good, he would let Luke have many minutes of a slow death to repent, rather than letting him be killed off instantly.

Both Irwin brothers also counseled Cal for having "perverted thoughts." He'd been dreaming of being married one day, but God had not said one word to Dan or Joe about finding a wife for Cal.

Determined to find out who did, Joe learned Naomi was behind it. She'd told Cal that he and his future wife would have a ministry together. Joe saw that as a big problem because it provided Cal an excuse to think about sex. Tiffanie set Cal straight by letting him know that Naomi preyed on his weak spots and did not speak by the spirit of God. Cal was instructed to get the perverted thoughts of marriage out of his head.

It didn't take much to meet Tiffanie's definition of perversion. Merely having a dream that included sexual desire made someone a sinner. Tiffanie had members detail their dreams in emails to her or include them in the handwritten journals they were required to maintain in spiral notebooks and turn over to her. The notebooks were to account for every minute of each member's day. If someone needed counseling from Tiffanie, they were to first send her an email outlining their issue. Nearly every communication was in digital form, including regular check-ins. She even kept tabs on her own family, and Linda, who she considered "extended family."

> **TIFFANIE:** *Where are you?*
> **DAN:** *deck*
> **DAVE:** *Sanctuary*
> **LINDA:** *Sanctuary*
> **JOE:** *My room*

Tiffanie assigned each member of her family a parishioner to watch, and her core team was to report on the comings and goings of church members.

> **LINDA:** *[Margaret] and girls just got here*
> **LINDA:** *Now Rick.*
> **TIFFANIE:** *Leonards just arrived...I knew it because I sensed demons.*

> **DAN:** *Whatever attacks, fight it off thru diligence...*
> **JOE:** *Yup. :)*

The leadership snooped on WLCC members when they were off church grounds, too, and monitored former members, mostly through their social media accounts. Jayden was no longer active in the church because his job took him out of state, but Linda was grossed out by a photo he'd posted online of himself wearing shorts that showed a normal bulge below the waist. He said it was just the wind, but Linda enlisted Sarah to get him to delete it.

Linda had positioned herself as an authority figure but not nearly as high-ranking as the Irwins. The hierarchy was clear—Tiffanie had the ultimate say-so. Even her family sought permission from her to do everyday tasks.

> **DAN:** *Is it alright if I lay down?*
> **JOE:** *Can i please play my drums?*
> **SETH:** *Can I come in about 10 minutes*
> **LINDA:** *Pastor Tiffanie may I pray and clean and listen to Bible on my phone tonight ?*
> **DAN:** *I've gotta take a shower I've got dog matter on me. is that ok?*
> **TIFFANIE:** *No...it's prayer time.*

Like her father, Tiffanie would command others to carry out her wishes.

> **TIFFANIE:** *Joe, and whoever else heard [Kathy] talk that way (who else did?)--go and patronizingly tell [Kathy] not to act that way, but to be respectful when I speak.*
> **JOE:** *I might yell if she gives me lip.*
> **TRACI:** *She won't give you lip*

TRACI: *She will cower*
TIFFANIE: *Firm, don't yell. Dave, go with him.*
JOE: *Ok*
TIFFANIE: *In front of [Brooke], since she said it to [Brooke].*

Tiffanie also adopted the confrontational tactics of her father. Claiming insight from God, she would accuse members of certain acts. If they questioned it, they were told their questioning was rebellious. If they said they didn't remember, it was because a demon was blocking their memory. The pastor would single out these members during the worship service or call them to a counseling session, either in front of the congregation or in a more private session. Members often came to believe what they were accused of doing; other times, they would confess simply to get Tiffanie to drop it. If she didn't let it go, Tiffanie's "counseling" could turn physically abusive.

Seth Wright, who was in his early twenties, experienced this. A common punishment was to make him stand for hours facing the front of the sanctuary, even as the cleanup crew swept around him. Seth became the Irwins' punching bag and was frequently counseled for alleged sexual aberrations. The sessions usually started with Tiffanie opening the laptop on her desk.

"You know what, Seth? You don't like being mocked, do you," said Tiffanie, phrasing it as a statement.

"No, I don't."

"Why not?"

Joe, who was there for Tiffanie's protection, or maybe just for kicks, joined in with a phony voice, exaggeratingly mimicking someone with a disability. The Irwins had taken to ridiculing the developmentally disabled, calling them "retards," and now lumped in Seth for the ridicule.

"Because it makes him wealize just how stoopid he weawy is," said Joe.

"What's that?" asked Seth.

"Whazzat?" Joe mocked. "Huuuhh?"

Tiffanie laughed, then put on the firm, staccato voice that meant business. "I said. Why. Not."

"It makes me think that my intelligent thoughts are not intelligent," replied Seth.

More than once, he was made to do pushups at Joe's command. Seth would drop and do twenty as the ear-shattering sound of barking dogs drowned out the count.

"So who's the last person you thought of murdering?" asked Tiffanie.

"You."

Forty more. Seth moaned and whined, his muscles shaking.

"You stop, you start over," Joe almost sang.

Seth cried out that his muscles felt like shards of glass.

"Then maybe you should stop lying," snarled Tiffanie, adding that her brothers should beat him to a bloody pulp for his wicked thoughts. "That's what you deserve for your sin."

Seth told Tiffanie he made up some stuff, because "I thought that's what you wanted to hear."

"No, you're a liar right now. You're making that up." Tiffanie continued degrading Seth, ranting about how worthless he was.

Linda was sometimes present for these counseling sessions. Whereas Tiffanie employed threats of punishment from the Creator, Linda brought threats of physical violence, on at least one occasion telling Seth, "If you don't stop, Seth, you're gonna get a beatin' from me."

Tiffanie found it amusing. "You have no idea what would actually happen."

"Don't you look at me with those demon eyes! You don't scare me!" Linda growled at Seth. "You understand me? Listen to me. . . . You touch Mrs. Irwin, you hurt a child, you do anything . . . I guarantee you . . . I will find you." When Seth didn't respond, she ripped into him, calling him a liar and a coward, a pretender acting like a fearful little boy.

Seth's tears did not move her.

"You're not a good man," Linda sneered. "You're a rotten man. You're a little demon." Her piercing voice could crack glass. "God was giving you a chance to get on your knees and say, 'No! I'm a wicked man! I'm a wicked man!' Go to your pastor and say, 'No! I'm a wicked man!'"

Linda was an A-lister lead in a terrifying real-life horror show, screaming like a raving lunatic that Seth must repent. "You're gonna die a gruesome death. Are you scared? Or you don't care."

"As much as I appreciate your heart for him," Tiffanie casually interjected, "I am having to bite my tongue to tell you if he looks at you with defiance again to smack him. Because I know you definitely will."

"And you can turn around and justify, 'I'm abused.' Are you abused? Are we abusing you?" Linda mocked in the voice of a whiny child.

Tiffanie asserted that Seth had something yet to confess but had been lying, stalling, dragging it out.

"If you just spit it out, I promise I won't hit ya," said Linda.

Minutes after no response from Seth, Tiffanie made her own threats. "I will take that box, and I will smack you upside the head with it, and hopefully it will cut you. And I'm not a sicko like you. I will do that. Because you do deserve that. And we're all nice people."

This had gone on more than an hour.

"If you put your arm up or anything, I'll just hit you over and over and over and over and over again." Tiffanie laughed. "'Kay?"

In the end, it would last three hours. Linda ordered Seth to stand up straight. "What's your name again? Seth what?"

Seth replied almost inaudibly.

"What's your name?" Linda screamed. "I can't hear ya! Loud!"

"Seth Wrong."

"What's your name? Loud!"

"Seth Wrong," he said, louder but not loud enough.

Tiffanie giggled.

"Seth Wron—"

"My name is . . ." Linda prompted.

"My name is Seth Wrong."

"Loud. I wantcha to yell it," ordered Linda.

"My name is Seth Wrong!"

Tiffanie laughed. "He's not yelling."

"My name is Seth Wrong!"

"Loud!" screamed Linda.

"MY NAME IS SETH WRONG!"

"Say it again!"

"SETH WRONG!"

"AGAIN!"

"SETH WRONG!"

Joe offered a suggestion: "Can we make him get on his hands and knees and say, 'I'm a little pig, oink oink oink?' Put some garbage on the floor and have him eat it?"

"I . . . I picture . . ." Seth stammered, "I pic . . . I picture . . . Pastor . . . I'm sorry, I picture Pastor . . . and me having sex with you."

Tiffanie giggled. "Okay, that's funny."

Guitar riffs blared in the background as someone practiced. Linda gritted her teeth. "You know what?" *Whack!* "You deserve it." *Whack.* "You deserve it. Okay?" she screamed. In another, bloodcurdling shriek, "Okay?" The blows kept coming.

"You wanna be beat up, Seth, by people who use knives and fists and intend to kill you?" Tiffanie asked calmly. "Is that what you want?"

Whack!

"I dunno," Seth answered wretchedly.

"You don't know? Did that feel good?" asked Tiffanie. "Linda, go do it some more."

"Oh, that feels good," said Linda. "You like getting smacked? You're one of those cuckoos."

Tiffanie ordered Joe to monitor Seth to see if he got an erection. She called Seth a moron, bastard, little idiot, stupid fool, wicked.

"I've been giving into the demons of masturbation," he confessed.

Tiffanie hit him. She would do it again and again and again, she threatened, and made him vow to die before he ever masturbated again. She had him repeat her exact words.

Joe might have been slightly more intimidating than Linda, simply because of his size. During these counseling sessions, he would sit by Tiffanie's side and play on his cell phone, get up and stroll around the room, or become an active participant. His presence always changed the atmosphere. Fear became tangible in the air. Joe participated many times in ridiculing Seth and promised the young man that if it came down to it, he would walk over and kick him in the face until his nose fell off.

Joe's lifestyle quickly matched his hardened tone. He and his brother turned into heavy pot smokers. They smoked cigarettes and got drunk.

Dan joined his siblings in feelings of desolation. Heading toward his twenty-second birthday, he was not eating well. He'd been keeping away from porn. He'd been exercising, trying to take off the extra pounds, and seeing modest gains. But in his writings, he attributed his lack of appetite to angst over family matters. He complained that his mother could act like a *nut job*. He expressed being tired of people not caring about things that were important to him and stressed over Naomi, whom he felt hated him and acted as though he were a great annoyance. But it wasn't just Naomi. He wrote that *everything and everyone* seemed to be against him. He felt as though he'd been engaged in battle his entire life—fighting to protect the church from some unseen threat and fighting to simply keep putting one foot in front of the other. For his upcoming birthday in June, Dan planned to get his guitar tweaked, as well as his hair. He wanted a Mohawk-type haircut worn by a main character in a shooter video game.

Dan and his brother, Joe, looked a lot alike. Aside from similar body types, they each had a close-cropped beard and mustache, sometimes shaped to a goatee, and each was going bald at the crown. But Joe's hair had red in it, and he had brown eyes to Dan's blue.

Naomi was a storm that needed to be quelled. She'd taken a job outside the church, had a car, and was openly swearing, drinking, and refusing to follow anyone's rules but her own. At twenty-three, she was not just having lustful thoughts but acting on them, without excuses or regret. The Irwins' younger daughter remained devoutly religious, although she interpreted Scripture differently than the rest of her family, a family that did not give her a sense of belonging. She was making friends in the community and coming and going as she pleased. It was confusing to parishioners. Why did she act this way? What was wrong with Naomi?

In the spring of 2013, Naomi began to unravel. Tiffanie called a late-night meeting, but Naomi was ornery and too tired to stay up for it. In the middle of the meeting, she sent her mother a text saying it wasn't fair—Tiffanie was abusing her power. Naomi was going to leave the meeting.

Traci begged her to wait, but Naomi said she was not Tiffanie's slave. She was sick of her sister dictating that they live their days just to sit and listen to her. Tiffanie's *super spiritualism*, she texted, was seriously impacting her life, keeping her awake after a long day at work, and Tiffanie's ways *put God in a negative light*. Naomi was just another sheep at WLCC, but the black sheep, becoming bolder with each passing day. She texted her mother that when it came to Tiffanie, she would no longer *grovel like everyone else at her royal feet and beg on her mercy*.

On Independence Day weekend, Naomi gained autonomy. She planned to tour an island castle with a friend and watch fireworks for the holiday. The next day, she sent her mother a good-morning text, but in response, Traci accused her of having been out all night with a man. Naomi argued that she'd been drinking and didn't want to drive home, so she'd stayed at a friend's house. It was an argument that escalated throughout the day, most of it by text. Then in the evening, Joe showed up in Naomi's room, taking the hostile stance of an old Western gunslinger waiting for the opponent to draw. Naomi stared into his eyes for a few seconds before dodging to one side and out the door. He gave chase. She flew down the hallway with Joe on her heels, and then into the stairwell, jumping every other step. She ran out the door, at some point passing Kathy in a blur, then passing Dan, Dave, and Seth, before making it safely to her car.

Naomi spent the rest of the night there. Just before midnight, sitting in her car, she sent her mother a text accusing her of orchestrating the confrontation. She believed her mother had sent Joe to remove her belongings, but Traci denied it and warned her daughter not to cut off those who loved her. Traci sent myriad texts baiting Naomi for a reply, but they were met with silence—until Naomi said she was going to go live with the imaginary boyfriend her mother had conjured up for her. Still with shattered nerves over the encounter with her brother, Naomi reminded her mother that she had promised a physical line would never be crossed with Joe. From her car in the parking lot of WLCC, Naomi then castigated her mother in text for a laundry list of infractions, including interfering with her attempts to go to college.

Traci fired back that Naomi had made quite the scene during her hasty exit and would have to do *damage control* and eat *humble pie*. Naomi would not be allowed to return until she sent a group text apologizing for being *foul mouthed* and *shocking*.

Naomi refused. The foul-mouthed part she couldn't let go and lay the blame squarely on Joe—he'd chased her down the hall screaming she'd better "fucking stop" and "fuck you" and "go fuck yourself."

It was almost 3:00 A.M. Naomi went to sleep in her car.

Upon waking the next morning, July 6, she texted her mother asking for her birth certificate and social security card, and when she went

to get it, she found the church locked and a chain on the door. Naomi
sat on the pavement. Her mother was not home. The two continued
texting, and Traci was firm: she would not allow Naomi to live with
them until she sent a group apology text.

Naomi threatened to call the police for help getting her belongings.
She and her mother whipped allegations back and forth like a dodge-
ball. Naomi brought the subject back to Joe—Traci had sent him to
physically attack her, she accused. But Traci continually denied it. *Just
like you didnt tell him to lock up half the house and barricade the
door*, Naomi texted. And Joe, she said—all one had to do was rile him
up and *he will go to extremes*.

Naomi asked if she could stay at the church until she found a place
of her own, but her mother said the window to return home had
closed. She would pack Naomi's stuff, and when she handed over the
first load, Naomi was to give her the church key and garage door
opener.

Naomi texted as the night wore on, sitting on the asphalt, a warm
summer breeze blowing errant strands of hair here and there. It was
clear Naomi had discussed her family with her friends outside the
church—the very threat the Irwins tried to evade. She now threw it
in her mother's face. Naomi should have listened to those *sinners*, she
texted, when they said her mother would stab her in the back and then
hide in self-pity and make Naomi out to be the bad guy.

Lame. Disgusting. These words were hurled by both sides. *Bitch.
Worse than a non Christian. Stupid. Childish. Drama-lover. A dis-
grace.*

Darkness enveloped Naomi outside in the early-morning hours. It
was 12:30 A.M. on July 7, two days into the fight. Naomi wanted to
retrieve her own belongings, but her mother refused. Naomi threatened to pull back the curtain on the Word of Life Christian Church,
telling the world about the *prison like conditions* her mother imposed
when she discovered Naomi was in a relationship. She would have a

lawyer force Tiffanie to hand over her school transcripts so she could go to college, she texted. A soundtrack of frogs, owls, and crickets made the biting messages with her touchtone keypad seem artistic: *Liberal New York plus liberal vicious lawyer equals you make the local, if not national news for your "cultish" behavior and i get my money and my stuff.*

Spiteful, nasty, vengeful bitch—more angry words were exchanged before Traci's battery depleted and she signed off, *I love you more than you can ever imagine...*

You have taken abuse your entire life, Naomi shot back. *Now you kick me out of the house for refusing to apologize for being abused.*

Unstable—the next shiny adjective from Traci.

Naomi accused her mother of gaslighting her, trying to make her out to be crazy. She said it was, ironically, a therapist who'd recommended she move out of her "extremely destructive environment."

Around dinnertime that day, still outside, Naomi watched the boys start a bonfire on the roof. As gray smoke spiraled to the clouds, she texted her mother that police would be calling from a blocked number. It wasn't Naomi who called police, she wanted her to know. The neighbors had. They were complaining about smoke from the fire. But Naomi planned to go into the compound and get her things when police arrived.

Meantime, Naomi was texting Dan, begging him to let her in so she could get some personal belongings, her money, and one outfit for work. Could he also drop a bottle of water out the window? She hadn't had anything to drink—or eat—since leaving work the previous day.

Traci, who'd packed Naomi's belongings herself, texted Naomi that she loved her and wished it didn't have to be this way.

Naomi's reply came after two hours of silence: *I ran from my brother.*

God *hates* to be around most of the people in this room. Because they think evil. You think evil in your hearts against other people. So God hates to be around you because of the air that you put off. Well, we want God to move in this place. We want his presence here. What else do you think we're here for? I don't care if there were five people here if God showed up. I would be happy. I really don't care. I care about each one of you. And that's why I've prayed my heart out for you. But if you made your own choice, and then God came, I would say, "I'm sorry they missed out." That's what I would say. I don't understand why anyone has to have a bad attitude about staying in this place. I do not understand it whatsoever. "We're all gonna do the hard thing and stay in this church." Why is it hard?

—PASTOR TIFFANIE IRWIN

TO THE CONGREGATION ON NOVEMBER 2, 2014

THEY COULD LEAVE

Church members waited anxiously for Tiffanie to address them. Naomi was gone, and they weren't given a why. They were instructed to keep her out of the building and have no contact with her. On October 26, 2013, Tiffanie did some personal housekeeping, emailing Naomi that the accusations she'd leveled against her family and the church were lies, and the real reason she left was so she could continue in sexual sin. Tiffanie put her on notice—refusing to send a group apology that day in July would come with consequences.

The hole created by Naomi's absence was quickly filled by one of the Leonard clan: Sarah. She fluidly slipped into the role of obedient Irwin "daughter." Church members helped move Sarah's clothes and furniture into the Clayville home of Bruce and Debi that Halloween, after she was evicted from an apartment in the same village. The arrangement was supposed to last about three months, until Sarah could find a place of her own. The two-story Leonard house was now bursting at the seams with people and objects. Luke and Chris had to share a bedroom so that Sarah and her kids would have one. The cramped quarters became even more of a challenge when Debi had to get around on crutches.

> **TRACI:** *I just found out Debi broke her leg!!*
> **LINDA:** *Good.*

The coming year would be one of significant transition for the Leonards, and for their church, and would ultimately trigger a catastrophe. WLCC's annual business meeting on January 19 was pivotal.

The meetings occurred on the third Sunday each January. Throughout the years, the policy changed on who could attend. When Jerry had been alive, he expected every member to attend, as long as they were "in good standing," something left to Jerry's interpretation. "If you have to ask," Jerry would say, "you aren't." So it was never clear who could attend. Jerry would rebuke anyone not present who he felt should be there. And if a member was present who Jerry deemed to be not in good standing, that member would be kicked out. Members of voting age (over eighteen) would elect trustees. The church leadership would discuss financial matters, including upcoming projects. Rick or Linda would usually bring up the subject of increasing the pastor's salary.

During the 2014 meeting, as Joe was preparing to speak, in a first-ever move, he demanded everyone stand for his remarks. There was no movement, not even on the puzzled faces that surrounded him. "What's it going to take to get you all to stop rebelling?" he barked.

That's when one member spoke up. "Pastor," replied Mason Bowden*, meaning Jerry.

Joe screamed to an audience of lost looks, "Do I need to invoke Pastor Jerry to appear before you and straighten you out?"

Slowly, they stood. Joe paced the line of parishioners. "How do you expect the church to keep going without money?" he shouted.

Tiffanie sat in her chair on the platform behind him, chin in the air with an undisturbed expression. As Joe's actions went unchecked, he told members that Tiffanie was his cover. If she approved his actions, it was justified in the sight of God.

The very next Sunday brought the first departure of several WLCC families in 2014. Mason and his mother, brother, and one of his sisters defected to a church in nearby Randallsville, into the presumed abyss of sinning. The WLCC congregation prayed for their souls and methodically wiped them from memory.

The following year, Mason's mother, Faye Bowden*, would reflect on her family's exit, and police would document it: *She advised that* *when Joe Irwin and Linda Morey took a bigger role she became concerned. [Faye] states that she felt the church abused their authority and states there was a lot of psychological coercion within the church. She advised that there was even isolation from others and that ofter families were seperated.*

Faye's husband had left the church the year before his wife left. Investigators interviewed him, too, and reported: *at several different times during his time with the church he contemplated leaving as he did not feel right with the direction to church was headed. [Faye's husband] advised that at no time did he ever see any physical abuse but states that in his eyes there was definitely phsychological abuse within the church.*

The couple's adult daughter, Brooke, stayed with the church, a steadfast Irwin supporter. A police investigator would later note Brooke's comments: *Pastor Tiffanie — not the kind of person who is mean, she is gentle.* A more structured police report would state: *[Brooke Bowden] advised that she is currently a member with the church and disagreed with her parents stating she never saw or heard physical or mental abuse within the church. She advised that she is very close with Tiffanie Irwin and states that Tiffanie is not the type of person who would do something like this describing her as gentle. . . . She described Joe Irwin as gentle.*

The Bowdens' departure cost the Irwins income, conceivably a catalyst for further strain on Irwin family relations.

In texts, Traci sheepishly criticized her daughter for creating *monsters* in Dan, Joe, Dave Morey, and Seth Wright. They'd teamed up against the Irwin matriarch. When Traci told Dave Morey that his mother had gone to urgent care, she found herself reprimanded by the men for not demanding Linda get permission first. They told her Linda had been "demon-led." Traci complained it made her feel like the *lowest person with the least right to speak.* When she left to sit in her chair and collect her thoughts, Joe stormed in and chastised her.

In February 2014, as Naomi prepared her taxes, she requested her giving statement from her mother, the record of her church donations. Traci was supposed to have sent it automatically. Naomi warned that her mother had missed the deadline for renewing the church's non-profit status and the church would lose its property tax exemption. The tax rate would be substantially higher. Plus, the town could go after the church to repay any rebates they had claimed but were not entitled to receive, as well as the full property tax amount for each year the nonprofit status was invalid.

Traci rang the alarm bells and told parishioners Naomi had launched an attack. The devotees vowed to pray. It was around this time that Tiffanie sent a message to her congregation during worship: God told her a member was going to donate a large sum of money to the church, and that person needed to obey. She told parishioners the church owed $4,000 to the utility company, $10,000 for work on the roof, and $1,000 for the building fund, because that money had been used to pay some of her father's medical bills.

Kristel, now married with two children, had donated so much to WLCC that the IRS once flagged her for an audit. Still, she hoped that she and her husband, Arthur*, were the ones chosen by God to give the money. Though Kristel was a stay-at-home mom, her husband had a high-paying job. Together, they could afford it. She prayed God would send her a sign to give the money, but none had come.

While Kristel was awaiting word from God, Luke was experiencing a spiritual breakthrough. He walked through his house on a hunt for movies that had no real purpose but entertainment. He collected them in a box and then grabbed a baseball bat and made a game of tossing them into the air and whacking them against the wall. His family had implemented a fast from games and movies. The Leonards also decided to memorize the book of Proverbs as a family, committing to memory at least two verses a day. Luke went beyond, memorizing more. On his own, he started a Bible search, writing down references and verses that contained the words "faith" or "Holy Spirit." He committed to two hours of prayer each day. When he wasn't praying, he was speaking in tongues under his breath, and that included when he went to the store. The distractions in public were sometimes too much for the teen, and when he caught himself not speaking in tongues, he would start over.

Chris, too, was speaking in tongues, and singing in the room they shared. Luke talked about it in an email to Traci on February 27, 2014: *2 weeks ago you would not have heard any of this except him reading the Bible. Chris is a very image oriented guy, note the perfect hair, dont touch, you might move a strand. Anyway, for him to be doing any of this is amazing. Grace has been such an encouragement to me, we rarely now have any talks that dont involve God and what He's doing. for example we were talking about the strongest we've ever felt the manifest presence of God and she starts going on this rant about how we cant work up the presence of God. there was not much to do but shut up and listen.*

On his way to church the Sunday before he wrote that email, Luke was overcome with anxiety. He sat in the van and practiced his smile. He curved up his lips. They fell down. As he selected each expression, he felt his facial muscles respond. He watched himself in the reflection of the van window. He was tired and miserable and trying to cover it up. But he soon became aware of what he was doing. Then, he felt ashamed for resenting having to go to church and suffer through a long, boring sermon.

When they got to the parking lot, Luke sensed the presence of a religious spirit and began praying. The presence grew so powerful he started to feel claustrophobic, so he stepped outside the van to pray. The weight slowly lifted. The church doors opened. He walked inside to rock-style music and people dancing their constrained, side-to-side sway. That everyone was moving, as he preferred to stand still as a stone, made him feel awkward and critical of himself. As soon as he sat down, a demon left. He was certain of it. And then, a revelation: *i can dance, i can walk with a spring in my step because im forgiven. i love how Mrs. Morey walks, she has such a freedom, its like every step is a separate dance.* He rose with the others and began crying like never before. He felt so . . . clean. The music got louder.

"The roof just ripped off!" shouted Joe, his arms stretched to the heavens. "Jesus and his angels are flooding into the room!"

Luke began to shake, first his hands, then his arms, then all the way down to his knees, quivering like they'd fallen asleep. He struggled to remain standing. It was, he thought, the presence of Jesus overtaking his body. *I actually opened my eyes to see if i could see Him! ive always thought i had to work up the Spirit of God, you know? pray a little louder, get myself excited through the music, i always ended worshipping the words coming out of my mouth. all i have to do is pray and focus on Him.*

Luke vowed to focus on God and improve other areas of his life. He would rid himself of every temptation feeding his porn addiction and end his dabbling in witchcraft. *i told you about where the interest in witchcraft came from and i just remembered something as i was writing that, a really long time ago, actually before we met [Olivia], Mother said something about a potion that you make somebody drink and it causes them to love you, i remember that it was intriguing to me because i had a crush on one of [jayden]'s friend's little sister and had hopes of marrying her.*

He would keep adult matters from children. *one time we were all in Graces room, Chris Grace [Ezekiel] [Olivia] and me, and we decided tell [Ezekiel] about sex because "its good for him to know these things" was our excuse. we were really explicit. thank God Mother found out about it and disciplined us. this was one of the really hard thing to beleive God could forgive me for because He said that who-ever causes one of these little ones to stumble it would be better if a millstone were hung around his neck and he were drowned in the*

*depths of the sea. in some way or other i have caused each of my
younger siblings to stumble. i pray God would forgive me.*

Still, no one knows if one word of what Luke wrote in his texts and
emails to the Irwins was true. Outside the church, around people he
was comfortable with, Luke's sarcasm was well established. And he
was tiring of his chains. He was eighteen, and though adolescents usually go through a normal process of breaking from their parents, Luke
was trapped. He would need to wage a final battle for independence.
Born into WLCC, there was little he could do. For Luke, there would
be no stepping off a precipice and having the wind catch his wings.
But he could fly in his mind. Creating fiction was one small way he
could break from the church's hold and resist authority, the crowning
of adolescence. It would be a protest waged in his mind, and it would
free him, but tragically.

As weeks passed, the Irwins' call for the mystery donor got more
urgent. This time, Tiffanie's message was that if the person God designated to donate did not come forward, serious physical harm or death
would come to someone close to them.

It rattled Kristel. God needed to get this person's attention. She
wanted to give the donation, knowing it would spare lives, but God
sent her no signs. If her husband was the one to give, he would need to
hear separately from God. She waited and prayed.

In early spring, Sarah was still in her parents' house, now settling
permanently. The friction with her bothers was getting worse. Matters
weren't helped when Chris was suddenly singled out at church for
rebellion. Though schooled at home instead of the church, the Leonard
boys still attended the WLCC after-school Bible study. Children were
seated in rows according to age, with the youngest in front and the
moms in back. Chris, however, was in none of these rows. They'd
started seating him behind the mothers' row, flanked by two of the big
boys, either Joe, Dan, or Dave. It was most likely he'd been accused
of some sort of sexual perversion, and his presence could contaminate

the younger children by emanating a sexually perverted spirit on them. But no one knew for certain.

The first week in May 2014, the Irwins went to a ministers' conference in Kansas, so they didn't have mass on Sunday. They held it on Tuesday when they returned. This particular service became a rally for the big money donation. People read different scriptures on topics of giving and being generous. A few told stories of how they gave money when God directed them, and in return, he delivered a miracle.

At the end of the service, Kristel was gathering her belongings and getting the kids ready to send home with their father so she could do the required after-service cleaning. There were no sounds but the rustling of chair legs and the clanking of a belt buckle against a seat. She leaned over to collect her jacket and bag and, upon straightening, was startled to find herself within inches of Joe, blocking her like a wall.

"Kristel." His voice was restrained but firm. "We know it's you."

It stole her breath. "What?"

"Don't play games with me. We know it's you."

Was he implying she had a demonic presence that she needed to get rid of? Not understanding, she repeated, "What?"

"Stop playing games with me. We know it's you. You're the one who needs to give the money, and we know exactly how much."

Kristel's husband, Art, was a few chairs away, but Joe said nothing to him. With no income of her own, Kristel could not fund such a donation alone. She panicked, recalling the warning a few months prior of harm coming to a loved one if the chosen parishioner did not donate. She was a mother, wife, daughter, sister.

That night, Kristel went about her business cleaning the church, but the worrisome news never left her thoughts. She prayed desperately, "God, tell me how much money to give and how to get it."

When she returned home, Art was sitting on the couch, waiting for her. "What did Joe say?"

Her eyes widened. "Joe says I'm the one who's supposed to give the money."

"I don't know how you're gonna do that," said Art. "You're not taking money from our account."

She was stricken with dread. And she wasn't entirely clear on why Art didn't want her to give the money—though he had shown signs of being fed up with the all-consuming projects he'd been expected to complete at the church, and the abuse their children had suffered in the school.

At different times, Kristel sought out Traci or Tiffanie for guidance. She could've written a check for the amount that was on her heart: $10,000. Her name was on the checking account. But it would cost her the marriage, and she had married under a mandate from God. If refusing to obey God meant harm for herself, she could weather that, but she was not okay with someone else getting hurt because she'd failed to obey God. She told the Irwins, "I could do $10,000." But the Irwins did not confirm that was the amount God had intended.

On Wednesday, May 7, Traci checked in with Kristel via text and advised her to wait to hear from God and pray. Kristel responded, *I am fasting at least through today... I just need to know the amount and how— if I write a check or sell some of my personal belongings.*

Traci advised her not to speak to Art about it, even if he brought it up, and then suggested there were ways Kristel could sneak money to the church without her husband finding out. Kristel thought it was an odd thing for a pastor's wife to suggest.

That very day, Linda had an encounter with Naomi. The renegade Irwin had just gotten out of work and was sitting at a table in a convenience store, talking on her phone and intermittently taking bites of a sandwich. She saw Linda walking into the store and, caught off guard, tried to remain calm. Naomi lowered her phone and, though apprehensive, greeted Linda pleasantly. Linda asked how she was doing.

"Up and down," said Naomi, forcing something other than a frown. "I just got out of work." The conversation was strained. She asked about Linda's Mother's Day plans, her kids, and how everyone was doing.

They were all good, said Linda, with a genuine smile. She asked again if Naomi was okay. She noticed she'd grown out her hair.

Naomi set down her phone and stood, facing Linda. Then, she fell into the other woman and wrapped her arms around her, tears wetting Linda's cheek as Naomi pressed her face to Linda's. "I love you, Linda. I miss you."

"I love you, too." Linda almost cried but walked abruptly from the embrace to spare the emotions attached to it.

The following month, Tiffanie tightened her grip on Chris. She wrote herself reminders to read him Psalm 36, per God's wishes, and to have a *private confrontation and apology.* Chris was to apologize to her for *perversion and rebellion/obstinacy, blatant sexual comments in the service,* leaving the church door open, and disrespecting church elders. She would deliver a final warning: he was not to talk in church unless he first ran his question by the person assigned to watch him, he was not to leave Luke's side when on church property, and he was not to speak to women.

Kristel learned of the segregation during cleaning crew, when she was told to assign her brothers chores together. She had no idea what Chris had done to earn such treatment.

Before Sunday mass, Art was hurrying to the bathroom when Tiffanie greeted him in the hallway, but he didn't catch it. He stopped and turned back, but there was no one there. From the restroom, he made his way to the sanctuary. That's where Joe and Dan accosted him.

"How dare you disrespect my sister," growled Joe.

"The pastor," Dan added.

Art tried explaining it was a misunderstanding. From afar, Tiffanie watched the exchange but did nothing to censure her brothers' behavior.

The next morning, Art was getting dressed and ready for work when he told Kristel about the incident. It had been on his mind all night. "I don't think I can go back to that place."

That got Kristel's attention.

"They claim their every move, their every word, is from the mouth of God, when clearly it's not," he continued.

Art left for work, but Kristel stayed at the kitchen table with her hands around a mug of hot coffee, deep in reflection. Maybe this was the answer to her prayers. She remembered something Jerry had said repeatedly: "Strong families make strong churches." Recognizing her family was not strong in the church, she reconciled, *We're not helping by staying, so we might as well leave*. It was the first time in twenty-five years that thought had crossed her mind.

The school year wasn't over yet, so for the next three weeks, Kristel stayed at WLCC while contemplating such a drastic action. What they were considering was very scary, but she knew it was right.

July 9, 2014, was Kristel Leonard's last day in the Word of Life Building.

Monday, July 14, 2014, 9:10 AM

Dear Dad, Debi, Luke, Chris, Grace and [Ezekiel],

Dad, thank you for texting last night to check in on us. I have some news that will probably be disturbing. We will no longer be attending Word of Life Christian Church and Academy, as we have withdrawn our membership. We are certainly not leaving our faith; we must have Jesus. For the sake of our family, we need to make this change. It is not easy by any means. My heart is breaking, but I know this is what we have to do.

I deeply appreciate how close you have all become to me. Brothers and sister, what a privilege it has been for me to watch you all grow and mature and become such beautiful, amazing people! I can only ask that you continue to grow and that I will still be granted the privilege of seeing that. I have no greater desire than to still be close to you all. I understand that you may very well be angry and hurt, and I apologize for causing you any pain. Please know that we would not do this unless we were convinced it is what we have to do. We will soon be moving closer to Syracuse. Our doors will always be open to you, no matter where we go. I shall keep the same phone number and email address, so you can contact me any time. If you feel that you shouldn't maintain contact with us, I understand; I surely hope that isn't the case, though. I love you all so much.

Yours Forever,

Kristel

(The Eldest)

Kristel, Art, and their children joined the same church the Bowden family had joined after leaving WLCC. It was little more than a half-hour drive southwest of Chadwicks. The sudden split from the Word of Life did not feel freeing or exhilarating. It was more like spinning in the wind, with no direction or control. Kristel struggled to find footing. Driving home one night, she hit a deer. After that, Art cracked her truck's windshield while installing a part. Little or big, Kristel attributed every bad thing to leaving the church. Were the Irwins right? Did she bring misfortune upon herself?

She sent Grace a simple text: *I love you.*

Much to Kristel's relief, Grace responded, *I love you too.*

Kristel sent the same text to Sarah but got no reply.

Within the WLCC community, Kristel and Art's departure triggered a cavalcade of panic. Luke texted Tiffanie asking if she was okay.

God had been preparing her for this, she replied. The pastor denigrated Kristel's choice to notify her family by email rather than in person and her failure to consult her before leaving, so God could let Kristel know if hers was a sound decision. Tiffanie sent a similarly worded text to Bruce, adding stinging commentary that Kristel's decision would have spiritual implications for her kids.

Bruce didn't reply to Kristel's letter until he ran his draft past Tiffanie, delivered in handwriting in a notebook. He told Kristel he believed she'd left because she was in some kind of sin so big she felt God couldn't handle it. He was concerned that Kristel failed to seek counsel for such a decision, one he imagined that Art had forced upon her.

This was God's plan for her life, replied Kristel. They were not rebelling. They were not sinning. She asked to discuss it with him.

The Irwins barely had time to sweep up that mess before another hit, this time from Debi and Rick's brother, Jeff. On August 17, he sent an email withdrawing his children from the WLCC school effective immediately, and his entire family from the church. He, too, made it clear that they were not sinning and planned to continue to serve God. In a respectfully worded note, he thanked the Irwins for their generosity and wished them well.

Reaction by group message was swift. Dave, Kathy, Linda, Joe, Traci—everyone in the inner circle—pounded out question marks and hurled judgments and presumptions. *They wanted sin*, Joe texted, *they got it*. Tiffanie said she'd known for weeks it was coming, because God had shown her, and she claimed Jeff's wife had threatened to divorce him if he didn't leave the church.

In reality, the tipping point for Jeff was that he'd begun to question things his son was accused of doing. Tiffanie once blamed the child for swearing at the top of his lungs in the entryway of the church, though the boy vehemently denied it. "My wife and I had a hard time believing our own son because we had been conditioned by the leadership of the church to believe only what they told us was true," Jeff later told police. His son didn't even understand the words he was accused of screaming. "We had to explain to him what it meant." The punishment Tiffanie handed down was one hundred sentences to be written the next day, and the boy had to stay up all night to complete it.

Jeff emailed his brother, Rick, about leaving. Margaret, devastated and disgusted, quickly notified the Irwins. While Rick was getting together a response that would go through Tiffanie for approval, Margaret was concerned that Bruce and Debi would also leave. She texted Tiffanie, *Where can any of us go? This is where we hear the words of eternal life- the truth that sets us free!*

Rick wrote his brother, blasting him for doing such a thing to the Irwins, who had done so much for his family over the years. He disparaged Jeff for not being *man enough* to talk it through with the pastor.

Jeff sent a note to his brother-in-law Bruce, too, but it was more personal. He didn't give him the news face-to-face because he was afraid it would be too emotional. He asked Bruce to contact him so he could discuss the reasons they'd left and pleaded with Bruce to allow them to continue a relationship. Jeff voiced his greatest fear: that Bruce and his family were expected to shun him. Jeff had shunned his youngest sibling when she'd left WLCC after only about a year, back in the early 1990s. He wrote to his oldest sister, Debi, that he'd lost one sister for the past twenty years and didn't want to lose another.

Meanwhile, Kristel's liberty was coming with a cost. A few weeks after leaving WLCC, she again sent her sisters an *I love you* text, but this time, neither responded. Kristel couldn't brush aside worries of the way Chris was being treated when she left WLCC. She emailed her father about it:

> *He is being isolated and apparently guarded from influencing others I guess. Why is he being treated like this? What has he done wrong? Is he being accused of sin? Are you personally certain in your own spirit that Christopher is doing what the leadership says he is doing? What scriptural basis is there for his being separated from the rest of the group and flanked by the big boys?*

From the safety of her keyboard, she dared offer a suggestion: *I'm going to go out on a limb here, but would you be willing to let Christopher come to church with my family? If he would like to?*

Her two-page email included a desperate pitch to get her father to see WLCC for what it was. *You really can stand on your own two feet before God. Have you ever truly believed you were hearing from God, gone to the pastor for a confirmation, and been told you were wrong? What if they were wrong? If God is telling you something, you will not be excused because your pastor did not confirm it. The Lord is your Shepherd. The shepherd is not to be your lord.*

In driving home the message that they were appointed by God to rule over the flock and that the flock must be obedient to them, the Irwins would regularly quote biblical verse Hebrews 13:17 (KJV): *Obey those that have the rule over you, and submit yourselves; for they watch for your souls, as they that must give account, that they may do it with joy, and not with grief; for that is unprofitable for you.* In quoting the passage, the Irwins would tell their followers that "unprofitable" meant detrimental, and that if they did not obey the Irwins, it would be detrimental to the member's spiritual health.

Kristel now cited the same passage in proselytizing to her father that Jesus is the only head of the church. *When pastors are lifted up into the place of Sovereign authority over men's lives, thus usurping the place of Jesus and God's word over the lives of their sheep, this is idolatry . . .*

God does not want you to feel like you don't measure up, that you need to work harder to be up to snuff. God is not performance-based . . .

Galations 5:1 'Stand fast therefore in the liberty by which Christ has made us free, and do not be entangled again with a yoke of bondage . . . '

(MSG) Gal 5:1 'Christ has set us free to live a free life. So take your stand! Never again let anyone put a harness of slavery on you.' (See, it is not in reference to sin holding you captive. It is in reference to man-made and imposed rules.)

Kristel tried, that same day, to get through to Sarah, too, but rather than serve as an olive branch, Kristel's message only incensed her stepsister, who promptly shared it with Tiffanie.

Bruce had also shared Kristel's latest email with the young preacher. It triggered a twenty-three-page response from Tiffanie. She told Bruce that Kristel was either insulting his intelligence or trying to teach him something contrary to the word of God. She argued Kristel's email line by line, breaking down Bible verses and providing her own interpretations, which she deemed to be the truth. Tiffanie reasserted her position as *ruler* in the church and asserted that her job was to lead the flock as God directed her: *Sheep choose to follow the human shepherd that the Good Shepherd has given them.*

The Randallsville church handed Kristel something she had left behind long ago: hope.

"And the free time on Wednesday afternoons had a feeling reminiscent of a snow day when I was a kid. Still, I ached for my family," Kristel later recalled. "I missed them fiercely, and my greatest fear was that they were hurt by my actions."

Those in the new church prayed that the rest of Kristel's family would be freed from WLCC.

"I recall one Sunday finding a verse in Psalm 107 particularly strike me, regarding how God would deliver any who called on him from the depths of their despair. I prayed that God would reveal to my father just how deep the despair really was, knowing that he was deceived and couldn't really see his own despair."

No longer under the Irwins' control, Kristel slowly began to find herself. But this brought its own set of issues. Art was not happy with the "new" Kristel. One day, he shouted, "You used to be a Christian, but now you're a liberal!" as though politics and religion were synonymous. He told her she should've stayed at WLCC.

Hi, this is Luke. I just want to say thank you, I don't remember a time when I've been truly happy and peaceful. Last night was the happiest I've ever been, thank you so much! God gave me three things: I have a starting place, I am empty of the sin now and God can fill me up, and God said, "It is done." To Luke Leonard! I'm not hindered now, I have a chance to be one of those radical Christians. I was thinking last night about two things, before, I was floundering in the ocean, now it's like I'm standing on a boat, the ocean is still there but I've got a place to stand now. The other thing is when a sinner repents his name is shouted throughout heaven, and Pastor heard it! Thank you so much, it's finally real!!

—LUCAS LEONARD'S EMAIL
TO TRACI IRWIN, SEPTEMBER 25, 2014

Odd, thought Sarah, standing in the empty downstairs of her Clayville home. It was morning. Everyone was gone, but no one had an appointment. Where were they?

It was three fifteen in the afternoon before Bruce got home and told her they'd gone to the library. More irritated than curious, Sarah wanted to know, "What was everyone doing at the library?"

"Chris is watching a movie." Bruce kicked away the clothes piled at his feet as he shuffled to the living room. "Ezekiel is playing a game." He picked up a dirty shirt from the floor and tossed it aside. "And Luke is waiting in the van."

Sarah's eyes popped. "On the Kindle?"

"Yes." He nodded. Once up, once down.

"Watching porn!"

Bruce continued into the kitchen as if she'd said nothing.

Since Luke and Chris shared a bedroom, Luke had taken the walk-in closet and made it his space. It fit a recliner chair, and that was where he slept. Sarah was living in the attic with her kids, and in the summer of 2014, at Tiffanie's direction, Grace moved up there, too. The attic was comprised of two large rooms, two exit doors, and a window with no screen, allowing insects to fly around the kids' heads and food area.

The sisters became their own kidnappers, pushing furniture and boxes in front of one door. They padlocked the other door on both the outside and inside, and added a key lock on the outside, which they jammed with aluminum and superglue. They rarely went alone to the lower part of the house, and never alone to the second-floor bathroom. They took their meals to the attic to eat, where there was a Crock-Pot, microwave, and mini fridge. No running water, but they used bottled water.

The space reflected what was often blowing around Sarah's brain—a windstorm of discombobulated, religious-themed thoughts whirring around all day and into sleepless nights. She repeated the mantra "I choose JESUS JESUS JESUS JESUS!" in her head. The floor was a sea of mattresses crammed head to foot and side by side, covered in mismatched comforters, blankets, and quilts. There was a drum set and two couches on a dark gray carpet sprinkled with crumbs. The wall that separated the rooms was painted black, and words were painted across it haphazardly in glowing white. The only legible word was "FACE" in gigantic block letters, underlined twice.

Canvas oil paintings were the bulk of the wall decor, done by Sarah, a gifted artist. She loved guitars, and there were two leaning against the wall, plus a painting of guitars and a wall hanging that read "music." There was a painting of horses, and a horse figurine on a dresser. Next to it was a cross made of twigs and another that looked mass-produced.

There was a dresser with the standard female toiletries—sprays, lotions, nail polish, a round hairbrush, Grace's eyeglasses—all crammed together and stacked. Three other side-by-side dressers were plastered with tiny stickers. One was decorated with blue and green finger-paint designs of hearts, stars, and nondescript blobs.

In one corner, there was a pile of loose clothing waist-high, and clothing in boxes stacked nearly to the ceiling. There was a handmade wooden half wall smeared with marker in Sarah's favorite color of tropical blue, and a handmade wooden counter stained with grape jelly and stacked with condiments, food staples, and a whole watermelon. Cooked sausages were left on an electric grill. Perishable food sat out beside pots and pans and plastic bags overflowing with bottles and cans. The place was overrun with bulk packages of paper towels, toilet paper, and baby wipes. In the middle of the room was a pink potty-training seat.

Sarah's four children stayed as captives in this space, their wider surroundings mostly a mystery to them. Grace and her nephew, six-year-old Gabriel, shared a computer and sat next to each other at desks with schoolbooks and Bibles, studying and praying for hours, often into the next morning. Behind them the carpet was littered with toys, cups, empty drink bottles, a broken cardboard box, a cupcake tin, and a ten-gallon storage tote filled with dirty dishes. And there was Ivy in her high chair.

Grace's move to the attic was a big adjustment for Sarah. Not because she was new to change—that had become a theme in her life. Sarah was new to settling down. She fought off melancholy from missing the party life, despite calling it a *horrible time of hopeless wandering*. And she was still legally married. Although she had picked up divorce papers and begun the process, it was stalled as she struggled with the complicated language on the forms. But Grace's presence threw a wrench into Sarah's life in the attic. Sarah was not Grace's mom, and Grace was not a little girl. She didn't know how to interact with a fourteen-year-old and found having her up there to be a huge responsibility. Plus, the close quarters made it difficult for the sisters to communicate about private matters. Little ears heard everything.

Sarah enlisted Grace's help in taking care of her children and then became frustrated when Grace couldn't do more. But Sarah was more annoyed with her parents, particularly her mother, with whom there had developed a clear divide—certainly not helped, and more probably aided, by the Irwins' decades-long insistence that Debi was possessed by a lying demon. One day at church, Joe preached about honoring and respecting parents, and on the way home, Sarah tried to practice it. She forced herself to pray for her mother. Debi hadn't been feeling well, and she prayed Jesus would heal her. She even offered to make Debi tea and get her ibuprofen, though she really didn't want to do either.

In Sarah's mind, her parents were always up to something, staging the room or discussions with intent to get Sarah angry, placing items on counters just to mess with her. If they were acting lovey-dovey, something was up. If they stopped talking when she came into the room, they were plotting. And she was convinced they were plotting in concert with Luke and Chris.

Sarah went downstairs one morning, and Luke offered her a cigarette. She thought she heard God say, "Use caution." Luke read Sarah his school report, a gung ho piece on legalizing weed. As he read, she ignored every word, instead leaning forward and peering into his eyes. She interrupted to say, "Your eyes are red."

"I've been smoking weed." He laughed, as if he were joking. "What do you mean they're red?"

She stared with her mouth half open, her eyes darting back and forth, looking at each of his pupils. "You're not the same Luke. You're a new creation."

Luke would turn nineteen on November 8, 2014. He was, perhaps, not a new creation but ready to break out and be the person he'd always been—the person hiding inside him for nearly two decades. He was growing into a man, and the church couldn't stop that. He would find ways to mature within the confines of church and home while secretly plotting escape from his tightly controlled world and mind.

Two days before Luke's birthday, Jayden invited everyone to his place for a celebration of Luke's and Ada's birthdays. Sarah wasn't sure it was a good idea for her to go, writing Traci that she worried it would *open the door to any agreements with the devil.* She prayed about it, solicited Traci's opinion, and finally reached peace. She resolved that if she went to the party, she would read the Bible aloud to everyone.

Luke got throwing knives as a present.

Thwack! It was a smooth release, not a flick. A flick made the knife spin too much. The ones that missed the wall fell to the floor with a clang. Luke's walk-in closet wasn't big enough for knife throwing, so he did it in Chris's space. One wall was half grasshopper green across the top and coffee-colored on the bottom. He aimed the knives at the top, which became riddled with slats. The lower wall got sliced up, too. Knife throwing took a lot of practice.

He'd written "LUKE'S ROOM!" on the green wall. Chris's space had an acoustic guitar, an electric guitar, and a vintage wooden tabletop piano. In Luke's walk-in closet, next to the filthy hunter-green recliner where he slept, a sinking gorilla helium balloon came to rest on a wooden nightstand fit for the dump. On the stand was a 1950s paperback book called *My Side of the Mountain*, about an unhappy teen who feels trapped in his parents' home with his eight siblings and so runs off to live alone in the woods, learning independence and survival. Next to the book were a two-liter bottle of orange soda, four lighters, and a bong. And a well-loved brown teddy bear. Behind the chair was a suitcase, an item for travel in a young man's world where there was none.

When the sound of knives could no longer be heard, and everyone in the lower house left to go to the library—or maybe the thrift store, or park—Grace and Sarah ventured to the cellar to talk privately. They'd been down there a while, and Sarah was starting to get nervous about her kids upstairs by themselves. She felt a physical pressure, which she attributed to Satan making her worry, so she talked herself out of giving in to fear. She rebuked the devil aloud and then thought she heard a voice whisper, "Demon setup."

Sarah remembered she'd seen a book in the house. She couldn't recall its name, or what it was about, but that didn't matter. It wasn't the Bible and, per Tiffanie, no one in that house should've been reading anything but the Bible.

Sarah rushed upstairs to check on the kids. Finding them all content, she went back downstairs to lead a room-to-room effort to cast out cowering demons. Grace went to their father's office and performed a spiritual cleansing. When Sarah got to the older boys' rooms, her sister joined her. They walked around the room and consecrated it to

Jesus, praying and speaking in tongues. They named demons of sexual perversion and immorality, cast them out and forbade them to return, and then proceeded to their mother's room.

"It's weird," Sarah commented, as she made her way around Debi's room. "There's this weird air in here, like . . . a sleepy, comforting air."

"It's okay," said Grace.

But Sarah didn't think so. She decided it was a demon and shouted, "I bind you, spirit of slumber and sleepiness!"

They headed to Grace's sleeping area.

"We take authority over sexual sin, sexual perversion, molestation, masturbation, fear, worry, and anxiety."

As Sarah quietly praised with her arms raised, she felt a hand in hers and pressure on her fingers. Peace overcame her. Then she thought she saw a black "X," as though marking a spot. The book! She went back to fetch it, and then rushed downstairs with it. The rest of the family had just walked in the door and quickly dispersed, leaving Debi by herself.

"Whose book is this?" Sarah asked her mother.

Debi shrugged.

Sarah marched to the laundry room after Chris. "Is this yours?"

Luke peeked out from behind the washing machine where he was smoking but didn't say anything.

"We need to get rid of it," she lectured. "No one should be spending time reading anything other than the Bible."

Neither boy said a word. They both walked upstairs to the kitchen, where Zeke had joined his mother.

Sarah was right behind them. "We need to get rid of it."

Luke, standing near a cupboard, now tucked his head to the side of it. Chris grabbed his Bible, sat down, and began reading.

"We can shred it," offered Debi.

Ezekiel's eyes lit up. He needed no further invitation to spring up and start tearing out the pages. As he did, Sarah repeated the words that she and Grace had been chanting in the upstairs rooms, the part about taking authority over sexual sin. That wasn't what she'd intended to chant, but it was stuck in her head from earlier. Once she caught her mistake, she kept chanting it anyway. Chris began reading louder, and Luke scurried out of the room.

Sarah later ran the scene past Traci via text, telling her Luke was acting *super weird*. He went past her, but way around her, and darted upstairs. She was afraid he was going to get his knives and bring them downstairs, so she ran to avoid him. She rebuked the devil. Then, out walked Luke from their mother's room, and he wasn't carrying knives but a Bible.

Sarah made her way back upstairs and sang in the stairwell and shouted, "Yea! I'm here for Jesus!" She praised her way to the attic and made up her own song. "Your name is a fine, fine wine on my lips, Jesus, Jesus, Jesus, Jesus. Your name is a fire! Your name is a fire! Your name is a fire branded on my heart, oh, your name is a fire!"

Later that night, Sarah typed her daily report to Traci, recognizing that it was filled with anger at her parents and Luke. Eleven-year-old Ezekiel wrote in his notebook, too. It was full of the teachings reinforced every day he was in that redbrick building: sexual immorality was the issue, stubborn rebellion made him stupid, and he must repent from witchcraft. He wrote that it was a secret that made him a huge target, and he would pay the price.

Bruce wrote in his journal, too, to be handed over to Tiffanie. He repented for giving in to his family because of *pouty face, begging etc.*, for accumulating and hanging on to stuff, and for not fully submitting to those who had authority over him. He repented for thoughts of wanting to have a normal life.

Midnight passed, and Sarah's oldest, Gabriel, was still at his desk, in plaid shorts and a muscle shirt, making corrections on his schoolwork. There were just a couple left. His mom asked him to break a few minutes to pray. After his hands were folded for several seconds,

Gabriel's dimple on his right cheek deepened as he looked up at his mother and, smiling, said, "I saw the side of Jesus's face, and then a car driving, and it went *screech!* and stopped."

Her son had had a vision. Sarah was so excited. "Remember what Pastor Tiffanie said on Wednesday—that if you see something like that, it might be a message, so pray right away."

Together, they prayed.

Luke and Chris were best friends. Luke was known to test the limits of his behavior for self-amusement, and he liked to do what he called "popping Chris's space bubble." He would come from behind and jump Chris and put him in a bear hug. Chris was a private, closed-off guy. Fully aggravated, he would wrestle from the hold, leaving Luke howling so hard he could barely catch his breath.

On one such occasion, neither boy noticed Sarah eyeballing them from across the room, her eyebrows inward and lips pursed. Her gaze lingered too long in a cold stare, until she screamed, "Leave him alone!"

Luke clutched his stomach with one hand. It was so amusing to him.

Sarah tore into him. "It's not appropriate. Get off him. Give him his space."

Chris walked away, and she followed, waiting until they were alone and no one else could hear. "Don't let Luke do that. You need to stand up for yourself."

Chris nodded. "Thanks."

Luke also pestered his littlest brother, Zeke, by shooting him with spitballs from a dart gun. Ezekiel would do a pratfall and roll around giggling like it was the greatest fun—until it wasn't. If Ezekiel was grumpy, he'd stop short and burst out in anger. That's what it sometimes took to get Luke to cut him a break, or Bruce would have to step in and tell him to knock it off.

Sarah couldn't stand that show, either. She hated the thought of Luke with any kind of gun. The atmosphere between the two grew so contentious that Luke began sidestepping Sarah. When they passed in the hallway, he avoided eye contact. Sarah asked her father if he would build a foyer at the bottom of the stairs, where they could put coats and shoes. It would be a completely separate, private entrance. She wouldn't have to pass anyone. Once her father agreed, she sought Tiffanie's permission to move forward with the project.

In February 2015, Debi suffered a heart attack, sending her to the hospital. Her estranged siblings attributed it to stress caused by the Irwins forcing the siblings apart by their practice of shunning. Tiffanie scoffed at that, attributing Debi's health problems to her rebellious, lying heart. The preacher prayed for her, though—prayed several days at the Word of Life Building—and Debi was convinced her surgery went smoothly because of it. Tiffanie sought a personal invitation to the hospital to pray for Debi, and when it didn't come, she invited herself and then reprimanded Bruce for having to do so.

Soon after Debi was sent home to recover, she was lying on the couch when Sarah bounded over and appealed to her to be a better person so the demons would stop making her sick. "Whatever it is you need to do to get right with God, you should get on it!" Her tight, black curls danced with animation. She squatted near her mother's head. "Whenever you're reading the Bible, really pay attention and listen in. On Sundays, really listen to what's being said so you can bring it home and apply it."

Debi's eyes were barely open and watching Sarah's bobbing shoulder, the only body part visible from her position on the couch.

"I really love you," said Sarah, "and I don't want you to die."

Just then, Bruce and the boys walked through the front door. Did her mother all of a sudden look sad? Subtle, thought Sarah, but she was sure her mother was putting on an act to get their attention. She leaped up and shooed them out of the room. "We're having a mommy-daughter talk."

In March, Grace celebrated her fifteenth birthday in the attic. Jayden was there, and he helped with one of her school lessons before they went downstairs for presents. Sarah longed for Jayden to get back into the church. She spent a lot of time trying to coax him, but he couldn't do it because he traveled too much for work.

At the party, Sarah's oldest boy was full of energy as everyone crammed into the living room for a spot. "Mom, can I sit with Luke?" Gabriel asked excitedly.

Luke was sitting right there, and he'd heard. Sarah was filled with apprehension but didn't want to hurt his feelings. She wondered if anyone noticed how long it took for her to say, "Sure." She would keep a close eye on Gabriel. What a relief when, after only a minute or so, he scooted off his uncle's lap to go do something else.

The beautiful spring weather outside their window that day got Sarah daydreaming. She longed for a trip to the ocean. She wanted to take the kids, and Grace, of course. They could go to Portland, Maine, or Virginia somewhere, maybe for a couple of days. Jayden got car rental discounts through work, and that made a summer trip to the beach feasible. Except—she would have to wait for Jesus to say it was okay.

That spring, the attic got a cleaning. As the kids pared down the toys in the toy box, Sarah went downstairs to do dishes. She was praising Jesus as she washed and got about halfway through the bucket when she heard noise from the living room. Sarah peeked around the corner and saw that the rest of the family had returned. Debi was on the couch with her eyes closed. Sarah rushed up and jiggled her frantically. "Are you awake?"

She wasn't sleeping, her mother mumbled.

Sarah tossed back her head and let out a loud *whoosh* of breath. She was worried that, with their mother asleep, Luke would sneak onto her phone to look up *whatever nasty*. She texted Traci about the scene. She frequently shared the minutiae of her days with Traci. Bruce did the same with Tiffanie. The pastor had been working with him individually and set a goal for Bruce to complete five hours of Bible reading a day. He was to text Tiffanie those Bible reading times daily, as well as details about family matters. Tiffanie counseled Bruce that he was the key for demon-controlled Luke and Debi to be saved. She hammered home the message that his *obedience* would be three-quarters of the battle needed to win his family.

April brought more illness. Luke was having a lot of knee pain in the spot where he'd broken it a couple of years earlier on the mini-bike. A medical scan showed an anomaly, and doctors said there was a slight chance it was cancer. They scheduled him for further testing. But one thing Luke did not schedule: time for Tiffanie to pray for him. Strike two. The Leonard family had slighted her again, and she would not soon—if ever—forget.

In January, Tiffanie had prophesized cancer, and this, she proclaimed, was her prophecy coming true. She took it as a personal affront that the Leonards did not consult her on a diagnosis and treatment plan. She let Bruce have it. *How many times have I said that shaking was coming . . . ?* she texted him, warning that God was stepping back and allowing consequences to come. These afflictions stemmed from Debi being a liar, she pounded into her phone, and liars cannot enter heaven. She reminded Bruce these edicts were not hers but God's. In a flurry of texts, she vented suspicions that Debi had been avoiding going to church, that she didn't want to be there and neither did Luke. She made an impassioned plea that Luke had *dangerous cancer* that was killing him, and reprimanded Bruce for not taking her seriously.

Luke had not asked Tiffanie to pray for him *as the Bible commands (James 5)*. There should have been weeping, fasting, mourning, a call for repentance. *Why is Debi treating me like I'm a prayer line that she doesn't even want to talk to?* Bruce's *precious son* was dying. Witch-craft and demons were involved. *I have the answers, and all you have to do is humble yourself a little!*

At home, Sarah reinforced the message, accosting her mother one morning as she rested on the couch. "You let them get away with everything!" She blamed her mother for failing to get a grip on the children's rebellion, which she believed to be the cause of the spate of illness and disease. "We have got to take what's being warned seriously because if we don't, it will come to pass just like every other prophecy that has been spoken to this family."

Debi looked at her daughter strangely.

"Something has to change!" Sarah sat facing her, and continued. "We have to wake up! The longer that nothing is done and the rebellion stays, the more death it breeds! Your actions are wreaking havoc in the lives of your children. You may think you've done a better job with these guys than with us older three, but I'm sorry, I just don't think that's true at all. They just know how to be a lot sneakier and manipulative and play 'the good boys,' all the while doing whatever they want to do." She stood and yelled a finale, flailing her arms. "And you're letting them get away with it! You can't live vicariously through sin anymore! It has to stop! You're breeding death and destruction! It's *murderous*!" She paced in front of the couch and muttered, "I knew you were doing that even as a young girl. I counted on it to help me get away with stuff."

"What do you mean?"

"What do you think I mean?" Her question was met with silence. "Maybe you call it something different. I call it living vicariously. Either way, it's sin! And is something to be repented of, and if that makes you mad, you have to realize it's a demon that you're hanging on to, so just repent!"

The next Sunday, after service, Bruce ushered Luke to the front of the small sanctuary to be counseled.

"What did you come up for?" Tiffanie asked, as though she didn't know.

Luke's head was slumped more than ever. "Um. I know I'm being rebellious and a lot of things. I think I know what it is, but . . ."

"You think what?"

"It's in the . . . in the reading and, um, grabbing hold of God's word." Joe's and Dan's electric guitars blared only steps away.

"Can you turn your head towards me?" asked Tiffanie. "Because I can't hear you very well. The reading and what?"

"Um, in reading, for, um, paying attention, for healing. And for not doing all three hours."

"Is that all you came up for prayer for?"

Bruce stood to Luke's right, Seth to his left. They formed a circle, with Tiffanie across from Luke and Linda next to her.

"For my leg, too. For the possibility for healing."

This was a slow process. Tiffanie waited long periods for Luke to speak, but most times, he didn't. She egged him on. "So why were you being stubborn and rebellious and not coming up?"

The only sound was the earsplitting guitars.

"Would you not just try to think of an answer and just tell me what it was?"

"Because I know that it's . . . um . . . I know it's, um, because of my rebellion, and I didn't want to open up and talk about my rebellion. I know it was . . . I know it has to do with the judgment."

Tiffanie quizzed him, and he eventually sputtered, "I was just talking about . . . as far as the sickness, um, three people have been sick in church so far."

"This tells you you've sinned *how*?"

"I think it's judgment for my rebellion."

"What rebellion? How did you know? What did you know? Who told you there would be judgment for rebellion?"

"From . . ."

"From?"

"Here . . ."

"Who?"

"Here. You," he said. "And in my reading, what I do, I know there is judgment for rebellion."

As the large men played their music, a handful of disciples were in the rows of seating. They could see the back of Luke, his faded blue jeans and black checkered shirt. Some were leaning over at the waist, heads bowed in prayer. One was standing, bowed and praying, her arms outstretched. Ezekiel was standing, too, but wiggling back and forth and whacking his hands against his legs. Sarah was off to the side, standing with Ivy on her back in a baby carrier. Her head, too, was bowed. She twisted her body to the music, but her feet stayed planted. Grace was in the last row on the far right, wearing a light blue jean shirt. Her head never lifted as she moved from sitting to standing. Her hair was twisted, tied, and pulled to one side.

"Okay," Tiffanie continued, "so you're telling me that you would rather die of a disease than discuss your rebellion. Did I get that right? Okay, I got that right?"

The pastor's derision worsened as the clock ticked. "What are you working yourself up for? If you're feeling something, that's one thing, but don't stand there and work yourself up. Just quit it. If you're feeling bad, I don't care how you act, but you came up here and you thought, 'I'm going to say something about God and about Bible reading so that I don't have to confess the real issues.' You stood there in front of me and thought that. Now you're going to mock me? If you're real, that's fine, but don't. It's not going to make the appearance look more believable to me. So you have a . . . a sickness that may be incurable by the doctors. We'll know more later. And all you care about is not wanting to discuss rebellion. Uh, does that seem normal to you?" When he didn't respond, she lambasted him. "What do you think is wrong with you?"

After some time, he spit out, "I listen to demons?"

"You listen to demons. Okay. What demons?"

"Telling me about other people. Listen and go with those."

"That sounds like a joke to me," Tiffanie ridiculed. "You listen to demons tell you about other people and you go with those. How do you go with them? You're not a little baby. Stop talking like one. You know what you do. The time for games is over. Do you understand? It might be too late. How many times did I tell you that God said it was the last time? It's time for you to quit this crap and really, finally, actually tell me what is the big deal. Before it's definitely too late. Because it might be already. But, you know, there's always a chance. But you're still acting like 'I'm gonna give her a little bit here. I'm just gonna throw her some crumbs so she'll get off my back.' Give me a break." She tossed back her head. "Give me a break. What are the thoughts you've been thinking? Give me a break here."

"That it's all . . . a joke," said Luke.

"Well, no one's ever heard that one before," Tiffanie sarcastically shot. "Okay, go on. It's really gonna be a joke when, you know, you think it's a joke what the doctor said, too. Because you can't see it, it's not really in you? Is that your point of view for that, too? That it was just a joke. It's not really there. You don't really have a problem. It's not really gonna take you out. Is that your mentality? 'God will fix me through somebody else, like he always does, and I'll stay in my rebellion.' Is that what you're thinking? Why? Who do you think God is gonna fix you through? Be honest." She paused. "Who do you think God's gonna fix you through? Who do you think's gonna fix you? Tell me."

"I'm hoping . . ."

"Come on, I know what you're gonna say. You might as well spit it out. You're hoping that . . . ," she prompted.

"The doctor will be able to do it. I won't have to repent."

"Well, yeah. What are you gonna do? Don't you realize these things progress rapidly? What happens when you go there—what happens if he says it's incurable? What then?"

"I don't know."

"No, you don't know, really? Really? After all this time you don't know? Are you serious right now?"

"I just keep on pretending it's not real, so I still don't have to repent."

"Why don't you wanna repent so bad? I mean, what's . . . what's so tempting about the other side? What's so exciting about how fast you're gonna meet your Maker? What's so exciting?"

"Nothing."

"Nothing? What do you think he's gonna say if you keep up with that mentality?"

Luke fished in his head for an answer. "I'm lazy?" But that only invited derision.

"I'm sure he thinks you're a bit more than laziness going on here."

"Please look at Pastor," Linda admonished in a sharp tone. "Please show her respect."

Luke seemed to not understand what Tiffanie wanted to hear. He was giving half answers, and she wasn't satisfied with them. Linda began chanting what sounded like the words, "You're gonna die. You're gonna die," in a cadence that sounded like buzzing flies, with the first two words strung together, and the accent on "die."

"What was the word that you got about this situation?" Tiffanie prodded.

"I'm not remembering," Luke said softly, unable to bring his head up to meet her eyes.

"Really? Someone prophesized about your life ending and you don't remember? Luke, what kind of game are you playing?" She glared at him with utter disdain. "Luke, let go of the hateful attitude and look at me. What game are you playing?"

"I guess that . . ."

"You're being ridiculous. You actually are one of those rare people

that gets to know their life might just end soon and you're acting ridiculous. You're standing here in stubborn rebellion. You actually get a
chance. Who gets that? You told me this is happening because you've
been rebellious. You told me that. Okay, well why don't you stop?
What's the problem? What game are you getting from your choices?"

"I don't, I don't understand why I'm staying in this. I don't, I don't
understand why I'm staying in this. I don't . . . I don't understand . . ."

"Do you know how many times you've lied to me? You're listening,
right?"

His voice quivered. "I'm not hearing it good, though."

"You've lied to me with almost every word you've ever spoken to
me. There's been some kind of lie in it. And I told you, like a year ago,
that God was saying that until you confess that one evil thing that had
been in your meditation, you are never gonna be free. And you refused
even then."

"I thought that was."

"You thought what was?"

"The—the hateful thoughts against you and Pastor [Jerry]."

"Oh yeah, that was it, but you surely didn't say what those evil
thoughts were, now, did you? Just like you're not confessing what
the real issue is now, even though you wanna give me some sort of
general confession. You're not actually being honest. Even in your
confessions, even in your most repentive moments, you weren't completely honest. And now here you are doing the same thing. I told
you, if you didn't repent and confess that evil thing, God told you—
you wouldn't be free. So you just decided to be rebellious again? Is
that what I just saw?"

Luke began to shake. His head sunk farther, and he wore a twisted
expression.

"Luke, stop it. Please stop it. You're putting on a face because you
know your dad will allow the face. You surely didn't have that look
on your face before he walked over. Stop it. Your life is at stake. Stop

acting like this. Stop it. That false demon of sympathy that you have wrapped around you is not gonna save you, do you understand that? You're gonna die if you listen to demons. Stop. I told you, you need to confess that one thing. That was six, eight months ago, a year ago. Joe gave you a prophecy a few months after that, about this! You told me, 'I think this is happening because I was rebellious.' That's what you just told me. You think it's judgment. That's what you just told me, right? Joe gave you a very specific word, a very clear, specific word with no two ways about it. And here it is happening and you're telling me you don't remember."

Bruce tried to help Luke find a response. "Look, I thought, okay . . . about . . . about six months ago, whatever it was, whenever you stopped texting Joe, Pastor texted something to you, and then you stopped at that point and then . . . Is that it?"

"I don't"—Luke tripped over his words—"I don't think so."

Traci joined the circle. "Can I interrupt for one second? Yes? Something that I see, something that I know is in you is a demon of rebellion. I can see it. I've seen it. It took me all the time that Pastor Tiffanie said, 'Come up front,' and you rebelled, because you knew that you felt it right here. When you rebelled, it took all the time I prayed my heart, gave it everything I had for that demon to lift off of you long enough for you to obey. But I'm telling you, Luke, if you don't renounce that thing, I don't know if you'll make it through this. Do you understand?"

Tiffanie joined in. "If you had not come up here, you would have died, do you understand? You're playing with fire. Listen, I don't even know . . . I told you, God already warned you, that there would be a point I was too late, and yet I'm gonna fight till the end. And you're still being a fool?"

"Listen to me," said Traci. "Listen. You have to renounce that thing. You have to renounce it, and you have to, you have to renounce it, and you have to turn away from it and walk the other way, because right here is where that demon wants to be. And right over your shoulder is the spirit of death. Do you understand me? Luke, I'm telling you, even if this comes back that this is not life threatening, they can deal with it, whatever, I'm telling you what I see."

"The spirit . . . I'm telling you what I see, too," added Tiffanie. "If this isn't it, it will be something else."

"The devil wants to take you out," said Traci. "You have to renounce it."

As Dave sauntered into the circle, hands in pockets, Linda walked away from it.

Tiffanie continued. "When you said you were confessing and getting your life right, you would not confess that one thing. You refused. You've said hatred towards me and Pastor. Okay, but you know full well that there were specifics about that that you refused to confess. You know it full well. And the Holy Spirit told you that if you did not confess that, you would never be free. And you chose not to confess, and you're still bound by the demon of rebellion. It's in you, Lucas. You have to renounce it."

Luke was biting his lower lip.

"It's inviting the spirit of death to you," said Tiffanie, "whether through this, or through something else. We've seen it a while now. And now this happens, and you've got a very specific word. And I cannot believe you say you don't remember what Joe told you. I just don't believe you. I'm not saying I think you're lying, but I'm saying I don't believe it in the sense of—that is unbelievable. That is unbelievable that you would let the demon control you so much that you can't remember," she taunted. "It's unbelievable. You have a problem, Luke. Don't stare at me with demon rebellion. Renounce it. You have to renounce it, and you have to renounce it by confessing the evil that you had in your heart first. And after that, then maybe you can hear from the Holy Spirit so he can renew your mind to what it is that he said to you, so that you can face it, so that you can get past this."

Tiffanie and Traci worked in concert to compel him to say more, but he struggled to find words. No words met their need for the correct answer, and he just didn't know what that was.

"You're gonna die. You're gonna die," the women chanted.

"So is it time, Luke? Are you gonna continue to tempt the spirit of God?" asked Tiffanie.

"The hatred against my parents?" Luke tried.

"I told you, it was about hatred against me and Pastor. There's been something that you refuse to confess to this day. Even though you've used your confession as something that it isn't. You still have confessed a lot of things, but you refuse to confess this one to this day."

He was motionless in front of Tiffanie's animation, her hands thrusting in front of him. "Luke, the spirit is telling me that in the next few minutes I have to transition to the next thing. You can't stand here, and just stand here, and just stand here. Okay? I can't stand here for much longer. I need you to do what you need to do. It's what he's telling me. You don't wanna miss your window of opportunity. Do you understand that?"

Luke's eyes welled with tears.

"So you're just gonna hold it out? That's all you're gonna do? We're just gonna stand here for five minutes until the opportunity for me to pray for you for healing is passed? Do you understand what you're doing?"

Bruce jumped in. "Luke, we need you. We need you in our family. You just gotta. Please, just trust God. Bring it out and trust God."

"You're gonna die. You're gonna die."

"So what was it?" Tiffanie goaded.

"Look at Pastor," snapped Linda. "Look at her when you speak."

"For crying out loud, Luke. Luke! Just say it," Tiffanie's voice elevated. "Would you stop this? I'm not down there."

"Sorry," said Luke, and burst out crying. "I thought you guys were being unfair as far as, like, the school stuff."

"Okay, just keep going, because that's not all. I'm telling you, don't try to, don't— If you wanna start with the easy stuff and work your way down, go ahead. But don't skip it this time."

"I resented that, uh, our family, uh . . . It seemed like our family was kind of singled out to . . . for, uh, for discipline stuff. Um, I resented being in the small room."

"Small room? What's that?" asked Tiffanie, her impatience mixed with disgust.

"The electrical room."

"The electrical room?"

"In the hallway across from the old learning center."

"Okay, when were you in there?" Her voiced dripped with condescension.

"Uh, I was in kindergarten, or no, um, first or second grade." Pastor Jerry made him study in the electrical room after accusing him of failing his tests on purpose, he said, adding, "Um, I resented that we, uh, were kept so late afterwards. Um, after our tests were done."

"Lucas," said Linda sharply, "are you afraid of what your father's going to hear out of your mouth?"

Luke said yes, but Tiffanie said otherwise. "He's not afraid, but he's afraid of, um, he thinks that if he tells the truth right now then his, his ruses won't work anymore. That's what he thinks. He's not afraid something will happen to him; he's just afraid he won't be able to control his father anymore." Tiffanie insisted Luke disclose more.

"Um, I . . . I used to try to, um, play games with Pastor [Jerry] as far as the schoolwork and get mad when they didn't . . . when he wouldn't go for them. Um, I uh, I used to rebel on purpose. I, I used to do things on purpose trying to get away with them. Um . . . and . . . um, I resented when I got caught doing them. Um . . . I . . . uhh . . ."

"*You're gonna die. You're gonna die.*"

"Spit it out, because I've got things to do."

"Uhh . . ."

Luke, with his head continually lowered, inspired Joe's wrath. He stormed into the circle and demanded, "Look at her when you're talking."

Luke straightened. "I used to wait until he left the room so that I could talk to Mrs. Irwin in the cellar. Um, uhh . . ."

"Just keeping talking, Luke," his father prodded.

"I tried— I would work up Mother and Dad to go against them, so . . . go against Pastor and you over the school stuff so that I could feel like I was in control. Uh, like tell them lies so that they would be on my side and go against you guys. Um."

"*You're gonna die.*" It got louder. More people joined in. "*You're gonna die.*"

"Jesus Christ wants you to live!" shouted Bruce.

"All right, I'm gonna have to leave in about one, two minutes, God's telling me," said Tiffanie. "Unless he changes his mind. If he says something good. But I'm just telling you, you deliberately said the things you thought would be the least offensive to your dad. You're still playing games. Say the rest of it."

"I just . . . I would try to make Mother and Dad feel guilty over, um, what they would allow, um, Pastor and you, uh, to do with the school stuff."

"So? Go on. What did you do as far as hatred toward me and Pastor? I'm telling you, I'm not gonna stand here much longer, and if you won't say it now, we'll just have to get together another time when everybody in the whole room isn't waiting. But you're not gonna get away with this, Luke."

"You're gonna wish them evil?" asked Bruce. "Like, wish they'll drop dead, or anything like that?"

"And when we were in the other schoolroom, I used to imagine that Pastor would, uh, while I was doing schoolwork, that he would be on the floor dead. And, uh, I would hope that's what would happen."

"Okay," said Tiffanie.

"Um . . . I would hope that, uh, you and Pastor would get really sick so that school and church would be canceled. Me and Mother would kinda side together against Pastor and you, and against Dad to get him against you guys so, so that we could leave, um, church and school."

"Right," mocked Tiffanie. "How did you guys do that? What were your words? What were your actions? What were your words and actions to try to make that happen?"

Luke's mouth was now spewing answers, but it didn't matter. Tiffanie accepted none of it. "You just told lies."

Lucas was still crying. "I thought you guys were, um, uh . . . talking, um, about us, like discussing . . ."

"No, rephrase that. You 'think' that we were."

"I think that you guys were, like, talking about us and discussing what, um, you were gonna do next week for . . . or, like, um, keeping us behind on purpose as punishment."

"That's really funny to me considering all the work I put in to try to get you up to par when you didn't wanna be. All right. Go on, though. That's not what I'm talking about. You thought very specific hateful thoughts, and you need to confess them. So you can go sit down. Maybe you'll, you know, I don't know, maybe later God will tell me to spend some hours with you, but I don't know. There was a window of opportunity today, and all you wanted to do was be stubborn and rebellious. God was here to heal and you stood back there for a half an hour, an hour, while he . . . while he waited. And all you have to do is confess and forsake sin and break free of demons before I can pray for you. And you don't want to do that because you're letting the devil tell you what you want."

"Please look at Pastor!" Linda snapped. "Show her the honor she deserves! Stand up straight!"

"Are you gonna say anything else? Because I'm going over there if you're not." Tiffanie pointed to the other side of the room. "Are you going to or not? Don't just stand there and stare at me. Tell me if you're gonna say anything. Or, at the floor I should say. Are you going to or not? You know you're not gonna get away with it."

Turning her attention to Bruce, Tiffanie said he needed to read his Bible and "push it down Luke's throat." Bruce was the key, she said. He needed to take charge. "You cannot allow demons anymore to run the show. You just can't. And you're dealing with a boy with a demon who's willing to let it. He's got it in him now."

Ivy was crying that mysterious baby cry; uncomfortable, hungry, or tired. Worshippers were crying and praying.

"Yeah, he didn't confess what he was supposed to," Tiffanie concluded, "and then he didn't need the other word. He didn't need the word, so I'm just gonna pray for you again," she told Bruce. "Okay?" She squeezed her eyes and outstretched her arms. "Jesus, I just ask you for strength. Strengthen him. Strengthen him by your spirit and his inner man, oh God. And rise, rise up in him. . . ."

Sarah was on a whirlwind cleaning expedition, and in the middle, it struck her—lustful thoughts of Joe. It was intense for a bit. She pushed away the feeling and then confessed to Traci. She sent Traci dozens of pictures of the cleaning that went on over several days. In almost every photo that included Grace, the teenager was sitting at the same desk, on the computer or writing in her notebook, but she was wearing different clothes, indicating she'd at least taken a break to change clothes on different days.

On the final day of cleaning, Sarah exhausted herself. Grace turned on the vacuum, and Sarah fell asleep on the play castle floor. Shortly after, Grace fell asleep, too, with Ivy. When she awoke, she realized the baby wasn't wearing a diaper. Reality hit—Grace had done something terrible. Lying with Ivy without a diaper was molestation in the eyes of the church. She told the church leadership about it but kept it from Sarah.

After their naps, the young women asked their father to take them to the store, because Sarah's license had been suspended. Debi offered to drive but didn't tell them she'd invited Luke. Sarah was uncomfortable with that. She pretended to be too busy to go when she found out and then waited for Bruce take them when he got home. Sarah threw on a pair of jeans and selected one of her several identical bohemian sling bags—blue, red, or beige—that hung on the wall and got in the car with her dad. Walking around in public never felt good to her anymore. She could sense gross eyes on her, lusting for her, making her, as she would say, "awkwarded out."

After getting home that night, to decompress, Sarah painted. She missed doing that. There was little time for it anymore. Then she watched online videos and learned how to do cornrows in her girls' hair. The rest of the night she filled with prayer, Bible study, and her report to Traci. She was awake all night, going to sleep after five o'clock in the morning, and when she finally did, Grace was still up studying. Grace had just spent three days studying two lessons, and Sarah was miffed, because it meant less help with the kids. It was the kids who always took the brunt of her discontent. Sarah was increasingly short-tempered and either silently seething or lashing out. Her daughter Ada was getting spanked harder and harder for being disobedient in any way. Even arguing would earn her a walloping so hard it stung Sarah's hand and reddened her palm. Sarah seemed proud of that, sure to include in her updates to Traci how Ada *got it good*.

With Sunday worship now lasting eight hours and sometimes into the next morning, Sarah wasn't getting the kids home until eleven o'clock at night or later. After that, Gabriel still had Scripture writing to complete. Sometimes, it would take the first grader until two thirty in the morning. At breakfast, Gabriel was up reciting Scripture from memory, sitting beside a pipe through the ceiling with foam insulation hardened in a spew at the top.

One day in early June, Grace came rushing upstairs. She had gone to the kitchen for a glass of water, but Chris was there, and they would've been alone, so she'd scurried away.

A bit later, Grace went downstairs again and did a look-around to let Sarah know what everyone was doing. She reported, winded, that their mother, Luke, and Ezekiel were in the living room, and Ezekiel was under a blanket, and it looked like he was masturbating. The two reported their findings to Traci.

Later, Sarah went downstairs. Her father was there and acting weird, she thought, talking down to her. She asked him directly, "Did I offend you in any way?"

Bruce returned her question with a quizzical look.

After Sarah went back to the attic, Grace snuck downstairs alone. She again relayed her findings: the boys were supposed to be cleaning, but only Ezekiel was, and he was talking back and being disrespectful. Debi was hollering about maggots in the garbage.

Sarah made an excuse to go downstairs. "It feels really fake down here," she came out and said to her mother, "like you're trying to cover something up."

"Maggots?" Debi responded.

Sarah texted Traci that everyone's *masks were tightly and securely in place, trying to lure me into their lie that everything is fine, but attempting to joke around with me.*

She bought paper plates and plasticware. Not having dishes to wash would mean fewer trips to the first floor of the house.

Frances Bernard was walking to the Leonard home at the same time Debi, Grace, Sarah and her kids were arriving with Bruce in his car. Bruce went straight inside, but Sarah stopped to say hello. She hadn't seen Frances in a while. As it turned out, Frances was coming to ask for a ride to the store. The grandma grinned widely upon seeing the four little ones.

"You need to get outside more often," she exclaimed. "It is so wonderful to be outside!" Frances stooped down to Gabriel. "Honey, you're old enough to ride your bike up and down the street all by yourself now."

Who does she think she is? Sarah simmered, her lips tightly shut.

"Grace! Look how lovely you are! But . . . so pale, honey." Frances drew her eyebrows together. "You're so pale. Everybody asks about you because they don't see you anymore."

Sarah hustled the kids inside. Grace followed, but Debi stayed behind to talk to Frances. Sarah was about to burst. As soon as she got out of earshot, she vented to Grace, "I hate how gossipy she and Mother get."

Sarah went to cook the hamburger Tiffanie had given her, a gift she had been reluctant to accept. But Sarah had little money, and her food stamps were on hold. She hadn't paid her parents the full amount of rent for the month, giving them just $85 of the $450 she owed. As she flipped the meat, she prayed loudly to drown out Luke's complaining about some chore he didn't want to do. That didn't last long before Bruce called the family together into the living room for devotions. It was time to read the Bible together and pray. Sarah did so in the kitchen alone. She texted Traci about what happened next:

> I went right into praise and praying and worship. i had the BEST time in praying, praise and worship. There was such resistance first but i kept focusing on Jesus and focusing on Jesus and focusing on Jesus some more—im saying the demons that try to rule downstairs were being so stirred up the cats started acting crazy and things were banging around for a minute lol i don't even know what it was but i was looking at Jesus and tehn at a point i knew the devil was REALLY mad at me, i saw while my eyes were closed off to my left a demon that looked like Luke when he's acting out that that demon possessed angry thing he gets just like staring at me with a stance of fury and like it was seconds from attacking me. i just decided against the fear that i felt to stay focusing on Jesus and focusing on Jesus and FOCUSING ON JESUS and then i saw the thing run scared. Shortly after Daddy must had dismissed them from Family Devotions because i heard a mass exodus out of there. it was really as if my praying and praise had driven them off. that's what it seemed like. . . it did hurt that they chose to go away instead of worship. like they allowed themselves to be run off with demons?? ? that's what it seemed like! Whatever. taht kitchen was a very free place for a bit. I had SO much real joy. im saying, it was awesome. so beautiful.

June 8, 2015, was Bruce's birthday. He turned sixty-five. Five foot nine and weighing just 145 pounds, Bruce had grown frail-looking, lean and slight, his skin hanging off hallow cheeks. Stark-white hair was pushed back behind his ears and covered his lower face with a mustache and full beard.

Debi was a year shy of turning sixty. Her hair long ago had lost its luster. Gray mixed with brown. It hung scraggly to chest level. She had bangs, and usually wore a barrette in the back that pulled the sides of her hair from her face, revealing tired jowls and dull blue eyes.

The couple called their daughters downstairs to watch Bruce open presents. Luke got him a hatchet.

Bruce announced, "Tomorrow, Grace has a doctor appointment, and I plan on having the boys in the way back, Ezekiel in the middle, and Grace up front."

Instead of everyone acting surprised, as Sarah thought they should be, it was the opposite, as though the car-seating announcement was standard. At the celebration, her father was nicer than usual, her mother looked "weird," and the rest were downright gleeful, observations that made Sarah think something sinister was in process.

Something was definitely up on June 26. Sarah's kids were conked out on the attic floor with a box fan blowing around hot air. She went downstairs to ask her father about getting air-conditioning.

Ezekiel came downstairs. He'd been spending a lot of time in his brothers' room and now looked nervous.

"Why are you acting so suspicious?" she asked.

He was too quick to reply. "I'm getting Luke's video game."

"Zeke, what are they doing up there?"

Bruce found it odd and began questioning Zeke, but the boy started crying hysterically. Bruce and Debi went upstairs to talk to the older boys. Once they were gone, Zeke told Sarah his brothers were smoking weed. They'd been doing it every day for about a month. They got it through a kid from the homeschool co-op and paid for it with Luke's dog-sitting money and money that Chris got from doing odd jobs for his father.

Bruce went back downstairs to call Zeke. "C'mon upstairs. The boys have something to apologize to you for."

Sarah was alarmed, afraid the boys would retaliate against Zeke for telling. She heard what sounded like Luke sneaking out the front door, either tossing something he needed to get rid of, or eavesdropping, and then sneaking back in again. Sarah next noticed Zeke had gone into the kitchen with his parents, but soon after, Bruce strolled into the living room without him.

"Why isn't Zeke with you?" she asked.

"Well, he's with Mommy right now."

"That's where all the bad happens!"

Bruce brought Zeke to the living room, and the boy fell asleep on the couch. Bruce sat beside him and wrote on paper what he planned to send to Tiffanie in a text. After some time, he set down his pen and looked up. "I forgot to get something at the store. I might have to go out again."

"If you do, you're bringing Zeke, right?" asked Sarah.

"No. He's sleeping."

Sarah was panicked. "What about the boys?"

"Well, they're in bed now."

"They're not sleeping," said Sarah, breathless. "They're plotting, planning, and scheming!"

Later that week, Sarah snuck into Luke's room when he wasn't there. She took a picture of his pill bottle and sent it to Traci. Luke was on antibiotics following knee surgery and what turned out to be a bacterial infection.

Another day, as Sarah was loading the kids in the van for a trip to the store, Debi came out to drive them. Luke was a few steps behind. Sarah was dumbfounded to see him. She tried to signal her displeasure to her mother. When nothing came of that, she waved her mother aside. "Can I talk to you for a minute?"

Debi walked in front of the van.

"I don't appreciate you blindsiding me like this," lectured Sarah. "It's important that I know who's going to be around my kids at all times, and you didn't so much as ask me if it was okay."

Debi said, "I'm sorry?" more like a question.

Without her mother's backing, Sarah was at a loss as to what to do. Should she act like nothing was wrong? Kick him out? Ask him not to go? She walked up to Luke. "Have you totally repented?"

"Of what?"

"Of sin!"

"I . . . think so."

"If it's only 'I think so,' then you haven't. And if you haven't, I can't go compromising and acting like nothing is wrong."

"I *knew* what this was about!" he said, exasperated.

"Humility is the key, and if you truly repented, your first reaction would've been to search your heart to find out if you've truly repented or not, and it would've catapulted you into the arms of Jesus and not anger."

"I'm not angry. I'm hurt."

"I don't mean to hurt you. I love you very much. But I care more about your eternity than your feelings right now. I was in the same situation as you. Momma came to the apartment when I lived up on the hill, and she warned me. It played a big part in putting me in the kingdom of heaven. Look in the deep place in your heart. What side are you on? Who are you for? Go into the arms of Jesus because he loves you so much. He's been pleading with you to repent."

Luke said nothing as he walked back into the house. Grace watched him. Her teeth together, she murmured contemptuously, "He looks smug."

You guys don't have any idea what's what in your criticisms and your judgments. You don't have any idea. You guys have not visited a lot of churches. You don't know anything. I'm telling you. You just— You're being ridiculous. This isn't normal. Okay? Please. You're not acting normal. What's normal is you wanna be in a church to hear the word of the Lord. To live it. That's normal. Okay? Please be normal here. You don't know anything. I mean, you all think you've got a better idea, but you don't know anything. I mean, you think you can tell me how to do this, and what you can and cannot do, but you don't even know how to control a single thought in your mind. Really. Give me a break. Time to grow up. Okay?

—Pastor Tiffanie Irwin

to the congregation on February 9, 2015

In the spring of 2015, Kristel was walking the aisle of a store when she noticed a familiar face she couldn't quite place. She continued to see this woman in several more aisles, and they stole glances. It was Helen, the friend the Irwins had ordered away from Kristel in adolescence. Helen had left the church in 2010, two years after divorcing the man the Irwins had forced her to marry. The impetus for her leaving had been a friend outside the church who couldn't ignore that Helen often got home with her children after 2:00 A.M.

"You're being abused," he'd told her. "That's not a real church. A church doesn't do that."

It was the first time Helen had heard that, or given any consideration to such a suggestion.

"For a congregation of people who seem to be so loving and protective of you," her friend had said, "they're very abusive. I don't even know why you go there. That's not a church. That's not what a church does."

It didn't take long for Helen to see her friend's point of view. She was tired of her children being told they were being rebellious, tired of having no proof of rebellion, of always being suspicious of her children. She called the Irwins the following morning and told them she could not be what they wanted her to be, and with that—she was free.

Now, it appeared to Helen that Kristel had made her way out, too. Helen had looked her up online, right there in the store, and discovered that Kristel was connected, through social media, to others who had left the church. She sent Kristel a message.

"I had to decide what to do with that message," Kristel later said, "because my last five years' knowledge of Helen was from the Irwins, which meant bad news. But I also could not forget how close she and I were as kids and wanted to see how she was 'for real'—in her own words—now that I was free from the Irwins."

It had been a tough year for Kristel as she found her way apart from WLCC. Running into her former friend kicked up dirt, but at the same time, the familiar face—and feelings—gave her solace. The two began communicating, and then spending time together. On August 6, they went to visit Kristel's grandmother at a Herkimer nursing home to celebrate her birthday.

It was not a complete surprise but certainly a delight when they ran into Bruce and Luke. It was clear by the tightness of his hug that Kristel's father had missed her dearly. It was the first he'd hugged her in years, and warmly. She and Luke teased each other. The interactions were brief but satisfying. When it came time to leave, they almost felt like a family as they walked together to the parking lot.

Three days later, on Sunday morning, Kristel got a surprise text message from Debi's phone. But it wasn't Debi. It was Luke. He wanted to know what time her church service began and asked if he could go with her. A shiver of excitement shot through her. This could be the answer to her prayers. Not only did he want to go to her church, he asked if he could stay at her house for a few days. Kristel and her husband decided they would not push Luke for information. It was a delicate situation, and the wrong approach could scare him. They would not ask what triggered this. He would see for himself that they were okay and that others who left the church were not only surviving but thriving.

Kristel, Art, and their two kids pulled up at the Clayville home, and Luke was outside waiting. So was Chris, and he looked angry. It was clear he and Luke were in a heated disagreement. When Luke stormed away and got in the car, Chris raced into the house.

Three other former WLCC families had been going to the Randallsville church. The hope was that Luke would recognize it was a healthier congregation. The parishioners of Kristel's new church greeted the newcomer enthusiastically after she proudly introduced him as her "baby brother," a label that Luke returned with a sour look. Though he was polite, and engaged with those who approached him, he appeared more nervous and withdrawn than ever. As soon as the service ended, Luke went outside and smoked a cigarette, out of Kristel's sight. He then went to the car and waited for them.

"So what do you want to do?" asked Kristel. "Do you want to come stay with us for a few days, or do you want to go back home?"

This time, there was no hesitation in his answer. "I guess I'll go back home."

On the thirty-minute trip back to Clayville, Kristel didn't bring up the service. She let it marinate in his mind. He'd seen that those who left WLCC were fine. The stories of all hell breaking loose weren't true.

At the house, Luke grabbed his bag from the back and Kristel gave him a hug. "You know where I live," said the big sister, holding her brother tighter, longer. "You're welcome any time."

It would be their last embrace.

———

The scene Luke had left behind on Main Street that morning was one of turmoil. As soon as Luke jumped into Kristel's car, Chris ran up to the attic and banged on Sarah's door. "Come downstairs! It's an emergency!"

By the time she stumbled to the lower half of the house, the rest of her family was assembled in the living room.

"Luke just left for church with Kristel!" blurted Debi.

"What? And nobody knew about this?" That's when Sarah learned Bruce and Luke had visited Grandma Leonard earlier in the week and Kristel had shown up. "With *Helen*," Sarah repeated the information with distaste. "Isn't that cute." Too on edge to sit down, she stood. "Did Luke talk to them while they were at the nursing home?"

Debi shrugged. "I don't know anything about it."

"I don't know why you're all shocked," said Sarah. "Your rebellion enabled this behavior in Luke. Change now, before it's too late for Zeke!"

Zeke panned the mixed-up faces surrounding him. Chris stared at the carpet, chewing his nails.

Debi offered, "I asked Luke why he was doing it, and he said, 'Because I'm not ready to repent, and it's better to go somewhere.'"

Sarah ratted out her brother, firing off a text to Tiffanie. The pastor then texted Bruce, demanding answers. Bruce told her he was in the basement feeding the dogs when Luke approached and said he was going to the other church. He told his father he'd been thinking about it awhile. Bruce told him not to go, but in a flash, Luke was out the door.

Chris and Zeke turned on a cartoon movie, and Sarah retreated upstairs to nap, emotionally spent. Grace joined the somber mood downstairs, where she overheard a phone call between her father and Luke. He was still at the service and apologized for taking his mother's phone.

Bruce hung up and turned to Grace. "I told him we didn't have a service this morning. He went dead silent." Coincidentally, WLCC's service had been rescheduled for evening. Luke would have to go and face everyone. "Luke's planning on coming home today."

Bruce and Debi went into the home office to talk, and it wasn't long before Sarah went knocking. She had to be kept informed so she could update the Irwins.

At WLCC, Tiffanie was forwarding the Leonards' text messages to the group and working herself up about Bruce not responding quickly enough. She implied the delay was intentional, for some nefarious purpose. Tiffanie deemphasized that Luke's visiting another church was the issue, telling Bruce the real problem was that Luke had blatantly disobeyed his father when he told him not to go. She accused Luke of skipping church the previous week by pretending to be sick, and asked Bruce if he'd dealt with that or simply let it go. Bruce said he thought Luke was legitimately sick. He had taken him to urgent care. Tiffanie argued about the absence. She counted each minute it took for Bruce to reply and then sent around group texts about the questionable delays.

Luke got home at 1:50 P.M. and headed straight to his room. His parents went in to talk and pray with him. Tiffanie knew what was going on, thanks to Sarah's up-to-the minute reports. While Bruce was in Luke's room, Tiffanie was attempting to direct the conversation via text, asking Bruce what he planned to say and what excuses Luke was providing. Not getting answers, she continued to badger Bruce for two hours, until he responded.

Luke, Bruce affirmed, did not prearrange the visit, did not want to go to that church, and did not want to leave WLCC.

> **TIFFANIE (6:01 P.M.):** *Now, before I got these texts, the Holy Spirit showed me that Luke was like a cat that drank the milk, and was satisfied there because of what he thought he could do along sexual lines . . . This is all lies, and also Bruce is obviously being very stubborn.*
> **LINDA:** *Yup I believe Luke now can have sex with someone.*

Shortly after 8:00 P.M., the Leonards went to church.

> **DAVE:** *Leonards just pulled in*
> **LINDA:** *Bruce has an attitude*
> **TIFFANIE:** *I want to see luke walk in*
> **TIFFANIE:** *Then, I'll need you to adjust it again.*
> **TIFFANIE:** *He's "happy he got away with it".*

At the close of service, at about 11:30 P.M., Chris handed a writing assignment to Dave.

"Where's Luke with his?"

"Um . . . ," Chris said, "Luke lost his assignment, and he can't find it. But he did do it."

At Chris's side, Bruce nodded heartily in agreement.

"Where is he?" asked Dave.

Luke was already gone, and though it would be close to midnight by the time he got home, he would not be going to bed. Tiffanie sent a scathing text to Bruce that scrolled for several pages, dictating Luke's punishment. He would have to write seven hundred times *I will not lie. I will not be rebellious. The rebellious will be cast out (Psalm 5:10).*

It was to be turned in by ten the next morning and posted on the school door for all to see. Tiffanie put Bruce on notice—if he did not handle this, he would forever be undermined in his own home. This disease of disobedience could result in his entire family leaving the church, Tiffanie forewarned, unless Bruce *decisively and quickly* established his authority. Bruce was to apprise her of any further measures he expected to take to bring Luke into compliance.

When Luke hung his completed assignment on the door, Traci took a picture of it and sent it to the inner circle with a message that Luke had been writing whole books of the Bible to save face.

What had he done? The fallout was inconceivable as the Irwins worked to regain the control they'd never actually lost.

Meanwhile, the reality was now bigger than ever of dwindling cash in the collection plates. There were only eighteen members left, plus a handful of children who weren't old enough to meet member status. And there was Luke, threatening to be the next escapee. Tiffanie gave a sermon asking for money, phrased to make it look like she wasn't asking for money. "Don't give more money until God speaks to you. You need a servant's heart." This followed what sounded more like a therapy session than a sermon, in which Tiffanie bemoaned the days of her childhood when she spent so much time worshipping that she didn't eat or sleep and everyone hated her because she was "upstaging" them.

"You may think I'm a nobody, but the Bible says you should honor me with double honor than you give anybody else, because I labor in the word to teach you. The Bible says you should love me, not treat me like I don't even matter at all."

Chris scribbled furiously in his notebook: *We should honor her with double honor because she labors in the word for us . . . She's not asking for our money.* [September 9, 2015]

Luke was merely existing, waiting for a vision to learn what plans God had for his life. In the interim, he was doing projects around the house, working for tobacco credit.

Bruce expressed to Tiffanie that he was missing Kristel terribly and had minimal contact with his brother-in-law Jeff. *Get an emotional ping every time I think of them.*

Four years earlier, Tiffanie had written in her diary that one of her greatest fears was that Debi's children would grow up and leave the church. Certainly she wouldn't soon forget that Luke had gone to Kristel's church. On September 13, she took aim at Debi during a sermon, her words likely engineered to stifle Debi's communication with outsiders who might lead her out the door. "The Holy Spirit is highlighting a relationship you know you shouldn't have."

Debi was confused. Was it someone from the homeschool co-op?

"There is a relationship that you have that you know that you shouldn't have. At least, when I say you know you shouldn't have it, I mean that you feel, in your heart, that you are doing something bad, being naughty, getting away with it, being in control."

It was a tactic Tiffanie used to find out if Debi had been communicating with anyone. But Debi was unresponsive for more than a minute as she pondered this.

"The spirit of death just came in this room," said Tiffanie.

Debi piped up. "Could it be my relationship with Luke?"

"Huh?"

"I mean, providing . . . getting cigarettes and . . . things at the store . . . I don't know."

Tiffanie issued a condescending laugh. "Yes. You do." She told her, "The spirit of death came in the room. Okay? Sometimes the spirit of death comes in on the face of persistent rebellion, and he intends to bring death and destruction with him. I'm just warning you. I know what the spirit of death is."

From the back of the church, Ivy loudly called, "Mommy," and Sarah shushed her.

"I'm telling you that it's coming to attach to you because of what you're doing right now. Okay? And the spirit of death manifests in different ways. It doesn't mean that I'm telling you something will immediately happen to you. But the devil brings death. And whenever that spirit of death comes, something not good is happening. And I'm asking you to stop opening the door to that demon. You know, if you wanted to come clean, or whatever you wanted to say, if you wanted to communicate about this relationship, you would have already. But that's what the Holy Spirit is convicting you about. And he wanted to give you the opportunity to speak the truth today."

"I'm speculating," Bruce joined in. "I'm wondering if I can ask . . ."

"You can talk to your wife."

He asked Debi if it was the man from the homeschool co-op who had gone to the hospital and prayed over her. Probably not. They tossed around other ideas.

"The Holy Spirit's the one speaking to you, Debi," said Tiffanie. "So I'm just being his mouthpiece here. He showed me what it is, and he wanted to give you an opportunity. That's it. If you don't want to take the opportunity, I'll just wait until God tells me to move on to the next thing."

Debi whined, "I do want to take the opportunity."

Tiffanie casually worked on her laptop in silence, head resting in her hand, as the entire congregation sat in the audience with their heads lowered. Eventually she asked, "Who's the person you've been talking to saying that we, as a church, are victimizing you?"

Her brother Jeff.

"Okay. And what were his words?"

"His words were—not in this order—but he said our constitution is not scriptural. He said, um, he is very upset with Seth, because Seth told Jeff's son to sit down and to stop looking at . . . Ada? I think? And that he was very seething. Very pissed-off. And how dare he talk to him like that. And, um . . ."

Tiffanie nodded with a sardonic grin.

Debi continued. "That you said some things that are very off the wall. He did not go into detail—"

"Oh, he didn't. Right? Are you positive, Debi?"

"I don't remember."

"Uh. 'Kay. When somebody doesn't go into detail, it makes me wonder if there is any detail."

"I didn't want to listen to him—"

"Debi. Don't say stuff that's not true. Okay? All right? It's better to say nothing than to volunteer a lie. Okay?"

"At the time, I felt very uncomfortable with what he was saying."

"Yeah, but how did you respond? And he said you are being victimized personally?"

"He said Chris was being victimized."

"He *is*?" Tiffanie smirked.

Debi threw up her hands. "That's what he said."

"Are you kidding?" Tiffanie turned to Chris and asked him if he was on church discipline. He said he wasn't, but that he'd heard Tiffanie say he had to stay with an assigned person while in church. Tiffanie asked Chris if he knew why.

"Because I can't be trusted?"

"You think you can't be trusted? That's what you just said. So that's what you think? I'm asking you. It's not a trick question. And I don't wanna know what you think sounds good. I wanna know if you think you can be trusted."

"Not really," he answered sheepishly.

"Okay. So. Doesn't it help you in the sense of, in the interest of doing what's right, to have somebody with you?"

"Yes."

"Are you telling me the truth right now? Yeah, I don't wanna hear any BS. I wanna know if this is true." Tiffanie's voice was the only one that vacillated, while everyone else's was level. She asked Bruce if he thought that was victimization. He turned his head to the side for a second or two, as if mulling it over, before answering, "No." He added that it felt like it, but—no.

She brought it back to Debi. "So you agreed with him that Chris was being victimized. Right?"

Eventually, Debi nodded. "Yeah . . . in my heart . . . I think I did."

Just one week before he would be beaten nearly to death, Chris wrote in his notebook, all underlined, *Rebellion only gets us to hell. Just stop rebelling. It's not our parents fault it's our own.* Tiffanie's sermon was about how sinners needed to be shamed in order to repent. Traci talked about how their church was different from the others, because other churches only cared about money. The Irwin matriarch said she didn't want any more people to leave the church, because she loved them and prayed for their souls.

PART TWO
THE CRIME

Children aren't gonna be molested in this church. The devil can go to hell, and I will not back down. Okay? So if I even see the start of it, you had better bet that I will put a stop to it. . . . Children are the treasure from the Lord that he's given us. And if somebody even causes one of them to stumble, it would be better for him to have a millstone hung around their neck and they were forcibly drowned right then, than to live longer and keep doing what they're doing.

—PASTOR TIFFANIE IRWIN

TO THE CONGREGATION ON SEPTEMBER 13, 2015

CRAPSTORM COMING

The Leonard family had a busy Columbus Day weekend planned. Ezekiel's soccer game on Friday got canceled, but Luke and Chris were scheduled to play on Monday. It would be a glorious day for the playing fields. Sunday and Monday were forecast to be bathed in sunshine. Debi and Chris spent Saturday at the library.

Luke was taking care of the Livingstones' dog. Their daughter was in the hospital in Connecticut, so they'd been driving back and forth, gone three or four days at a time. Frank would give Luke his key chain—mailbox key, house key, toy cap gun. Every Sunday night, after the Livingstones returned, the teenager would walk down and trade in the key chain for his pay and the Sunday paper.

As noon mass on Sunday drew near, Chris was aware of his brother's detachment. Luke pulled up a pair of gray denim jeans over plaid boxers, slipped on clean, white socks, and laced up his red, white, and blue sneakers, all on autopilot. He used a black tank top for an undershirt and, though it was unseasonably warm, chose a gray thermal top and hooded sweatshirt. Chris was also dressed casually, black pants and a gray crewneck sweater draped on a scrawny body of about five-foot-six. Luke was slightly taller, thicker.

The Leonards split up the family, loading some into Debi's van and the rest in Bruce's. It was about eleven o'clock in the morning when they made the three-mile drive to WLCC. Though the gate to the parking lot was unlocked, the door to the church was locked. They waited for someone to let them in.

The family docilely made their way to their assigned seats, third row back. Chris and Luke were bookends—Chris on the far left, Luke

on the right. In between were Bruce, Ezekiel, and Debi. Grace took
her seat in the row behind her family. And behind Grace, the video
recorder was rolling, up on a counter on a tripod. Chris had noticed
the red blinking light when he walked in. Traci was in the sound booth.
Sarah was in the church, too, in and out of the small sanctuary with
her children. There was the usual cast of characters, including Rick
and Margaret Wright and their four adult children in the second row.

"One of you," said Tiffanie, her eyes black holes scanning the audience, "is practicing witchcraft."

Chris took notes as Tiffanie went along rehashing the usual sermon
about witchcraft. His notes repeated how God spoke to Pastor. If
anybody had gotten that message by now, it was the Leonards. They
needed to look at themselves as evil in order to see the need to repent.
He jotted that down, plus, *If people had obeyed and honored Him he
wouldn't have the people wipe them out . . . God will take the biggest
crap storm and turn it into the biggest blessing.*

For the last time, behind a cheap pulpit setup of school desk cloaked
in cloth of red—the color a universal church symbol of the blood of
martyrs—Tiffanie hammered home the message that rebellion makes
you stand for nothing. "It's time for the devil to stop being protected."

Dan was in and out of the service. There was work he'd rather
do, and every service was long. This one was six hours in before Tiffanie called a dinner break. Everyone had their usual spots to eat.
Some brought food into the sanctuary, while others took it outside.
Tiffanie would occasionally go into the dining room but mostly ate at
the desk that doubled as a pulpit. Luke didn't have time for dinner. He
had to get home to take care of the Livingstones' dog. Because Luke
didn't have a driver's license, Bruce would have to take him, but they
would need to run it by Tiffanie first. The request ruffled feathers; Joe
thought the whole thing was made up. He'd previously made an issue
of it, insisting Luke was "full of crap," that nobody pays someone to
watch their dog two weeks out of the month.

Bruce and Luke went to let out the dog and feed it and then stopped home to get a drink. They got back to the church at about 7:00 P.M., just as the sun was setting. The day had been hot, but darkness would bring chilly October air, and the church furnace was broken. It would start to get very cold inside. Evening temperatures were expected to dip into the forties.

Traci went upstairs to the apartment to use the bathroom and noticed her Yorkshire terrier, Truffles, was in labor. The dog had one pup to deliver, a large one, and it was breach. Traci would be absent for the rest of the service, so Dave took her seat in the sound booth.

After another hour and a half of preaching, at about 8:30 P.M., Tiffanie sent a group text: *Crapstorm coming in Leonard family. Luke can't wait to say something--say he's not coming back, I think.* Should she have them stay at the church and address it? Her mother voted to have them stay. Linda agreed. So did Dan.

Make him air it here, texted Traci, adding that Luke enjoyed having power at home, where he could easily control his parents. Grace and Sarah should sit in, too, she advised. And Joe—he should be there. Maybe even Dan, in case it turned physical.

Near the end of service, Tiffanie announced that God wanted her to address something. "Who has been practicing witchcraft? Please raise your hand."

All three Leonard boys shot up their arms.

"Raise your hands. Who among you would like to confess and forsake that sin now?"

Again, the boys raised their hands. Tiffanie first addressed Chris, goading him into listing his sins. She then asked if he'd involved another family member in his witchcraft.

Chris was silent for a solid minute or two.

"Why won't you say?" she pressed. "Is the reason because you're not quite willing to let that one go?"

"Yes."

"You have to let it all go, because if you don't, that sin will have a hold in your life. And you can't be forgiven of something you're not willing to let go of." Tiffanie waited a long time for Chris to come forward with a name, and when he didn't, she turned to Debi. "Did you raise your hand, Debi, and I just couldn't see?"

"I didn't raise my hand. I know I used to, but I don't do it anymore." Debi started to get emotional. "We talked about . . . my dad. You told me I didn't kill him by the way I thought and felt about him." Her voice cracking, and her eyes wet, she continued. "I felt that way about him, but he told me he loved me, and I forgave him just before he died."

"I'm glad for you, Debi," Tiffanie said without the emotions to match. She moved on to Luke. "How do you believe you have practiced witchcraft?"

"I thought . . . doing this would have a . . . negative influence on you and the church." The others strained to hear what he was saying. "I read things in books and experimented with them." He was using Ouija boards to perform rituals, doing black magic, and trying to make the church elders sick.

Tiffanie laughed arrogantly and asked if he'd made a voodoo doll. He said that he had, and that the voodoo doll was of Tiffanie. He'd poked it in the leg with pins to break Tiffanie's leg. His head was not lowered, as he confessed this. He was looking straight at her.

"Well, that backfired," said Tiffanie, with a toss of her head before leveling her gaze at him. "No, actually you're the one that ended up being injured." She was going to win this—whatever *this* was. "It bounced off me and goes back to you. And that's why you had the knee injury back in April." Again, her sadistic laugh. "The only one hurt by this is you, because demons don't touch the righteous."

"When you're preaching," Luke continued boldly, "I use my mind to try to make you stop. I try to get you to break for lunch quicker."

"Oh, do you," said Tiffanie, mildly amused.

"And when you're playing songs, I try to get them to end faster."

"What songs?" She smirked.

"This morning, during worship, I wanted a song to end, and I thought about it being over, and a couple minutes later, it ended."

"When you think of the name of the song, raise your hand and let me know."

She moved the discussion forward with other parishioners, and a short time later, Luke's hand went up. "'Humble Thyself in the Sight of the Lord.'"

"Can you think of any other examples where your thoughts seemed to have an effect on actual events?"

"A couple weeks ago, the service ended right after I was wishing it would end."

Tiffanie addressed the congregation. "This kind of belief, and practice, is absurd." God wrote for each person how their days would look before they were born, she told them, so the Holy Spirit already had planned when Sunday service would end. "It's not influenced by the whimsy of someone's thoughts." She asked Luke to stand so she could talk to him and not the demon possessing him. "God told me something. God said you have plans to leave and go to Kristel's church and that you have a reason behind it. What is that reason?"

"I want to do what I want to do and not get caught."

"What do you plan to do?"

"I want to abuse people and get away with it, so I can feel in power and control."

"How do you want to abuse people?"

"I want to molest little girls."

In that usually expressionless sea of faces, there were looks of shock. But not one of them said a word, except Tiffanie. "Are you hearing this, parents? He just said that of his own will." She zeroed in on Bruce. "So, Bruce, please don't let him go to Kristel's church. I know you love your son, and this must be very upsetting, but you need to face this."

As Bruce struggled to find words, Tiffanie prompted him, "Did you have something to say?"

"I have three questions," said Bruce. "What? How? And, now what?"

Instead of answering directly, Tiffanie did Q and A with Luke, asking him why he wanted to do this and not repent. He told her he liked feeling in control.

"What good is a feeling when, in reality, it's just a deception of the devil to destroy you?" Tiffanie speculated he would be found out and go to jail. "And they don't treat people there, who are guilty of those crimes, very well, because they're viewed as the worst. Is this what you want? Or would this make you feel in control?"

"No."

"Would you at least try to be sorry for your sins?" Tiffanie stared, unflinching. "You probably liked that place because it was more of a positive, feel-good environment. You hear what you want to hear, and not what you need to hear. Do you understand that even if you were to leave this church and get away from me, the Holy Spirit would still be after you? The Holy Spirit would always be there convicting you, and drawing you, and making you uncomfortable in sin."

The pastor abruptly stopped and closed her eyes and nodded her head. A vision had purportedly come to her. It was of Luke in an abandoned, concrete building. "I'm not sure if it's a finished building that's gone into disrepair after being abandoned, or an unfinished building project that was abandoned. But, Luke, you're sitting right in the middle of it, having lost everyone and everything as a result of your life's direction. But even there, in that very alone place, the Holy Spirit is still there, gently putting pressure on your heart."

"This place you're describing is my bedroom."

"I'm not sure about that, Luke." This was not a comforting tone but a cold one. It was not a discussion but a lecture. She appeared to be reaching deep into the recesses of her mind, recalling, "The building has holes where windows should've been, bare concrete framing and I beams. But I'm not sure if it's literal or allegorical, just that the Holy Spirit is showing you that his love is yearning for you still, in a way that's so deep I don't feel like I have the words to express it."

She turned to Debi. "Debi, I sense deep waters in you regarding these issues with Luke. Do you know what I mean by that?"

Debi nodded, cleared her throat and said, "I think so."

"Can you talk to me about this afterwards?"

It was about 10:00 P.M. when Tiffanie announced, "God says the sinning has to stop. Everyone's free to go, but I would like the Leonard family to stay." Her requests were more than that—they were obligations.

Sarah was on her way from the nursery to the dining room when Tiffanie caught up with her. "I've asked your parents to stay. There are some things I want to talk to them about. Would you and Grace mind staying, too?"

Sarah's kids happily went with Kathleen Morey, one of their teachers, to the dining room, as Sarah and Grace returned to the small sanctuary, where they saw Linda and Dave. Joe was there, too. His mother had asked him to stick around in case things turned volatile and to text her real-time updates.

Already at her desk with the laptop open, Tiffanie started by talking about code violations on the Leonard house. Joe sat on a chair only a foot away, dwarfing his sister's petite frame. He swiped on his cell phone, one knee up on the chair rung.

The pastor intermittently drank water from the green tumbler as she smoothly transitioned topics to the boys picking on Zeke. They'd hit him, pinched him, knocked him into furniture. It was impossible not to notice Zeke's progressive discomfort as Tiffanie made these accusations. His face crinkled. The room tensed. The older brothers had been mercilessly picking on him. They didn't include him in their play. Zeke's eyes darted from the floor, to the door—everywhere but in the direction of his brothers. He began sniffling.

"I'm sorry— Do you want to go with the other children?" Tiffanie asked.

Zeke nodded, and out poured tears. He quickly rushed into the dining room and fished out a deck of cards. He could still hear bits and pieces of the conversation. The yelling would come, and talk of pornography, though Zeke didn't know what it was. He would hear his brothers say they had touched him inappropriately. He would catch glimpses of Joe doing something very bad in a fit of anger.

Tiffanie moved the discussion to pornography. Luke's parents were supposed to help him confront his sin and rid him of his addiction. She advised they keep him out of stores and places where he could access it, "or possibly don't pay him for chores until he's no longer addicted to it." She asked Luke where he was getting it.

His face reddened. His jaw clenched. "The store."

"Where else?"

"The library."

The evil needed to go, she said. Repent.

"I like my sins." Luke again raised his head—a challenge.

Joe now lowered his phone. He stroked his beard as he eyed Luke and then scratched his forehead in slow motion as though trying to guess Luke's next move.

"Do you have a stash of pornography?" Tiffanie asked. And when no answer came, she asked another. "Are you repentant?"

"No," came the snappy reply.

Was he indulging in weed? Taking oxycontin? Tiffanie knew Luke was on medication, because of the picture of the pill bottle that Sarah had sent Traci. She used this information to suggest Luke had become a drug addict. Her questions turned to statements, and she accused him of sexually fantasizing about her. The next allegation was more preposterous: he'd plotted to kill his parents.

Bruce and Debi, still seated, stopped craning their necks and instead swung their legs around their chairs. It was Luke's turn at center stage, usurping Tiffanie, and his response only deepened his parents' expressions of horror. Despite Joe placing both feet on the floor, ready to spring, Luke said he'd taken knives and stood over his parents' bed. Right there with a knife over his mother's heart, something had startled him, interrupting his plan.

Unperturbed, Tiffanie asked Luke to explain why he'd gone to Kristel's church. Toying with consequence, he answered, "Opportunity." He was able to molest Kristel's daughter as he rode in the back seat on the way to the service, he said.

At Tiffanie's direction, Chris left his seat to go stand next to his brother. He shuffled over to Luke with shoulders hunched and straggly curls flopping over his eyes. But before he'd gotten a chance to stand fully at attention, Linda tromped up and slapped him, the hot sting lingering long past the sound of the crack.

Tiffanie took a gulp from the tumbler, seamlessly continuing from the slap to a series of calmly worded questions that went down a deep, dark path. How—she asked—did the boys sexually molest their sister Grace? Did they do it do it over her clothes, or under?

Joe's feet stamped the floor, simultaneous with a frenzy of shrill voices. The women were hollering questions in a hysteria. Debi—calm Debi—was irate. The aged mother's tone showed no indication of diplomacy. Luke flicked his head to the floor, and Chris went numb, dodging all questions. No one could hear any one, specific question. It was all noise, a surround sound of inquisition.

Emboldened, Grace walked up behind Chris. She'd been praying, moving her lips with no sound, but now spoke forcefully. "Tell the truth." Offering it as fact, she demanded to know, "How did you molest my niece?"

It was as though every person in the room held their breath. There was not a shuffle of a chair leg, not a scratch to an itch, or a clearing of the throat. And then, the first punch was thrown, landing square in the middle of Chris's back.

It wasn't enough to get the teen talking, and that sent Joe out of the gate like a bull to a red flag waving, all 275 pounds of him thudding after Chris. From over the top of the skinny boy, he warned, "You have three seconds to answer," and then turned to Bruce. "If you tell me to stop, I will."

Bruce may or may not have shaken his head, may or may not have answered, his voice and actions equally muted. Joe grabbed Chris by the shirt and gave the introverted, glasses-wearing child a "one . . . two . . . three." He delivered a shot to the stomach that made the boy double over. If the bowie knife was strapped to Joe's calf, he did not take it out and use it that night, despite his fists eventually absorbing shocks many times their capacity.

"If he doesn't answer," said Bruce, in his even keel, "hit him again."

Joe punched the kid again, same spot, right in the gut. Chris nearly spat out saliva but instead swallowed the pool of it.

Linda ordered him, "Take out your earrings."

The update Joe sent his mother at 11:39 P.M. said that Linda was going to *take care of* Chris.

Blackness enveloped the church outside, but no one inside could tell. They were sealed from the rest of the world. Some of the doors were chained. One exit door near the altar of the big sanctuary, as always, had a chain around both handrails and was secured with a bolt.

———

Worry was mounting on Main Street in Clayville. Neighbors wondered why the Leonards weren't home. Frances thought they had gone visiting. As the night wore on, Pamela Murphy got a feeling something wasn't right. Usually, the Leonards would be returning the same time she was getting home from work, at about eleven o'clock. But at eleven thirty, the house was still empty.

Down the road, Frank and Brenda were confused by the family's absence. Luke hadn't come over to get paid for dog sitting. When he didn't show up after a while, Frank walked the Sunday paper down to Luke's place and dropped it on the porch. He would never get his key chain back. The newspaper—"It's still on the chair on the porch," Frank said, three years later. "Shriveled up a little bit. I walk around the block and I see it there all the time."

Linda made Chris take off his glasses. He fumbled with them nervously, almost dropping them. Before he could lower his arm all the way, Linda hauled off and punched him in the face. Blood spewed from his nose. But that wasn't the end—she pummeled him madly, all over the head and chest, sending the blood from his nose flicking against the wall. Debi, who'd gotten out of her chair heaving and panting, walked up to Chris and punched him. Weakened by her recent heart attack, her face flushed as her temper raised, and she balled her fist, squeezed, and whacked. Though frail in appearance, the father was stronger, and he threw much harder punches, offering no protection for his boys—just fear.

Then Joe delivered repeated kicks to Chris's upper thigh. It sent him hurtling to the floor. Chris lay still and stared at the ceiling tiles, the fluorescent lights shining on him like a flood of interrogation. Joe dropped to the floor and forced Chris's arms to his sides. Though the boy didn't struggle, Joe held his arms firmly, allowing any takers to get in their shots free and clear. And they did. The cold floor almost felt good in contrast to the heat the beating was generating, and the blood dripping from Chris's nose was warm as it slid into his mouth.

Luke stood petrified, unable to help his brother. He must've known he was next, watching his mother's ratty hair beading with sweat at the roots, and his father flailing inexorably, focused on Chris as if wearing blinders. There were his sisters, Sarah and young Grace. And there was Joe, Dan, Dave, Tiffanie, and Linda, everyone having lost common sense and reason.

The oldest Irwin brother, Dan, had not taken a swing. He'd been coming and going, wandering from room to room. At this time, he was not in the small sanctuary.

Joe's face was purpling as he held down Chris, and his phone was going off. It was his mother texting about the next day's prayer meeting. Monday was supposed to be the last warm day of the year, and they had a ton of work to do. It was getting late. Traci was thinking her kids would want to move the time of Monday's meeting.

Tiffanie hadn't struck anyone but now redirected the chaotic scene. She wanted answers. The next questions were about Sarah's oldest daughter, Ada. How did Chris molest her?

When he didn't answer, it took everything within Sarah to rein in her fury. Joe again stepped up. "I'm going to give you one more chance," he said, and then began the dreaded countdown. "One . . ."

Chris couldn't speak.

"Two . . ."

Chris started to answer but stopped.

"Three." Joe knocked him with his knuckles.

Chris kept starting to speak but always stopped. He didn't know what to say. It went on until Tiffanie turned her attention to Luke. "It's your turn."

Her voice gained intensity, but not volume, as she directed the same questions to Luke about molesting Ada. He was now not so brave. The boys were outnumbered, and the rest were becoming more empowered. After having a front-row seat to the viciousness leveled upon his brother, Luke knew the drill—speak or get it. He wanted an answer to come to him. He tried so hard. But like his brother, finding no words, he would start, and then stop. The gang's impatience was palpable.

Tiffanie moved to the front of her desk and leaned against it with her arms and feet crossed. She asked Grace, "Is it if okay with you if I can talk about the molestation, so they can be made aware?" She was referring to Chris and Luke molesting Grace and making their parents aware of it. Grace had confided it to Tiffanie the year prior. Now, having gotten her consent, Tiffanie brought it up.

Luke's breathing was shallow as he awaited Joe's countdown. Perhaps more anxiety-provoking was that it didn't come. Tiffanie's inquiry triggered yet another frenzied scene, an onslaught of questions from everyone circled around the boys like feeding sharks.

Without warning, Joe punched Luke in the stomach and chased it with a kick to the gut so powerful the boy lurched forward. Before he went down, disciple Dave grabbed hold of Luke and held him back to be hit some more. Joe went in for a one-two punch, but after a throw to Luke's shoulder, it wasn't just Luke who felt a snap and flood of pain. Joe's wrist ballooned. His already thick fingers swelled like sausages ready to pop, forcing him to switch hands. Joe finished the job left-handed, whopping the boy's ribs from the backside. Under Luke's shirt, his pale chest was taking on colorful hues of pink and red, and he was queasy in a way that felt like his insides were going to rip a hole clear through his stomach. That's when Luke's mouth became a sieve. He admitted to molesting his nieces and nephews, all the children in the neighborhood, and a few from his co-op. One of the men yelled, "Liar!"

Truffles gave birth to a single puppy, but it was stillborn. Traci decided to stay the night with the terrier. She lay in bed, but her aching back made her toss and turn. And then eight dogs climbed in with her. Unable to get comfortable, she moved to the recliner in her room and texted Joe for the latest.

Luke was acting like a *subdued spoiled dog*, said Joe, likening the boy to a furious dog wearing a shock collar. *i cannot believe my eyes. I haven't even seen a dog this rebellious.*

Dogs have brains, replied Traci.

Sarah wondered aloud, "Couldn't we go to the police?" Because Linda's husband was a corrections officer who used to share stories of what happened to child molesters in jail, they decided against it.

Unable to contain her bubbling fury, Debi again lunged at her sons. "How dare you?" She swung her fists like windmills, yelling, "Those are your nieces and nephews! Those are my grandchildren!"

Joe responded to a text from his mother asking if the camera was still rolling so there would be a record. He confirmed it was.

"Confess it!" Debi shouted.

"Just do it," said Tiffanie, her words intense.

Taking his brother's lead, Chris admitted to molesting Grace, Ezekiel, and other children. He confessed, in graphic detail, to molesting Sarah's kids. But the attic was a fortress. How did they get access? When?

Joe, phone in hand, updated his mother. The confessions were coming so rapidly now, he could hardly keep up.

Linda hastened to a storage room in the back of the sanctuary and snatched a computer power cord hanging on the wall. One end had the plastic plug that went into the computer, and the other end the metal-pronged plug that went into an electrical outlet. She handed it to Bruce, who folded it like a cow rustler and began a relentless flogging. First, the strikes hit Luke in the back, the boy wincing every time. Every person in that room—every single seething, mad, uncontrollable, irrational member of that riotous gang—heard the *snap, snap*.

"They've been lying to me this whole time," said Bruce. "Pretending to my face." He went back and forth, lashing each of the boys on the back and chest, one unforgiving strike after another.

Questions rained down like a hail of gunfire, peppered with explosions of the whip, and Chris heard someone say, "You better start talking." When the boys recoiled and withdrew, it only got them beaten more. Ask a question—not answer—whip. Repeat.

The boys changed tactics and tried talking again, voices shaky, giving all sorts of details. They'd raped Ivy in her crib the night before, right there with Grace and Sarah in the room, but nobody heard because they had their hands over Ivy's mouth. She bled into the crib. But answers weren't satisfying the angry mass. Bruce hit the boys while telling them to repent. Speak louder. Stand taller. Chris struggled to speak at all. He was shuddering from cold, fear, injury. He was sobbing, choking. "I . . . it . . ." Words came slowly, and with them, astonishment and outrage from those in the room.

Debi had the cord next and hit one boy, then the other. Ten times? Twenty? Someone pulled off Chris's sweatshirt. In the frenetic scene, one of the women told Sarah to go check on her children for signs of sexual abuse. When she returned, Dave was pushing Luke up against the wall to field more blows. In the middle of it, Tiffanie had a question: "Does anyone have anything else that they would like to bring up?"

Sarah did. "Do you know anything about a peephole in the bathroom?"

Chris said, "Yes."

"What is it for?" asked Tiffanie.

"It's to watch family members take showers."

"What do you mean?" Tiffanie asked. "Who were you watching take showers?"

His mother, father, Grace, and Sarah.

Sarah's mouth was drawn open, and out poured the fury she'd been holding. "Do you watch my children taking baths?"

When no answer came, Sarah yanked the cord from her father's hand and erupted. Tears of unbridled rage streamed down her face. She flogged both teens in the chest, arms, legs, and groin, and not with the plastic end that the others had used. She hit them with the metal prongs. The sound of the whip snapping against their clothing interspersed with their screams.

"Please stop," begged Luke.

"How could you!" she bellowed.

"Ah!" he screamed as the plug drove another notch in his back. Every crack of the whip made his body contort. He didn't have meat enough to deflect the battery. "I— Please, stop!" he cried. But his pleadings went unrecognized by any Word of Life member in that room as he stood, just barely.

Luke was turning and flinching, covering his privates, crying out in pain. There was blood on the floor, blood on the backs of his hands— defensive wounds. When he used his hands to protect himself, they were pulled away. When the boys tried to turn away from the cord, Joe ordered them to "turn back, or I'll make you." Sarah gave the same command, whirled her arm to Luke's groin, and slashed away. The force tore the guts of the cord from its sheathing, exposing tri-colored wires. The prongs bent. Sarah's brothers cried, their wails echoing in the sanctuary.

Sarah was wild. She aimed at Luke's groin, thrashing heedlessly. Blood poured down the front of his pants from the zipper and ran down his leg. Linda's scraggly, salt-and-pepper hair almost touched Luke as she leaned into him and ridiculed him like a schoolyard bully. "Oh, little boy peed his pants. He ain't so tough now." Saliva flung out of her mouth when she emphasized "tough."

Most everyone, at some point, was either hitting Luke or holding him back so he could be hit. But not Tiffanie. She did not lay a finger on either boy. Dave threw at least three or four punches to the gut. Chris fell at least five times. He was ordered back up, and when he couldn't get up, Dave yanked him into position. Debi was sobbing. Grace went to the nursery, where she prayed her brothers would tell the truth. Dan, who had been going between the nursery and the third-floor apartment, made his way to the sanctuary for an update. He found Joe standing outside the room, talking to their mother on the phone. Joe and Dan went into the sanctuary in time to see Luke fall into a chair, toppling a cup of coffee.

"Get up off the floor!" screamed Sarah, to Tiffanie's cool instruction of the same. Dave gave the order, too.

Luke may have prayed. Were these the last five minutes of his life? Would he repent? Was there a God? Maybe, just maybe he thought he deserved this. He struggled to get up.

Joe and Dave loomed over him. Was it over? Had they come to help? Bleary-eyed, Luke looked at the door to his right. It led straight into the big sanctuary. Through it, just steps away, was freedom. It was an indescribable burn that jolted Luke back to the place he'd never left—the Word of Life Christian Church. His oversize attackers hadn't come to aid him but to hoist him back to his feet. Sarah struck him again with the whip. Again, he fell. And again, he was ordered to his feet. When he couldn't do it, Dave jerked him up, Luke's legs scrambling to catch up. The blows kept coming, focused on his groin, though Sarah was a cyclone, whipping from all directions.

Luke pleaded with them from under the highway of tears that wetted his cheeks, "I'm bleeding." The blood had saturated the crotch of his pants and flowed to the rear.

"We have to stop," said Bruce. It may have been 3:00 A.M.

Dave ordered the boys to clean up the spilled coffee and blood. They were handed paper towels and cleaning solution, and wiped down the walls and carpet. Chris wiped his bloody nose.

Bruce went to each of his sons and, as Tiffanie looked away, pulled open the waistband of their pants to check the injuries. The little kids had been moved to another location, so he and Tiffanie went into the dining room for a private meeting. "No more hitting on the back and chest," Bruce advised.

Together, they developed a plan to get to the truth. They separated the boys so they could not collaborate on their stories. They moved Chris to the big sanctuary and had him wear earplugs and headphones so he could not hear what was being said. Since the small sanctuary, where Luke remained, was just on the other side of the door, Chris could still hear but only mumbling. They sat Chris in a chair facing the corner and told Dan to guard him, but it was Dave who took the closest seat.

Sarah was walking around the first floor, sometimes in the nursery, and sometimes in the dining room and small sanctuary. In the nursery, she and Grace prayed together. They talked. Both started to doze while sitting on the floor. When Grace felt herself nodding off, she quickly woke herself by shaking her head and body.

Sarah went to the dining area, wrapped a blanket around her body and head, and huddled over the table. She fell asleep. At some point, Dave woke her up and handed her an energy drink. She took a couple of sips and fell back to sleep. The next time she awoke, it was to screams.

Tiffanie continued questioning Luke in the small sanctuary, but he wasn't answering. Bruce was asking questions, too. Why did they molest the children? How? After about half an hour, Linda went into the big sanctuary and asked Chris more questions. What were he and Luke planning as far as killing their parents?

Joe went upstairs, where his mother was, to eat. Traci hadn't been able to get comfortable in the recliner because all the dogs had left the bed and climbed into the chair with her. She was back in the bed when Joe came in. He only wanted to rest but, exhausted from his one-sided boxing match, fell asleep.

Dave brought a bag of ice to Chris, and the teen held it against his privates. After some time, Chris was made to swap places with Luke. Chris was questioned in the smaller room, but only for a few minutes before Tiffanie told him to stand in the middle of the big sanctuary. He was so tired, and in so much pain, that he could barely stand. He was falling asleep standing up, eyes closing, bent over. He tried desperately to stay standing, because he knew they would force him back up if he fell. Chris was mutilated. Sarah, alone, must've whipped him fifty times in the genitals. His body was reacting with edema. He'd taken so many strikes that his organs were shutting down, leaching poisons throughout his system.

Bruce and Debi left to spend the rest of the night in the small sanc-tuary. Bruce went in once to check on Luke and found him talking, dazed. Debi drifted off to sleep to the sounds of Luke crying.

Luke remained in the corner of the big sanctuary, his bleeding so profuse that it completely soaked the rear of his jeans, the entire pant leg, and his sock and shoe. He was falling over in the chair, shaking violently, mumbling incoherent.

Just after 6:00 A.M., Debi made phone calls from the small sanc-tuary. She needed to let the parents in her car pool know she wouldn't be able to drive to the soccer match that day because of a "family emergency."

At about 8:00 A.M., Dan went to the back of the big sanctuary to catch some sleep. He dozed off and on for a few hours. Where was Joe? He was supposed be back to relieve Dan. With the furnace not working, Dan was uncomfortably cold. He tried getting ahold of his brother.

By this time, Luke's body had involuntarily slid off the chair, col-lapsing onto the floor. His bleeding left a trail of stains on the carpet.

Joe responded that he would be right back down. And what about Luke? He wanted to know if he was *still in the hot seat.*

No. It's a bucket, Dan replied.

Why didn't he get the chair?

So he didn't soil the chair.

Ok, Joe texted. *What about the rug?*

Yeah he the drama queen soiled the rug.

Joe went back downstairs and surveyed the scene. Luke was in the corner of the room, moaning and writhing on the carpet, smearing blood all over the place.

Upstairs, Traci was pushing the dogs off her bed so she could get some sleep, when she got a text from Joe. Could she send down a sandwich and the steam cleaner?

Sandwich for who? she answered. *What kind?*

Me. Meat and cheese sounded good to Joe. He'd worked up an appetite. *I also need water for me.*

A lot of bloodstains meant a lot of cleaning. Joe tried to minimize the mess by protecting the carpet. He had Dave get the cloudy white tarp that was over a blue barrel catching water from a leak in the ceiling. Joe had been riding on adrenaline, so the pain in his hands wasn't too intolerable. He needed them, and Dave's help, when he pulled Luke's body onto the tarp, the hood of his sweatshirt tangling around his neck as they dragged him.

From the small sanctuary, Debi heard someone say, "He's getting blood on me! To try to get me!"

As the hours ticked by, the mound of wet clothing on the tarp went from moving to motionless.

From the third-floor kitchen, Traci appealed to Joe, via text, to get Linda to *babysit* Luke, because she and Joe had work to do. Traci offered to make her kids a hot pot of coffee, mixing in some ingredients to make it special, how they liked it. It'd been a long night.

CODE BLUE

It was just before noon on Monday. Chris had the earplugs back in and the headphones on, but it didn't keep him from hearing Tiffanie shout, "Bruce! Debi! Come quick! It's Luke!" Fearing the worst, Chris willed himself not to look.

Bruce and Debi rushed into the room with Grace behind them by a few paces. Luke was on his back on the tarp. His parents shook him, trying to get a response, but there was none. Debi checked his fingernail beds. His parents stood back, perhaps in shock, or maybe not knowing what to do.

In the upstairs kitchen, coffee was brewing. Not wanting to wait, Traci had made instant coffee for herself and was on her second cup, making a mental list of things to get done around the house, when Dave and Joe raced in, yelling, "Mom! Luke's hurt! Come now!" She bounded down the three flights of stairs, and then pushed on the double-door entrance to the building before realizing the doors needed to be pulled. She flew down the handicap ramp, grabbed the railing to swing around to the sanctuary doors, and burst inside.

"He's not breathing," someone said.

"Why hasn't anybody started CPR?" asked Traci.

Bruce said he didn't know how.

"Well, I do." Traci got on her knees, listened for a heartbeat, and checked for a pulse.

When Chris finally worked up the courage to look, he saw his motionless brother and people crowded around him. He pulled off the headphones and ran over. Traci showed him how to hold Luke's mouth and tilt the head to open the airway. As she did chest compressions, Chris tried to breathe for Luke but was having difficulty.

Grace watched inquisitively. She thought Luke had held his breath to make himself pass out. Sarah stood watching, too, and Linda and Dave were off to the side.

"I need deep breaths," said Traci, after realizing Chris could not produce them, so Tiffanie took over breathing while the rest of them prayed. "If we're going to save him, we need to take him to the hospital."

Bruce thought and thought. It took him a while to decide, pondering the pros and cons. The time frame was too rushed.

"You got to decide now!" yelled Traci.

"Got to take him," Bruce said flatly.

"We need to get him into the car," said Traci.

Chris, hysterical, grabbed his brother's legs. Completely overwrought, Dave made a failed attempt at trying to help Chris pick up Luke. That's when Dan, who was going for Luke's arms, whisked him up entirely and carried him to the Leonards' van. Joe tossed out the seats so they could lay him flat, and others were throwing trash and other items to clear the van floor. Debi got hit by a flying packet of mayonnaise. There were stains and crumbs in the van, and it smelled like garbage. Luke's head went behind the driver's seat near a swarm of flies, his feet behind the passenger seat. Bruce got behind the wheel, and Debi next to him. Chris tried to get in, but they wouldn't let him.

Traci climbed in through the rear passenger sliding door and shouted to Tiffanie, "Get in the van!"

Tiffanie jumped in the back and closed the rear hatch.

Grace, Sarah, and Linda stayed behind with the children. Chris was frantic, helpless. Dan called him over to help move scaffolding that was blocking the garage door. They pulled out another van, a dark blue one, and Joe took the driver's seat, shouting to Chris, "If you're coming, come on!"

Chris climbed in.

"Are you okay?" Joe asked him.

He nodded. "Yes."

The Irwin brothers, Chris, and Dave drove to the hospital, a bit behind the others. The Faxton Campus of St. Luke's hospital in Utica was a ten-minute drive north. Tiffanie breathed for Luke, and Traci did compressions while hanging on to the back of the driver's seat for balance as Bruce sped to the hospital. At the emergency room entrance, he flew down the exit lane, narrowly missing two pedestrians. He raced onto the concrete walking path in front of the emergency room doors and slammed the brakes. The car jumped and rocked. Before it came to a stop, Debi opened the door and ran into the hospital. It was 12:22 P.M.

"My child is dying!" she yelled to the security guard at the front desk.

"I think he's dead," echoed Bruce, steps behind.

Alan Rahman was at the desk. He'd been working at St. Luke's for almost four years since retiring as a corrections officer at nearby Mid-State Correctional Facility. The fifty-nine-year-old security guard was used to seeing people rush into the hospital and sometimes exaggerate, but because Debi did an about-face and bolted out the door, he gave chase.

On his way out, Rahman signaled to an assistant nurse. She took off out the door along with Nurse Gwen Romano*. People in the waiting room jumped out of their chairs, lookie-loos rushing to see what was happening.

Through the van's open sliding door, they could see Traci working on Luke. So fast it seemed like one fluid move, the nurses and guard climbed in, hauled Luke out, laid him on the pavement, and took over CPR. Romano did compressions while the other nurse cleared the airway. They checked for a pulse. There was none. His lips were blue. They noticed the tops of his hands were covered in bruises.

Debi was pacing several feet away. Traci sat in the open door of the van in a pink T-shirt and jeans, her elbow propped on her knee. She watched for a fraction of a second before turning away and covering her face with her hand. Bruce rolled up a shirtsleeve and walked a tight circle. He mostly stayed in one spot, shifting his weight from one leg to another, and at one point shouted, "Child molester!" Then, he went right up to where they were doing CPR and stood to watch, bent over with hands on knees.

Her energy spent, Romano called for help, and another nurse, Mila Graf*, took over. Seeing the dried blood in the crotch of his pants, one of the nurses asked, "Where is the blood coming from?"

They needed to find the source in order to stop it. Romano unbuttoned Luke's pants and lifted his boxer shorts. There was serious bruising, and it was apparent the bleeding had stopped a while ago. Romano turned to Bruce. "What happened?"

"I think he got beat up last night," answered Bruce.

She continued asking questions like "Was this drug related?" and "How long has he been not breathing?" But all she got were blank looks. "When was the last time he was alive and well?"

Nothing.

"How long did it take you to get here?"

Bruce said they'd been doing CPR for about ten minutes until they got to the hospital.

"He was breathing at one point," said Traci, throwing up her hands, "and then, he stopped. I did CPR the whole way here."

Romano again turned to Bruce. "Who beat him up?" But he didn't answer. "How did he get beaten up?" she asked the others, but no one was talking.

Debi would only repeat, "I am his mother."

By this point, the nurses knew they'd been working on a dead body. Still, more staff came with a stretcher and transferred Luke to a trauma care room. As the team raced into the hospital, Bruce followed. But before he got inside, he turned and headed back toward the van. Rahman caught up with him and ushered him to a bench.

ABOVE: The Word of Life Building on Oneida Street. The gated driveway entry is on the right. **BELOW:** The Word of Life Building parking lot. It shows the Irwin apartment third-floor deck and the "Jesus Saves" sign at the base of it. The van that Bruce Leonard drove to church the day of the beating is parked under the window. Parishioners entered the big sanctuary using the doors on the right (just out of frame). The photo shows a corner of the white peaked roof that is over the sanctuary entrance.

ABOVE: The big sanctuary in the Word of Life Building. Two doors on the left of the photo lead to the small sanctuary. **BELOW:** The small sanctuary in the Word of Life Building. A checkered hooded sweatshirt that Christopher and Luke shared is on the back of Christopher's assigned seat. Luke sat on the right end seat of that row.

ABOVE: Police encountered this unusual structure inside a room of the Irwins' third-floor apartment. They believe the Irwins were trying to build a soundproof room made of engineered wood and egg cartons. **INSET:** Police found a drawer full of knives in one of the Irwin boys' bedrooms.

ABOVE: Police found a trap door leading to an underground shooting range. **RIGHT:** The hyperbaric chamber found in a second-floor room of the Word of Life Building.

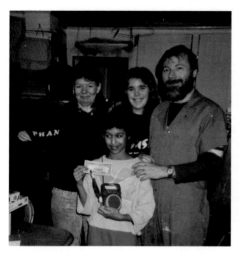 

ABOVE LEFT: *(from left to right)* Jayden, Debi, Kristel, Bruce, and *(in front)* Sarah at the Leonard family farm in December 1992. *Courtesy: Jason R Leonard of Kickin' L*
ABOVE RIGHT: Sarah, 14, holding Luke, 1, in their Clayville home in 1996.

Traci and Jerry Irwin at Kristel Leonard's wedding at the Word of Life Building in November 1999. *Courtesy: Jason R Leonard of Kickin' L*

(from left to right, back row) Traci Irwin, Jerry Irwin; *(from left to right, front row)* Tiffanie Irwin, 13, Sarah Ferguson, 17, at Kristel Leonard's wedding in the Word of Life Building in November 1999. *Courtesy: Jason R Leonard of Kickin' L*

ABOVE LEFT: Bruce and Debi Leonard in 1992, soon after marrying, before moving into their Clayville home. **ABOVE RIGHT:** Joe Irwin, 3, in the kitchen of the Leonards' Clayville home in March 1997.

LEFT: Bruce and Debi with Luke, age six months, in the kitchen of their Clayville home in 1996.

BELOW: Luke, 12, with his siblings and nephew in 2008.

ABOVE LEFT: Oneida County district attorney Scott McNamara addressing reporters after a court appearance involving the Word of Life case. **ABOVE RIGHT:** Former New Hartford police investigator Brad Pietryka in 2019. He was the lead investigator on the Word of Life case. **LEFT:** Intern Anthony Sokolowski working on the Word of Life case in April 2016. **BELOW LEFT:** Helen Lehrer and Kristel Leonard in August 2016, one month after Sarah Ferguson's guilty verdict. **BELOW RIGHT:** Inspired by this tragedy to testify about the word of God, investigator Dave Cady (pictured here in 2018) began writing and performing contemporary Christian songs.

MUG SHOTS

Bruce Leonard

Deborah Leonard

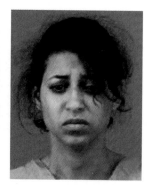

Sarah Ferguson

Tiffanie Irwin

Traci Irwin

Joseph Irwin

Daniel Irwin

Linda Morey

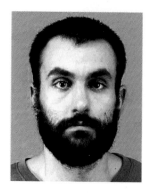

David Morey

Lucas Benjamin Leonard.
Courtesy: ReePoses

Rahman tried to get information from Bruce. "Who are you? What happened?"

"They jumped him," said Bruce tersely. He wouldn't give his name. He seemed shaken and disoriented.

"Who jumped him?" asked Rahman.

"My son is a child molester."

"Are you sure you want to say that to me?"

"Yes. He is a child molester." With that, Bruce prayed loudly, "Lord, forgive my son and forgive me."

"Do you want to see a pastor?"

"Yes."

Bruce kept asking the status of his son. Rahman knew the boy was dead, but it wasn't his place to tell Bruce. By now, Graf, in her pink scrubs, had come to help seat Bruce on the bench. The guard placed his hands on Bruce's back to direct him, but Bruce resisted, straightening himself. The father eventually walked into the hospital with the two workers guiding him, one on each arm.

With everyone gone, Traci stayed in the same spot. After a time, she leaned back and talked to Tiffanie, who was still in the van.

Joe arrived at the hospital, pulled around back, and parked in a handicap spot. He alone got out and walked quickly toward his mother, but as he approached, she stood and waved him away. At the same time, Tiffanie was texting Dan rapid-fire:

Stay away now
Get away
Hurry
Turn around . . .

Joe peeled out of the hospital grounds, driving so erratically that Dan told him to pull over. He parked in the back corner of a parking lot of a retail store, and Chris threw up in the car. He got out with the rest of them, and then threw up outside the car. Dave went in the store and brought back candy bars and twenty-ounce sodas for everyone. Within minutes, he went back in to purchase water for Chris. They left the lot just sixteen minutes after they'd arrived.

Staff asked Traci for identification, but she didn't give them any, instead burying her face in her hands when a paramedic arrived to talk to her. She stayed that way and did not respond when Graf walked back out and tried to reason with her. One by one, hospital staff tried gently to persuade her to talk. All she did was rock a few times and wipe her tears.

Graf put her arm around Debi and guided her through the hospital doors.

Over the intercom, Joseph LaClaire, in charge of the nursing staff, had announced a code blue, a call for assistance for an unresponsive patient. The fifty-seven-year-old nurse entered the triage room when staff was working on Luke and noticed the teen's ashen skin. It meant Luke's heart was no longer pumping blood through his body. His shirt was open, but his pants were still on. LaClaire had staff take off the pants to find the source of the blood. He saw extensive clotting and swelling in Luke's upper thighs and groin, and a hole that looked like a gunshot wound to the side of his penis, near the tip.

Dr. Mohammad Anwar shined a light in Luke's eyes, but they were unresponsive. The echocardiogram showed a flat line. This was not a living person but a dead body. Luke was quite cold, and Dr. Anwar believed he had been dead for some time. At 12:28 P.M., the doctor ceased lifesaving efforts and made a declaration of death.

A shot in the groin could cause a bullet to travel to different parts of the body. The doctor ordered a chest X-ray to see if the cause of death was a bullet that had penetrated the chest cavity.

Having worked at the hospital for more than twenty-eight years, LaClaire knew exactly what to do. Given the suspicious circumstances, he stepped out of the room and asked another employee to call the police.

The call came into dispatch: "Yeah, Luke's emergency room. Somebody just dropped off a patient that's coded here, and it's a possible shooting."

LaClaire blocked off the area and treated it like a crime scene. He called Nurse Sasha Newman* to the triage room and told her about the death and then went to look for Luke's parents to put them in the quiet room, a secluded room off the emergency department.

Newman went to the parking lot with another nurse to speak to the women at the van. Tiffanie was still in the vehicle, Traci still seated on the sliding door runner. The nurses crouched beneath her on the pavement. They touched her tenderly. But she wouldn't speak to them. All she did was pray.

Nurse LaClaire went to the hospital's resource room, a room with information and educational materials, where he found Bruce sitting with a resource attendant. LaClaire tried to speak to him, but Bruce wouldn't even look in his direction. The hospital's medical director came into the room and told Bruce there was no heartbeat, but they were doing all they could.

That time, Bruce responded, "Just get him out of here then."

Nurse Newman moved the parents to the quiet room. By then, hospital staff had led Traci and Tiffanie into the waiting room. When New Hartford police showed up, they waited for hospital staff to find enough rooms to separate everyone. Eventually, Traci was guided to an office, where Newman and social worker Chelsea Esposito* sat with her. Traci cried the entire time and uttered disconnected thoughts. Esposito thought Traci might be in shock and trying to figure out the series of events in her own mind. As Traci became increasingly nervous, Esposito tried calming her.

"Where are you coming from?" she asked, trying to navigate the dizzying encounter.

"I was running to the car. I had to do CPR, and Tiffanie breathed for him."

"What's your name?"

"Traci."

"And who is Tiffanie?"

"My daughter."

Traci was also blurting out spontaneous statements, like, "He raped a baby."

"Was it your baby?"

"No."

Newman left the room to notify police.

Inside the office, Traci repeatedly asked to speak with her daughter, who was in the hallway. Esposito opened the door and called to Tiffanie. When Tiffanie went in, the social worker left to give them privacy, but on her way out, Tiffanie asked about the hospital's confidentiality laws and regulations, an odd and possibly significant request that would later spark the interest of police.

Esposito returned and handed Tiffanie the phone number to a legal-aid group, but Tiffanie said she was going to use a legal-aid website she'd accessed in the past and stepped back out into the hallway. That's where Angela Belmont saw the young preacher praying. Belmont was the hospital's assistant vice president of emergency services and psychiatry. She approached Tiffanie and diplomatically told her, "You need to help police learn what happened."

Tiffanie looked up, and her eyes met Belmont's.

"As a pastor," Belmont continued, "it's your duty to help keep people safe."

"It is my job to pray," Tiffanie replied coolly, and went back into the office with her mother.

Belmont made her way to the quiet room and also tried to impress upon Debi the importance of cooperating with the police. But Debi just cried, shook her head from side to side, and muttered, "No, no, no."

Esposito was still trying to get information out of Traci, who'd begun making scattered statements about the church and her late husband, Jerry. The anniversary of his passing was coming up, Traci volunteered, and this was bringing back those memories. She told Esposito of the stroke he'd suffered and how he'd died in a hotel room. She said she'd been questioned by police at the time, so she was familiar with the process, and understood they were just doing their job.

"Tell me about what happened, Traci," said Esposito compassionately, bringing the topic back to Luke. "You said he raped a two-year-old."

"I didn't say it was a two-year-old. I said it was a baby." She then tearfully asked, "What would ever cause someone to want to hurt or touch a child?" Her tears stopped, and then started over again when she said, "It's their son. What are they going to do without their son?" Traci would repeat this phrase throughout, along with, "I'm the only one who knows CPR."

Traci asked if Lucas was breathing yet. "I was trying to give him CPR. Obviously, that didn't help."

Esposito tried to get Traci to walk her through what happened, but Traci started with the ending. "I ran and ran. I never ran faster in my life."

"Where were you running to?"

"Downstairs and out to the van."

"How did you know they were out in the van? Did someone call you, or did you hear yelling? How did you know they were outside?"

She closed her eyes. "I got up at ten o'clock. It's a lot later than I normally get up, six or seven. I slept in because my dogs kept me up all night. They kept pushing closer to me in my bed. They took over the whole bed, so I got out and went to the chair. But they followed me to the chair and kept me awake all night. I got up around ten. Made a pot of coffee with cinnamon in it, because that's how Tiffanie and Joseph like it. It was gonna be a little treat for them." She next remembered running down to the van. That was it.

"Were Lucas and his parents inside the van when you got there?"

She didn't remember, she said at first, but eventually said, "Of course they were."

When New Hartford police investigator Jason Freiberger arrived, Traci repeated the events to him. The investigator told her that Debi claimed she and Bruce had gotten a phone call to pick up Luke on Oneida Street that morning because he was hurt. "Could this have happened at your house?"

Traci gasped. "No . . . no . . . not at my house." She then cried out, "I can't believe this is happening. It's a nightmare!"

At 3:00 P.M., Traci signed a police statement. This included the information she'd previously left out, like the part where Joe hollered to her and she ran downstairs to find Luke on the tarp unconscious, his parents by his side.

In the social worker's office, Bruce had been mostly mute, making only a few comments to Patrolman Thomas Hulser, who documented them:

Mr. Leonard, what happened to Lucas?
They whooped him.
Who whopped him?
No response.
Why did they hurt Lucas?
He's a child molester.
You knew that, or you found out today?
I knew before, and he told me again today.
Where did you pick up Lucas today?
On Oneida Street in New Hartford.
Where on Oneida Street? The big church that looks like a school?

Yes. In the lawn there. They carried him out.
Who carried him out?
No response.
Mr. Leonard, did you hurt Lucas?
I... I... I... (no response)

Officer Hulser gave Bruce a pat-down and found a spent shell casing, a .223 round, in his pants pocket, as well as several jackknives. He handcuffed him and took him to the station for questioning. Debi was transported, too, after being equally uncommunicative in the quiet room. She just kept mumbling that Lucas was her son, and "God forgive us."

I do not understand what you want. What do you think you're doing? I'm serious. What does anybody *think* they're doing? Because, if you think you're serving God, it's not the way it looks.

—Pastor Tiffanie Irwin

to the congregation on November 2, 2014

SCRAMBLED. DEAD. PERIOD.

Back at the Word of Life Building, Sarah was picking up the junk that had been tossed from the van, now scattered across the parking lot. Grace went out to help. When they were done, they went to the second-floor guest room, where Grace fell asleep.

Joe drove back to the church. On the first floor, the men talked while Chris managed to get his aching body into a chair so he could try to fall asleep. But after a few minutes, they took him to a filthy second-floor storage room. There were no ceiling tiles but sheets of plastic in their place. Amid stacks of dog cages, Chris tried to wiggle into a comfortable spot on the cold, hard floor. The men cleared out the room and put in a mattress, blanket, and pillow. Chris threw up twice more in a box. Dave brought him food and water, but he was suffering too much to eat. He could barely breathe. His body was shutting down. He kept falling asleep and waking.

Everyone else, including Kathy, Zeke, and Sarah's four kids, were in the guest room on the second floor. This was a large room, a former classroom, where they'd installed orange carpet and put in two beds, a nightstand, and several couches. Beside one bed was a chalkboard that ran the length of the wall. They'd set enormous framed pictures in the runner at the bottom meant for chalk and erasers. There was a flat-screen TV at the opposite end, a vanity in the middle of the room, and a keyboard. After a time, Linda got Chris, and moved him to this room with the others. Chris dragged along his blanket and carried his pillow and uneaten bowl of pasta. The younger kids were at a circular dining table decorated with a white doily tablecloth and chairs with blue-and-white country-pattern seat cushions, chomping

on apples and crackers as Chris lay on the couch and drifted in and
out of sleep.

New York State Police searched the Leonard home in Clayville to look
for other possible victims. Staff at local newsrooms heard the activity
on the scanners and flooded the area almost as quickly as law enforcement.

Residents on Main Street had awakened that morning and realized
the Leonards were still not home.

Frances Bernard later recalled the worry she felt. "I thought—oh
my God. I hope nothing happened." Her first thought was that Debi
had another heart attack. "Then—" She took a deep breath before
words flooded like a burst dam. "All of a sudden, there's state troopers
here. Social Services was down there. All of this business. Fifty million
reporters. And it was like—my God. What the hell is going on?"

Then, they found out.

"It made me sick," Frank Livingstone recalled.

"I couldn't even talk to any of the reporters. I had to shut the door,"
Brenda recounted, still affected years later. "I started cryin'." She's the
one who called Olivia, Luke's childhood friend, and broke the news.
Frank walked to Frances's door.

"And he told me. It's like—" Frances inhaled deeply. "I don't believe
that."

Next door, Pamela got a visit from police. "The officer told me
Lucas had died. My heart just dropped." That the parents had anything to do with it never crossed her mind.

After police left, the door to the Leonard home was open. The
neighbors knew the family had pets, so they went to check on them.
What they discovered was stomach churning.

"It was dirty in there. Bugs," recalled Frank.

"Filthy," added Brenda.

"Cobwebs."

"Flies all over the whole place."

"Dirt all over."

There was an emaciated dog tied to an old, unused kitchen sink on a foot-long leash, standing in excrement with no food or water. Two other dogs were in small, mold-covered cages in the basement. "Just waiting to die," Brenda later recalled. "We never knew they were there." They had foot sores from walking on excrement. There was a dog running loose in the house, "and then the cats—there were eight cats—they left them in the house. There was hard cat crap stuck everywhere on the floors." There were three birds: a macaw and two parakeets that looked like ones the Irwins had raised and given to members.

"You wouldn't believe the conditions these kids lived in," Pamela recounted. "I was totally amazed in disgust. It was heartbreaking." There were baskets and loose mounds of clothes, and half-eaten food all over the kitchen counters. The stove was covered with rotting food and the table piled with dirty dishes. Upstairs, there were mounds of clothes all over the floor. The kids didn't have beds. It looked as though they'd been sleeping on the clothes. There was only one mattress. The parents' bedroom didn't have a mattress, just a box spring.

"It was despicable," Pamela said. "It was just ungodly. It stunk in the house." The stench of urine and feces was so bad, it was all the neighbors could do not to vomit. On the lower level in the back was a bathroom with just a commode. No bathtub. No shower. Not even a flush toilet—just a commode sitting over a broken toilet.

The neighbors fed the animals, and then called an animal rescue group.

At the hospital, New Hartford police called New York State Police to help with the investigation. But where was the crime scene? Until authorities could establish that, NHPD didn't know if they had jurisdiction.

NHPD investigator Brad Pietryka was among the first to respond when the 911 call came in for a possible shooting victim. Pietryka was new to the department's Criminal Investigations Division but not new to the job. A twenty-three-year veteran of the force, he'd started as a patrol officer. After six years, Pietryka was promoted to narcotics investigator and assigned to a multiagency drug task force in Utica, made up of seven different police agencies working to combat mid-to-upper-level narcotic and gun-trafficking groups. He stayed with the unit for fifteen years, until his promotion in 2012 to head of the Criminal Investigations Division.

Police Chief Michael Inserra and Lieutenant Timothy O'Neill, of the New Hartford Police Department, called Pietryka into the office for a briefing and tasked him with interviewing Debi at the police station. Pietryka's job was to identify the crime scene.

The problem was that Debi's story was fiction. It went something like this: Bruce had argued with Luke the previous night over allegations that Luke had molested a child. Luke took off walking to the church, or maybe got a ride. Someone called Bruce the next morning and told him to pick up Luke at the Word of Life Building because there'd been an emergency. It was apparent right away the story had holes in it. Debi wouldn't say who called Bruce, and then she shut down altogether. But the statement served its purpose. Police now had a crime scene: the Word of Life Christian Church. New Hartford police called more officers into work. State Police brought more troopers. Right away, police set up a perimeter around the Word of Life Building—no one in, no one out—to preserve the crime scene.

"We were not going to make entry into that church, just because of the fear that there possibly would've been some gunfight, like a Waco type of situation," Pietryka later said, referring to the 1993 police siege of a doomsday sect compound in Texas that led to dozens of deaths. In that instance, cult leader David Koresh had a large cache of illegal weapons. "Based upon past cases, these types of groups are known to be armed and would be willing to possibly die for what they believe in." Pietryka had been aware of the shell casing found on Bruce. Police would not make entry until they had SWAT teams in place.

Across from the Word of Life Building, Stacey Brodeur, who'd long since moved from Oneida Street, was visiting her parents in her childhood home. It was a beautiful, warm day, and because it was a school holiday, she had her grandchildren with her.

"Dad, let's sit on the porch. It's nice," she said, and scooped up her three-month-old grandson.

They'd barely gotten settled when she saw a man pull up to the gate at the Word of Life Building and try to open it. She laughed out loud at what had become a common scene over the years.

"Good luck with that," she quipped, and watched the man look around before going to the front door of the church and knocking. "Like they're gonna open the door for somebody," she joked with her dad. She did find it odd, though.

Four hours later, two detectives showed up at Stacey's parents' door. "Then, all of a sudden, the troopers were coming. The detectives were coming."

"Sheriff's. Troopers. I've never seen anything like it in my life," Stacey's mother, Meredith, recalled.

"Then the SWAT went in," added Stacey.

Police were knocking on doors. "It's better for you guys to go spend the night somewhere," they warned the neighbors. But not everyone left.

"My wife was excited," a father across the street recalled. "We had somewhere to go, but my wife wanted to stay. She wanted to see what was gonna happen." They left the doorway but watched through the windows.

An investigator asked Meredith to have everyone go to the back of house. Police didn't know who was inside the WLCC building and what might happen.

She later recalled, "He saw the kids, and he said, 'Please don't let the kids be in the windows.' Well, I'm gonna tell you the truth—as soon as he said that, my kids and grandkids all ran upstairs and went to the front windows." It was heart-stopping. Tankers rode right up on the lawn. There were snipers and uniformed police. "They were all over the place."

News crews showed up. That's how Stacey's aunt learned what happened. "I was in Florida, and I was watching the news, and I see my niece," she later said. "They're interviewing her about what was going on. I almost fell out of my chair."

The sleepy community had awakened.

"They came from all over," recalled Stacey—satellite trucks, television cameras, news reporters. "Every national network was here."

"It was chaotic," added Meredith. "You couldn't even get out of your driveway. Reporters were all over the place day and night, and sometimes they'd still be out there. You'd wake up in the middle of the night, and you'd see cars here and cars there. It was a zoo."

Within a half hour of the 911 call, police were interviewing possible witnesses and persons of interest. They learned there was an Irwin sibling who had been excommunicated. A State Police investigator tracked down Naomi by phone. She was living out of state, working and going to college. Naomi told the investigator she hadn't spoken with her family in years.

[Naomi] stated the reason why she was kicked out of the church was because she wanted to have an education, the investigator documented.

The investigator provided Naomi with few details, telling her only that it was a male who had died. After hanging up the phone, Naomi tried desperately to get ahold of her mother. *You are going to make our family another Waco Texas if you don't stop avoiding the police!* she texted. *Its not the time to lock up in your isolated world and shut down.*

But Traci wasn't answering.

Developing information was a slow build. The Word of Life members believed to be present during the crime were tight-lipped. It was immediately clear to Pietryka that Tiffanie was trying to control everything. Right from the get-go at the hospital, she'd been pushing the family to retain attorneys, a sign of a guilty conscious. Why was this person telling the parents of a dead child to lawyer up? It raised Pietryka's suspicions. And when police tried to interview Tiffanie, she refused and hid behind pastor-parishioner privilege.

NHPD had two interview rooms with recording capabilities and several offices without. When all the rooms were filled, they brought the possible suspects to the State Police barracks for questioning.

Officer James Hyatt drove Traci to the New Hartford station. Because the rooms were full, he took her to the other side of the building with the justice court.

Pietryka came into the room and observed. Occasionally Traci's phone would vibrate. She would look at it and say, "Oh, that's Naomi," or "That's Joe," but not pick up.

"I wanna talk to Joe," said Pietryka. He asked Traci to call Joe and see if he would come in.

Pietryka left Hyatt alone with Traci, and after about four hours of dead ends, he went back and called the officer out of the room. "Did you tell her Lucas passed away?"

He hadn't.

"When you're ready, you can let her know. I want to see what happens."

Hyatt went back in the room and approached her solemnly. "I just got word," he said, then cleared his throat and started again, "Investigator just came and told me that I have to tell you that Lucas Leonard has died. He's been confirmed deceased."

Traci's face dropped with genuine disbelief. "He's dead? He's dead? How could he die?" She looked off into space and asked, "How could he die from a beating?"

At that point, there had been no mention of a beating. Hyatt asked, "Who beat him?"

She froze.

"Well, who beat him?"

"I don't know."

"Well, how do you know he was beaten if you don't know?"

After a noticeable number of seconds ticked by, Traci replied, "When I saw his injuries in the hospital, it appeared to me that he was bruised from the waist down, and it looked like he'd been beat. That's why I assumed he was beaten."

It was at the police station that Pietryka briefly came into contact with Tiffanie. To him, she appeared emotionless. She carried herself as a person of authority, with a sense of arrogance, in stark contrast with the others they had interviewed. Both current and former members of the church struck him as very submissive people. Pietryka later reflected on the young pastor's presence: "One of my coworkers said, 'It's like looking into the face of evil.' Because there's nothing there. It's deep. She's got that mile-long stare. And you look into her eyes and it's like there's no soul there."

Pietryka was assigned to draw up search warrants, and there was much more work ahead. New Hartford didn't have a large police force, and this case was growing. They had to decide whether to keep the case or turn it over to State Police. The chief and lieutenant called Pietryka into the office to gauge his opinion. Should they turn it over?

"No. Absolutely not." Pietryka was adamant. "We're quite capable of handling the case."

It was a small police department, fewer than thirty members, yet one of the busiest in Oneida County, second busiest for serious crimes. The court attached to it was the second busiest behind Utica.

Chief Inserra had another question for Pietryka: did he want to be the lead investigator? Indeed, he did. State Police would provide support personnel, but NHPD would take the lead on the case, and Pietryka would be in charge. Pietryka set up a "lead desk," a command center to receive tips and through which all information would flow, and he would assign officers to chase down each lead—in the end, 337 files, many of them with copious documents.

On the day Lucas Leonard's body was driven to the hospital, police made short work of the massive task of questioning individuals possibly connected to the case, knocking off nineteen interviews in a single afternoon. More interviews were done in the days that followed and would continue over the course of a year.

Frank Livingstone told police, "I don't know why anyone would want to hurt Lucas. He's a great kid." Bruce was odd, he said, but he'd never seen signs of abuse.

Defected WLCC member Jeff Wright agreed, calling his brother-in-law passive and indecisive. "It is very hard for him to make a decision, which, I believe, leaves him open to the influence of someone with a stronger personality." Jeff had spent twenty years at WLCC but now called it "mentally abusive" and said the members were "brainwashed." In the police report, Jeff was documented as saying, *I do not really know anything about what happened in the church to my nephews, but it would only take speculation for this incident to occur. There would not need to be evidence. Their word, specifically with Tiffanie Irwin and Joe Irwin, was all that was needed.* Nothing, he said, happened in that building without Tiffanie's knowledge. "Tiffanie would've initiated this counseling session and would've been there at the start of this punishment." Even if she wasn't present, she would've been kept informed, he told police. "The mind-set of the leadership of the church would be to protect Tiffanie at all costs. The leadership would, without hesitation, lie, even under oath, to protect Tiffanie."

Kristel's husband, Arthur, warned police there were guns in the building. Joe had shown them off to him. "He's kind of like the bulldog of the place."

A friend of Jayden's contacted him around the dinner hour to tell him to get in touch with his family because something serious had happened. He drove to Clayville to find the Leonards' property teeming with troopers. "Lucas is a typical kid," he told them. "He doesn't have any enemies. I don't know why anyone would hurt him." Jayden said his parents had always been supportive, never abusive.

Investigators wanted to speak with Caroline Dibble. She had a story to tell. The mom was part of the homeschool co-op with the Leonards, and about three weeks before Luke's death, she'd been at the co-op site, Crosspoint Church, for a meeting. Debi had been there with her three boys, but Chris was off sitting by himself, as usual. Caroline's son had reached out to Chris and tried to include him, but Chris wasn't receptive to it. *Debi then mentioned something about going to a soccer game and Christopher not wanting to hang out with the boys [who were] going to check out the girls, as he did not want to be tempted,* read Caroline's statement to police. *Debi then mentioned that they, she did not say who, found out Christopher had committed sexual sin, and he would not be allowed to use the computer at the library anymore.* There were never any signs of abuse, she added, and *Debi always seemed very nice, kind and loving. I could not believe that she was capable of what I heard was done to her children. I never saw any anger in her.*

Authorities learned that Grace, who had gone once a week to the homeschool group and was involved in its skating and soccer programs, had stopped attending the co-op two years earlier. At that same time, the homeschool families stopped meeting at the Leonard house. Prior to that, they would meet there once a month, as the families were on a rotating schedule to host the co-op. The house certainly hadn't been in squalor then. Everything—and everyone—changed when Sarah had settled in, especially Luke. One homeschool parent told police he'd become "very rebellious."

Bruce's brother Jason Leonard talked to police about his three or four visits to WLCC when Jerry was pastor, visits he did not recall fondly.

Once, when he tried to talk to Jerry, the preacher walked away. Bruce said Jerry wouldn't talk to Jason because the preacher was modeling himself after Jesus and didn't want to engage in idle talk. "Every time I pointed out what I didn't like about the guy, my brother would defend him," Jason told police. "Around five or six years ago, my mother and I said something that was critical of the church, and after that, I was not privy to any church information at all." Jason didn't like the preacher's tactic of public humiliation. "He would call people up to the front of the congregation and name off all the bad things they did."

But about his brother, Jason said, *I just can't see him hurting his kids like this. He is just not assertive. And his first answer is not violence. It is usually prayer. I don't know if my brother witnessed this, if he would be scared to stop it, or if he would be off in the corner praying . . . I don't know how brainwashed he is.*

There it was again—"brainwashed." Same word, different police report. It would come up in others.

Jason told police that Bruce hadn't been visiting him like he used to, and whenever Jason would ask why his nieces Grace and Sarah weren't visiting anymore, Bruce would give only vague answers.

The Leonard patriarch was also giving hazy answers back at the police station. His incomplete sentences were difficult to understand, and he was slow to speak, to a painful, confusing degree. His speech was restrained to the point it seemed something metaphysical was clipping his words. But one thing out of his mouth was clear: Bruce wanted to talk to his wife and Pastor Tiffanie. Pietryka was not in the room with Bruce during questioning but watched him on a monitor from another location. He got the impression Bruce couldn't say anything unless it was approved by Tiffanie.

Despite having been told at the hospital that his son no longer had a heartbeat, Bruce seemed not to grasp that Luke was dead, and continually asked, "How's my son?" in a forceful, demanding voice that did not match his appearance. He sat curled in a red vinyl office chair at a cold metal desk, his head wrapped tightly in his arms.

"It's not looking good," said the investigator in the room with Bruce. The investigator needed to know where Bruce had picked up Luke in the morning. "Not cooperating—I'm going to be honest with you—is not an option, being a parent myself."

By failing to respond, Bruce turned down a request to lead police to the supposed location. He asked again, "Do you know what's happening with Luke?"

His statements were inconsistent with his actions, and police, who were trying to find the killer of his boy, were frustrated that this father wasn't interested in helping them. The investigator's approach reflected his sheer puzzlement and aggravation. To Bruce's question, he replied, "Unfortunately, we're stuck here dealing with you. All right?" He added, "Mr. Leonard, you know, if you're not concerned with how this happened to your son, unless you did it, then, uh, it's not worth our time to call the hospital to get you that update."

After a few more questions, police left the room. For more than an hour, alone, Bruce mumbled to himself, sang, and prayed. As in a salute, he stretched his arm high toward the ceiling with an open palm. "I thank you, Jesus, for bringing . . . bringing good to an impossible situation."

The officer returned and stood in front of Bruce, who had tucked himself into a corner on the chair. In response to Bruce's seeming disinterest, he informed him, "Mr. Leonard, listen . . . uh, your son passed away, just so you know."

This time, those words were received with excruciating reverberation. Bruce's body coiled, and a visceral wail erupted like that from a wounded animal.

Investigator Todd Grant had been working a few of the interviews all at once. He would try to question Bruce, and then move on to Debi's room to ask a question or two. Now, he was back with Bruce and trying to relate on a religious level.

"The devil is out there," said Grant. "Do you think he got himself ahold of your boy? At least a little bit?"

"Maybe more than a little."

"Have you looked evil in the eye? Have you looked at your boy and not recognized him?"

"Yeah."

"Do you think your boy deserved what he got?" asked Grant.

Most of what Bruce said could not be understood, but this answer was clear: "Yeah." He wouldn't say who was responsible for hurting Luke but did say he hoped that at the end, his son asked forgiveness.

"Do the rest of your family, does any of 'em know what's going on?" asked another investigator, Stephen Kubat.

"I don't know."

"Do you need to talk to any of 'em and just—"

"I don't!"

"I'm sorry," said Kubat.

All that could be heard from Bruce's mumbling, as though he were participating in a conversation with some unknown person, was, "Oh, by the way, Luke died today." He spent more time crying than talking.

They tried to get him to talk about the good things about Luke, like what he enjoyed doing.

"He liked fixing things," Bruce offered.

No amount of prompting would get him to share what sorts of activities they did together.

"I'm sorry. I don't really wanna talk about this."

Grant tried again. "You don't think I understand? We see the devil every day. We work about as close to the devil as you possibly could." Sometimes, the devil takes our kids, said Grant. "I've been doing this fifteen years now, and when I was young, I was like, you know what? The devil won. But I have a hard time believing that now."

"How come?" asked Bruce.

"Well, 'cause I think . . . a couple different things. One, how can the devil win, when we have the ability to just ask forgiveness? I believe that when we die, we see the light, and we hear the voice of God, and we ask for forgiveness . . . Do I think there's evil people in this world? Yes, I do. Do I think he gives the most evil people the chance to be forgiven? I do. I don't know what makes people evil. I don't know what makes people do what they do. I have two little girls, and I don't know any way better to do it. And that may not be the right way. I go to bed every night, I'm so afraid that they're gonna make a decision . . . they're gonna do something that's gonna put them in the hands of the devil. And there's nothing I can do to stop it."

"So you pray," said Bruce.

"So you pray. And you know what, though? How many times can you pray, and you see things happen again and again and again? See people lose their kids? See people injured? Injure little kids? Beat on each other, and do horrible things to one another, and go home and just—pray? That's a lot of faith. And you're an old—You spent more time earth than I have, so I got a long way to go. I have to imagine you've seen your fair share of things that you've had to pray about. And—"

"Children aren't supposed to die before their parents."

"They're not ever. Ever," said Grant, and offered to pray with him. But Grant continued to try to find out who did this to Luke, and after a time, said, "I may even think that you might have possibly said a prayer for those people . . . You look, you look at me and you see how I treated you, and I gave you my word." He tried to get Bruce to look up, but he wouldn't. "I want you to look at me. I gave you my word. I'll give them every respect when I talk to them, just as I talked with you. And I'll sit down, and I'll pray with them, as well. But if you don't tell me who I need to go sit and pray with, I can't tell you who's gonna be the person talking to him. They may not have the same belief system you and I have—"

"I want you to get my wife," Bruce insisted, starting a verbal tug-of-war over it.

"If I go get you your wife," said Grant, "and get her to come in here, will you tell me the people I need to go pray with? Will you make me a deal?"

"I don't know. We'll see."

At 4:23 P.M., at his mother's request, Joe walked alone into a cluttered office at the New Hartford police station. He took the middle of three brown office chairs against the wall, not noticing the one to the right had a contraption behind it, built into the wall, for locking up those taken into custody. He sat with his hands folded in his lap, like a schoolboy in the principal's office waiting to be scolded, his mood matching his clothes—black cargo pants and a couple of gray shirts, one inside the other. He sometimes hung his head, but not like the Leonards. This was different. It was hung in gloom rather than compliance. More often, he sat upright, facing forward but not looking at anything, deep in thought.

State Police investigators Dennis Dougherty and Susannah Rose introduced themselves.

Right off the top, Joe had something to volunteer. "May I just make a statement?" Joe said he wasn't there the whole time. "I do not understand how that happened. I . . . I do not understand how that killed him."

"What did you see?"

"Well, what I saw was his father beat him. On the back . . . with, like, a rubber power cord." And his mother was hitting him, too. "Debi was in complete agreement."

Earlier, Joe had run down a list for investigators, names of those present when Luke had been beaten, and Chris was on that list. Investigators now asked if Chris had been involved in hitting Luke.

"No. He was spanked, too."

Throughout five hours of questioning, Joe would refer to what happened as a spanking, and when anyone used the word "beating," he would correct them. The investigators asked why Christopher was "spanked." After a theatrical display of appearing to search for the right words, Joe said the teen was "inclined heavily toward child molestation." Luke, on the other hand, was giving graphic details and wasn't remorseful, according to Joe. He said Luke had confessed to Pastor a year ago that he was a porn addict, but Joe gave the story some flair: it was child pornography. Luke had basically checked out as far as church, said Joe. "My guess is the peer pressure of his family going to the church is the only reason he went to the church."

Why did this happen now?

"Today was the day that Tiffanie believed that God spoke to her to confront him." Joe recounted events, ones that didn't mesh with what police were hearing from the others. "I was told that the bleeding had stopped, but there was blood on the rug. So I don't know . . . I don't know what happened there. There was blood on the rug—"

"Where? In the small room?"

"In the big room."

"The main sanctuary?"

"Yes. We had moved—we had put him over—" Joe paused, touched his nose, shrugged, and said in a tone as though his story had been challenged. "Well, we didn't put him. He walked. He walked over to the corner and sat down. Maybe on the floor. I'm not really sure. That's probably why there's blood on the floor." Luke then "plopped," he said, they "freaked out," and Joe went over and asked him what was wrong. "I'm pret— I'm gonna try to quote him exactly. I'm pretty sure what he said . . . was . . . 'I'm sorry. I was lying. I just like to feel sorry for myself and feel pity. And be in control.' That's what he said in response to us asking if he was okay when he fell over. When he plopped over. Then he proceeds to—"

"What was he saying he was lying about?" asked Dougherty. But

Joe looked puzzled, so the investigator continued. "About raping the kids? Like the whole thing was a lie?"

"About . . . ?" Joe tipped his head. "When did I say lying?"

"Just now, you said that he said he was lying."

Recognizing his error, Joe tossed his head back. "Lying about that he was actually falling over." Joe was gesturing a whole lot, but not with his right arm. He kept it dangling between his legs as he sat in the chair with his knees apart. "He was asked repeatedly by me, 'Are you okay? Are you okay? Are you okay? Are you okay?' He said yes." Joe said he walked away, and next thing he knew, Luke didn't have a pulse. That was his story, but it was phrased unnaturally, his words too deliberately chosen.

Investigator Pietryka came in, and Dougherty filled him in on what Joe had told him, finishing with "and they started CPR and took him up to the hospital."

Joe hurried to tack onto the summary, "We, um, he willingly moved over to sit on a tarp. 'Cause . . . he had gotten blood on the rug. He willingly moved over onto the tarp. That's why the tarp is there."

Investigator Grant returned to Bruce but without Debi. "Okay. Um . . . Your wife can't come in right now. But can I tell you why?"

"Why?"

"Okay, because there's a guy, Joe, named Joey, that's here. And Joey's telling the other police officers—and I haven't talked to Joey yet, but I just went out to try to get your wife in here—and they said, 'You have to hold on,' 'cause Joey's telling the other police officers that you were hitting your boy with a belt in the sanctuary while your wife was punching him. And that's how he died."

Bruce said something under his breath.

"I don't know," continued Grant. "Joey's an awful big kid, like a . . . he's the— And forgive me if I'm wrong. I didn't talk to him. He's the, the brother of somebody and the son of the supreme . . ."

"Hm?"

"What? Pastor? Is that— Am, am I talking about—"

"What?"

"Does that make sense, or no?" asked Grant, fishing for answers.

"No. No." Bruce shook his head.

"Okay, well, so . . . so help me here. 'Cause I just wanna . . . 'cause we gotta sit tight here for a second 'cause Joey's down here saying a bunch of stuff."

Investigator Kubat asked, "Do you know Joey?"

"Yeah," said Bruce. "Yeah. A big guy?"

"Big. Yeah," said Kubat. "Real big kid."

"Okay, who . . . who is Joey?" Grant asked. "Can you tell me who he is, just so I know?"

And Kubat wanted to know, "Why would Joey make things up about you like that?"

Debi walked into the interview room at 6:56 P.M. the night of her son's death, asked for a cup of coffee, and handed her heart pills to the investigator, who explained he couldn't leave her alone in the room with them. It was a precaution, should she decide to swallow the entire bottle.

"No, that's not good for my heart," she said, ending on a laugh. She laughed again when assuring the investigator she would remind him to give it back. And it wasn't a nervous laugh. Debi appeared relaxed.

State Police investigator Jason Nellis chipped at her previous statement but took a calm and friendly approach. He asked what time Debi went to the church that morning to pick up Luke. She sat staring at the floor, still wearing her raspberry-colored winter coat. The investigators gave her a protein bar, and she ate it without answering. Had Bruce picked up Luke before lunch? She didn't know. Before breakfast? Couldn't remember. She sat for a long time at the wood-veneer conference table. The white-walled room was completely bare, except for

Debi's mug on the table next to sugar packets, and the investigator's documents in front of him. He pushed them aside and appealed to her— it was just the two of them, just talking. He only wanted to hear the story. He leaned in. "When did you find out Luke was doing things?"

"Last night."

She'd finally cracked. He wanted to know her part. He waited to hear it. And waited.

It took a lot of massaging to get Bruce to give up information. "He deserved a whooping," he finally said, and emphasized that he preferred it be called a whooping.

"It was excessive," said Grant.

"What he did was excessive, too."

"But did he deserve to die?"

No, he didn't deserve to die, said Bruce, and "God have mercy, too."

Investigator Grant tried to get Bruce to give up Chris's location, but he wouldn't. They put up pictures of Luke on the computer screen.

"Did you know his injuries looked like that?" asked Kubat. "Did you guys ever check and look and see what his injuries were down there?"

"I mean, he must've cried," added Grant. "He must've been begging to stop, right? How bad was he crying?"

"He, he cried . . . and . . . and then he stopped crying."

The investigators mentioned Joe had injuries on his hands and that he was capable of inflicting that kind of damage. But Bruce refused to implicate Joe. The investigators wondered aloud why Bruce was protecting him. They thought Joe might have been the father of one of the children that Luke had claimed to molest.

Grant said, "Bruce, I'm telling ya, I'm giving you my word, man. If you tell me, I'll . . . I'll treat this man with the utmost respect, just like I've treated you."

"Okay. All right," said Bruce, clearly frustrated, "but I've asked to see my wife—I don't know how many times."

They never did bring Debi but instead offered a pizza, a candy bar, or something else to eat.

"Today," remarked Bruce, "probably qualifies as my most miserable day in my sixty-five years."

Grant began typing a formal statement. "Anybody threaten you or, or make you feel afraid, or scared, or anything along those lines?"

"You mean the police?"

"Yeah, while we've been talking here. Have you felt like, like we've intimated you at all?"

"Uh, yeah. You've used your advantage to keep me from talking to my wife."

"Did he repent in the end?" asked Grant, meaning Luke.

"He said he was sorry, but that was it."

"The truth's gonna come out. Debi, look at me again," said Investigator Nellis. "You're Christian, right?"

"Mhm."

"I'm Christian. I appreciate the truth. There is a tactic where you can smudge things a little bit and mess with people a little bit to get 'em to talk. I don't do that. 'Cause I go for the truth. Everything I tell you is true. So what I want from you is the truth. I know you may wanna cover for somebody—"

"I hit him."

Once she was warmed up—and even then, it was tepid—Debi was more forthcoming with information, acknowledging that Bruce had hit Luke, too. She told about the cord but would not implicate others. She admitted staying at the church the previous night. That lined up with neighbors' accounts. Over many hours, at a tedious pace, she fed investigators bits and pieces about Luke's confessions. She appeared to appreciate the empathetic investigator at the table with her. "He also admitted to plotting to kill Bruce and I," she volunteered.

"That had to be hard to take," said Nellis. "Did he say why?"

"He had gotten interested in—in involving, like, dabbled in witchcraft. And, to the point where he actually, you know, made a voodoo doll. And, um, he wanted to get rid of us, and also Ezekiel."

"Who's Ezekiel?"

"My youngest son. Because he woulda told." She was referring to a hypothetical situation in which Ezekiel would tell on Luke for molesting him. Debi told investigators that after the service, Tiffanie called on Luke to confess. "Pastor's a prophet. So she saw in the Spirit that he was doing it."

When the investigator began to type the report, Debi apologized for lying when police first questioned her. "You'll have to rip up the bogus one," she said, a slight laugh through the sniffling and tears. "I'm sorry."

And what about Chris? He'd confessed to doing horrible things to a child, she said, but they checked that child and there was no evidence of it. Chris made it up because he got off on it, she claimed.

"How was that dealt with?" asked Nellis.

"The same way."

"Why did Luke get it more?"

He wasn't truly remorseful and repentant, "and he admitted to teaching Chris how to molest, how to rape."

Over six hours of questioning, more details emerged, bit by bit. Through clenched teeth, Debi said, "Luke pimped my fifteen-year-old. Daughter."

"To who?"

She named one boy, and then stopped herself. "Well, Grace stepped in. She said no, that she didn't ever do anything with [that boy]. He wanted to, so . . . She wouldn't do anything. But this other kid—she

did. He lives in Florida or somewhere." They were twelve years old at
the time. Luke "whored" her out to as many as four boys, she said. As
for the beating, Debi portrayed it as a suicide wish. "Unfortunately,
I think he wanted to die. Because he didn't want to repent. He didn't
want to go face jail, either." Luke admitted to growing marijuana in
his room. She never saw it, because she didn't go in there. She trusted
him. She also trusted him with using her tablet at the library, only to
learn in the last twenty-four hours that he'd supposedly been using it
to watch porn. "You know, we had warned him . . . It was years—
about five . . . I'm trying to remember . . . maybe five years ago. I don't
remember how many years ago. But he was caught watching porn."

As the beatings continued, Luke was saying things that were "totally
off the wall."

"Like what?" asked another investigator, Jamie Gallagher.

"Something about . . . Daddy. You know—Bruce. Something about
him. I'm not even sure what reference. But he was saying things that
were just, like, totally insane things to say."

"Could you give us an example?"

She thought for a while. "I don't even think Bruce was in there at
that point, but he said, 'Oh, look. Daddy's over there on the floor.'"

"Hallucinating?"

"It wasn't, like, hallucinating. It was just . . . you know, he was just
totally unrepentant."

They asked if she'd heard Luke's nonsensical comments directly,
but she said no—someone had told her. Nellis glanced at his partner.
Debi had just said Bruce wasn't in the room, yet someone passed along
what had been happening in the room. Others had been present.

As Nellis typed the report, Debi whispered, "Thank God for the
Holy Spirit."

Nellis stopped and turned to her. "Yes. Because without him, we'd
be lost."

"Oh, God is good," said Debi, as Nellis turned back and continued typing. "He's . . . good. All for except one patrolman, they've all been Christian today."

"It's hard to believe. Isn't it?"

"No. It's God. I mean, one even handed me his Bible. Pulled it out of his bag and says, 'I carry this everywhere I go.' He says, 'Hold on to it for me for, you know, for support.'"

"Well, like I told you," said Nellis, "I married the pastor's daughter. God had his hand on me a long time ago."

Nellis left the room, but Gallagher stayed and tried to get Debi to admit others' involvement. He told her they already knew Joe had played a part.

Investigators went over a time line with Joe. It took a while. As Joe gave his spiel, one of the investigators, Dougherty, slouched back in his chair, glasses on top of his head, one arm across his abdomen and the other propped under his chin, not just listening but observing. He brought his hands forward and touched them at the fingertips. He folded them and then casually stroked his tie until there was an opening, when he slipped in, "What happened to your hand?"

Joe's answer was a run-on sentence. "My hand, I was working before I changed out some of the old light fixtures and I slipped and I fell."

"What about your other hand, Joe?" asked Pietryka. "You got some marks on your knuckles there."

Joe looked at his left hand and pointed to the knuckles. "That's a bugbite. And that's a scraped knuckle from the same . . . d— Uh . . . I was workin' on a brick wall. 'Cause I was on a . . . the scaffolding that's out in the parking lot. You'll see it—"

"Did you hit him or whip him?" asked Dougherty. "Have any contact with him at all?"

"No."

Dougherty lost his relaxed look, leaned forward and talked to Joe about the importance of being honest. After all, these were sickening admissions from Luke. Hearing them would make anyone lose control.

"I did not hit him." Joe shook his head vehemently.

"Never once," said Dougherty flatly.

"No. I . . ." Joe released a loud sigh, covered his face with his left hand, and squeezed the bridge of his nose. Looking down, he said, "I have a very high amount of self-control."

Dougherty asked Joe to hold out his arms, and as he inspected them, asked, "Who's at the building now?"

"Daniel, who didn't see anything. David Morey, who didn't see anything. Linda came over with her daughter, Kathleen. They didn't see anything."

Joe said there were four people at the church and never mentioned Chris, who was still there, dying.

"Here," said Grant, handing Bruce a piece of lined notebook paper, because Bruce wanted to write the statement himself. Grant and Kubat then walked out the door, leaving Bruce at the table. He was to knock on the wall when he was done.

When that knock still hadn't come after about twenty minutes, both cops returned. "Are you done?" asked Grant. Bruce handed the investigator his paper, and Grant read it aloud: "'Sunday after church, we had a special family meeting to talk about issues in the family, especially porn, witchcraft, and sexual. My son Lucas 'fessed up to porn, witchcraft, and some very debased things he had done to.'" He handed it back to Bruce. "So you just started."

Dougherty was gone from the room on a break. Rose sat at a desk with her back to Joe, typing a statement for him to sign. A uniformed officer was in the middle of the room, sitting in a chair with his arms crossed. Investigator Pietryka stepped into the doorway. "You said there's another young man who may have seen something. Who is that?"

Joe told him it was Luke's younger brother Christopher. But when pressed on his whereabouts, Joe clammed up. "That, you're gonna have to talk to Brue and Debi about. He's a minor."

Dougherty reappeared two minutes later with a sense of urgency. "Do you know where Christopher is right now?"

"You have to ask Bruce and Debi."

"You don't know where he is?"

Stroking his thin beard and looking the investigator in the eye, Joe said, "I can't . . . I don't . . . I can't take any responsibility for him. He's a minor. So . . . you gotta talk to them about it."

Dougherty walked farther into the room. "Obviously we just wanna make sure he's okay, you know."

Joe looked at the floor and nodded. "Right."

"Do you know that he is okay?"

Joe looked up during the question but looked back down to answer. "Yes."

"Do you know where he is and that he's fine? I understand where you're comin' from. I just need to know that he's okay."

"He is okay," said Joe. He asked about his sister. And he brought up the tarp again, this time saying he had asked Luke to sit on it, but only because Luke was concerned about getting blood on the carpet. Joe admitted to texting his mom throughout the night to give her details of Luke's confessions.

"Do you think that he was murdered?" asked Dougherty.

Joe sighed heavily. "I don't think so." He couldn't understand how this had happened, he said, because Luke didn't have a single mark on his face.

"The way this has been described to me is that he was severely beaten," said Dougherty. "Okay? Which, to me, means murder."

At the very time Joe was covering for his brother, Dan was implicating Joe. At 8:00 P.M., he signed a Miranda waiver, agreeing to talk to police. Dan said he'd left the church service early and had heard about the counseling session secondhand. When he later walked in on the session, he heard yelling and ushered the children to another building. He told police his brother had been updating their mother via text messages and phone calls, and at one point, he noticed his brother's hand was swollen and shaking while using the phone.

"I asked Joe what happened to his hand. I think he told me he hurt his hand when he hit Lucas's brother Christopher." He saw Bruce hitting both boys. He told police he was assigned to watch Luke in the main sanctuary at one point. "The way Luke was acting and what he was admitting to, I didn't want to be around it. Lucas was completely unrepentant." He gave the critical details on who was where, at what time, and who did what.

Dougherty wheeled over his chair within a foot or so of Joe and reminded him that all the suspects were separated and the truth would come out.

"What I'm telling you is this: what you're telling me right now, this thing with your hand or whatever, we'll do whatever we have to do to verify that, but I have concerns that there was a little more going on with you." The investigator cautioned Joe that he needed to be up front. "I'm not saying you did a lot or caused all those injuries. This is problematic."

"I might have done *that*," said Joe, holding his hand up like a claw and making a pushing motion, "on his shoulder. I don't remember."

Dougherty mimicked Joe's hand movement. "This isn't it," he said. "That's not what you did. That's not all that you did."

There were certain parts Joe couldn't remember clearly, he said, but "I did not hit him." He was working with his mom when he hurt his hand, he insisted. But after investigators let him know they would question her about it, Joe told them she wasn't aware that he'd gotten injured.

"So there's no one who's gonna verify that," said Dougherty.

Joe held firm. He did not remember hitting anyone.

"You remember very clearly," said Dougherty. "I watch your eyes as you're recalling. I know what your eyes do as you recall. Because you've seen me sittin' here staring at you. Right?"

Joe eventually caved. "Okay, okay, okay. I'm sorry. Yes, I did lie. I'm gonna be honest. This is what I left out. I punched him in the . . . I punched him in the shoulder. That's how I did this to my wrist. I didn't do it on the scaffolding." He said he then used his other hand to punch him on the back of his shoulder. "That's all I did. I swear."

Dougherty had a problem with that version, too. He knew the actions Joe described were not capable of causing Luke's injuries. His relaxed demeanor worn off, Dougherty told Joe, "There's gonna be a judgment on all of you. And it starts with what you do right now. Because that boy was murdered."

No amount of inflammatory language could get Joe to give up imperative information. Four hours later, he was still holding out on disclosing Chris's location. Dougherty and Rose put up pictures of Luke's dead body on the computer screen.

"When you first came and sat down here, I thought that you were a good person," said Dougherty, exasperated. "I thought that you were somebody that has morals and values. You look at that"—he pointed to the pictures—"and tell me that you can sit here and play these games with me, which is what you're doin' right now. That is a boy," he said, his arm is outstretched, finger pointing to the picture, "who was murdered. And you"—he swung his arm forward to point at Joe—"know exactly what happened. And you're gonna sit here, and you're gonna *lie* to me about it, and then you're gonna play games about where his brother is? Is *that* who you are?" He stopped long enough to let it sink in. "Is that the type of person your mother raised?"

Joe looked at the floor, motionless, Dougherty within inches of him. "Is that what your church believes in?" the investigator pushed. "That that's okay? To act like that?"

Joe, his head still hung to his chest, said, "See, it's not working. You can just knock it off."

That ignited Dougherty, who now sounded downright furious. "I don't care if it's working or not, because I'm gonna get this off my chest." He pointed straight at Joe, who wouldn't look at him. "Because you're a no-good son of a bitch. That's what you are. All right? You can hide behind this religion and whatever you want all day long. If you were raised to truly be a Christian person and you have any morals and you have any values, you're gonna stop playing these games. Look at that boy!"

"I did, thank you."

Playing games. It was a favored phrase in Tiffanie's repertoire, the one she'd used many times while interrogating church members. Dougherty used it on Joe again. "All you care about is yourself and playing these stupid little games with me. I'm saying that *is* what you did to this boy—"

"No, it's not," Joe cut in with the voice of an untouchable, his pitch rising and falling.

"Yes, it is—"

"No, it's not." Joe shrugged casually and repeated himself, looked the detective in the face, and then barked, "It's the wrong side of his body." This voice was different, deep and vengeful, almost like a different person was speaking. He added with disgust, "For cryin' out loud."

Joe reached past the investigator's face and grabbed a paper cup of water from the desk in front of him, and as he brought it to his chest, he scoffed and said, "You can't even get your lefts and rights straight."

But the last word went unfinished, a heavy breath replacing the *t*. Joe turned from the investigator to face forward, clutched the cup in his uninjured hand, and released another big breath. He flicked his head down to his cup, exhaled again loudly, and again, sunk his head, and in a softer voice said, "I think I want the lawyer now."

In one uninterrupted move, Dougherty used both his feet to shove back his chair, stood up, and said, "I think you need it."

"Yeah," mumbled Joe. "I need to talk to someone else. I need to talk to somebody."

Dougherty got halfway out the door before turning to grab something off the desk. He stopped for one final message: "You need the kind of help a lawyer can't give you."

Police stationed outside the Word of Life Building needed to make contact with the people inside. There were two cars in the back parking lot, so they looked up the license plates. Both were registered to Steven* Morey, Linda's husband, a corrections officer Pietryka had known for many years through police work. State Police drove to Morey's house, and he agreed to ride back with them to try to reach his wife, who was presumed to be inside the building along with their two adult children. Steve warned police that he'd had no luck earlier. He had gone to the Word of Life Building at about eleven thirty that morning and tried to get in. He was the one Stacey Brodeur had seen banging on doors. But no one would answer the door and, of course, the gate was locked.

Morey told police that the last time he'd heard from his wife was a text message at six the night before. Police wrote in their report, *Morey stated that his family has been members of the church for over 15 years and that their life is centered around the church. That the church is run by Tiffanie Irwin who is the self ordained pastor and her mother Tracy Irwin. According to Morey no one does anything without Tracy or Tiffanie's approval. It is not uncommon for his family to go there and stay all day and even spend the night on occasion. He has tried to contact his family but they will not answer his calls or respond to his text messages. While Morey was on scene he did receive a call from a Joseph Irwin who is the son of Tracy Irwin and brother of the pastor of the church Tiffanie Irwin. Joseph Irwin advised that Morey's family was safe but that no one was going to come out until he received word from his mother.*

Eventually, through Morey, police were able to call Linda, learning Chris's location and how many people were in the church.

Someone woke up Grace. Bleary-eyed, she didn't notice Chris on the couch in the same room with her. Then, she was herded along with the rest—Chris, Kathy, Ezekiel, and Sarah's four kids—to the learning center, where Dave and Linda informed them that police were outside the building. The children would have to walk outside, into the arms of police. As they prepared to leave, they were also concerned that police were going to storm the building. The adults tried to keep the children calm by telling them they would see guns but they weren't real, just water guns.

Sarah looked well put together in gray boots, black boot-cut stretch pants, and a lime-green button-down sweater over a black top. Her hair was in a high bun. On the way out, Dave handed her a gray hooded sweatshirt to wear. It had turned frigid. Grace didn't have her shoes. She went back to the nursery to get them, and then she and Dave collected the kids' coats and got them dressed. Meanwhile, Tiffanie was texting someone in the building, telling them that the police would want to question Sarah, and Sarah was to tell them she did not want to talk, she wanted a lawyer.

SWAT teams dressed in camouflage approached, guns drawn. Ada cried. But they were as gentle as police could be with chambered rounds.

That concrete walkway to the front door of the old brick schoolhouse, the one that no one walked anymore—Sarah and the others now paraded down it, almost single file, with their arms raised. Sarah was at the head of the line holding Ivy, her other children directly behind, their breaths creating white puffs. They crossed the street under a dark, starry sky lit up by the lights of police cruisers and television news trucks. An officer took Ivy from Sarah's arms. The police were calm, and the children seemed to sense it. If they were frightened, it didn't show.

Police took Grace, Ezekiel, and Sarah's four children to the nearest fire station to wait for Oneida County Child Protective Services. They took Chris and Sarah to a nearby gas station, where they were handcuffed and put into separate squad cars but both driven to the New Hartford police station. They were turned away because the interview rooms were full, so they were taken to the Whitesboro police station and put in adjacent holding cells. Sarah overhead an officer asking Chris about his bruises. He had the same marks as his brother.

Chris gave his first statement at 11:31 P.M. Tiffanie had called the counseling session, he told investigators. "I can't remember exactly what happened, but after, we got around to Luke wanting to leave the church. Then we started talking about Luke and I confessing about what we had done. I believe Pastor Tiffanie brought this up concerning our nieces, nephews, and brother. Luke and I did not want to tell, so they began telling us to say what we had done."

Dave Morey also signed a statement around this time, but getting there was a challenge. When police tried to question him, he was very animated and hyperventilating, rocking in his chair, breathing heavily and mumbling, pounding his fist into his hand the entire time. It got to the point where they felt he might be having a medical emergency. They allowed Dave to call his father, and when Steve showed up, his presence calmed Dave a little. His dad proofread the statement and told police he wanted anything that implicated his son stricken. The investigator ripped up the statement. Dave reviewed the next copy and said he wanted his name to be paired with any mention of Joe's involvement, because if Joe got in trouble for something, he wanted to be right there with him. They tore up that one, too. Then Dave said he wanted anything implicating Joe stricken. That one also got tossed. Dave finally agreed to sign a version that included: *Lucas and*

Christopher began talking about sodomizing young children at the house . . . . This was an attempt to counsel Lucas and Christopher due to the sick actions they were talking about. Dave made a point to say he wasn't there the whole time and neither was "Joey," and that "Pastor Tiffanie was not the one doing the confrontation." She had no physical involvement, he told police, but Sarah was giving them "a good beating."

Kubat returned to Bruce's room without Investigator Grant. "How we making out?" He looked over Bruce's shoulder to see if he'd gotten any further on writing his statement and then changed the topic. "A little, uh, more information that I just found out that you should know. We have your daughter and Chris. They just came out of the church. Okay? So there's nobody to call at this point. They've got everybody. Apparently somehow they—"

Bruce mumbled something ending with "daughter."

At 11:00 P.M., Investigators Grant and Dougherty went to see Debi in her interview room. Grant told her that Bruce had admitted to Sarah's involvement, and he wanted Debi to confirm it. She did but said none of them should go to jail, because Luke's death was an accident.

"Did you see the photos?" asked Grant, referring to the pictures of her son, dead.

No, she didn't want to see them. She sobbed.

"Where was the proof he did something to a kid?" asked Grant.

There wasn't any, just his say-so.

The investigator wanted to know if Luke could've been acting like a normal teenager, puffing his feathers and making stuff up.

"Well, he said that he . . . um . . . um . . . abused the little girls across the street," said Debi. "Brought them in the backyard and fondled them."

"Well, did anybody talk to them?" asked Grant.

"I don't know."

"So he could just be saying that. If we go talk to those girls and they say, 'No, that never happened . . .'"

"He said that he threatened all his victims that he would kill them."

"Well, now that he's dead, if we go talk to them, and they don't have any worry about that, what if they say that never happened?"

Debi rubbed her forehead and sighed heavily. Still looking at the floor, she slowly acknowledged that was a possibility.

"Do you think it was wrong, what you folks did?"

"Yes."

When Grant left the room, Debi crossed her arms on the conference table and laid down her head, as though she were going to sleep. Then she lifted her head, uncrossed her legs, and fluffed her bangs. She leaned forward, put her elbows on her knees, and watched herself press up her toes in her black sneakers. She flipped over her feet and looked at the soles of her shoes, over and over again. Sometimes left alone in that room, she sobbed as if in deep emotional pain. There was no way to know if it was for the loss of her son, for the shocking so-called admissions she'd heard that night, or for the strife the ordeal had brought upon her church family.

She picked up the napkins the investigator had brought with her coffee and shoved them in her coat pockets.

Kubat was alone with Bruce, who was still in his chair, in the corner, at the desk.

Bruce remarked, "See, everything in my life is just . . . in one day, went upside down. Scrambled. Dead. Period."

"The truth is, I understand, but we—"

"This truly is—" Bruce stopped before continuing. "I've had bad days."

"This is the worst day of your life," said Kubat.

"Yeah. Everything."

"No doubt, this is by far the worst day you've ever had in your life."

". . . God."

"I know," said Kubat. "You probably feel like you're losing everything and you've lost control."

"This is true."

"Tell me this: is everything that you've told us been truthful?"

"Yeah, after you needled it out of me."

Investigator Gallagher asked Debi about hearing her son crying. "You musta had a motherly instinct to—"

"I did. But I didn't wanna see."

"You didn't wanna see him bein' in so much pain? . . . But you could hear him crying. Did you put your hands over your ears?" She didn't react. He continued. "I mean, that musta been torture for ya. To hear what they were puttin' him through and not bein' able to help him. Right? It's gotta go against every motherly instinct that you have."

"I didn't see him again till he was dead."

Debi said that when she heard Luke crying, Tiffanie was talking to her, asking what confessions Luke and Chris may still be withholding. The police wanted to know: was Tiffanie to blame for this? Debi didn't want to answer that one, even after it was asked repeatedly. Whose idea was this?

"It had to be somebody's, Deb," said Gallagher. "Somebody had to bring this out. 'Cause. Just—listen." The investigator shook his head back and forth. "It just doesn't happen. Me and my brothers and sisters aren't gonna be hanging out on Christmas and find out something and just . . . all become . . . beaters over—in the matter of ten minutes. It just doesn't happen. Is it something the church talked about? Be honest with me, please. So we don't have to do this again. I'm asking you this for a reason. Okay?"

"Mhm."

"We're usually asking 'cause we already know." He asked her plainly: "Did Tiffanie order this?"

Finally, Debi said someone told Bruce they would stop if he wasn't okay with it. "It was either Pastor, or it was one of the boys."

"Okay, well, Pastor's a girl, right?"

"I don't— Well, yeah."

"And the boys usually have deeper voices, so . . . who do you think said, 'If you want us to stop, we will'? Was it the pastor?" Tiffanie was running the show, he told her. They knew that.

"I am not confessing to doing anything more," Joe said to Rose, after Dougherty's grand exit. He expelled deep breaths and began to whimper and then calmed himself with successive deep breaths, like a runner trying to lower his heart rate.

He asked how long she'd been in law enforcement.

"Fifteen years," she said, before warning that he couldn't speak to them because he'd "lawyered up."

Joe didn't want a lawyer, he said. He just wanted to talk to someone other than Dougherty. A uniformed officer replaced Rose, and Joe took out a Bible and thumbed through it for more than an hour until State Police entered with a warrant to photograph him. Nearly twenty minutes after Joe was called out of the room, Investigator Grant escorted Sarah into it, her hands cuffed behind her back. A deputy photographed her. Sarah took the same seat Joe had just vacated. Her wrists now freed, she sat pressing her hands into her thighs and, in slow motion, rocked the upper half of her body back and forth. Her only spoken words were as she left the room: "May I bring my water?"

One minute later, Linda walked into the same room with an air of confidence, dressed in blue jeans and a black long-sleeved shirt. Her hair, freshly dyed black, was in a low bun. She wore glasses on top of her head and an expression that reflected not a care in the world.

No sooner did she sit—in the same seat Joe and Sarah had previously occupied—than she pulled a cell phone out of her pocket and, in a sugary, high-pitched voice, asked, "May I call my husband?"

"No. I'd rather you not at this point," answered the officer. "Because I don't know why you're here."

"Me either," she said. She brought her legs together and folded her fingers in her lap like an obedient child, chin up and grinning at the officer. That lasted a moment before she moved it to a closed-mouth half grin. Then she began squeezing one eye in a nervous habit that looked like repetitive winking. Soon after the officer turned away, her right eye appeared to be full-on convulsing. But that voice—charming like a fairy-tale princess. "I was, um, at the Chadwicks firehouse watching the kids," she said delicately, and then more squeezing of the eyes, and she tightened her interlocking fingers.

The busy investigator Todd Grant made an appearance and apologized to Linda for everything she was going through. Dougherty was with him.

"The children . . . can I have them . . . where— Who— What's going on?" Linda's pleading voice cracked.

"Well, that's what we want to talk to you about," Grant jumped in.

"The *kids*," she croaked.

"We wanna talk to you about this."

"Do I need a lawyer?"

He read her her Miranda rights and said that at any time, she could ask for a lawyer, and police would stop talking to her. But as they tried to question Linda, she whimpered and repeated, over and over, "I'm worried about the kids." She wanted to talk to her husband. "He's a parole officer. He knows a lot of stuff about this." She shrugged. "I don't . . . you know . . ."

Grant asked, "Have you done something that's wrong, that you considered—that you would think you committed a crime tonight?"

Her eyebrows lifted. "Absolutely not."

Grant eventually asked if the littler kids were around when they had the family meeting with Luke.

"No, we were in the nursery. My daughter, Kathleen, was in the nursery watchin' 'em. I've been—I was ricochet rabbit. Makin' popcorn. Gettin' food. Running upstairs. Get—you know, I— I'm basically the goer. I'm all over." She was gesturing broadly and kept rattling off about dashing around and making popcorn.

She had, in fact, brought the younger kids snacks that night, and did occasionally leave the counseling session, but she withheld from investigators her more prominent role in the beatings. Grant asked if anyone got physical when the boys made their unspeakable admissions.

"I stomped my foot, and I just screamed," Linda said, and then she "took off to get the popcorn."

"When you came back down, what did you see that was going on?"

All that could be heard was the ticking of the clock's second hand.

Grant leveled with her: someone said she hit one of the boys.

Linda caved and admitted to hitting Chris but said it was a slap and he didn't feel it. "I don't wanna keep talkin'."

"Is it because you had something to do with it?" asked Grant.

"Absolutely not."

Did she do anything to protect the boys?

"Yeah. Yeah. At . . . at one point I said . . . um . . . it, you know . . . we've gotta—we've gotta . . . yeah, we've gotta get 'im to a hospital. To do something. Absolutely."

What made her say it?

"Because I saw some blood." She gestured by stroking her leg. "His pant leg had, like, blood. I was concerned."

"And who did you say that to?"

She thought for a while, stammered, but got nowhere, and the only thing she could come up with was "I think I just said it in general."

They tried to pin her down on where she was when she saw the blood, but she wasn't clear on locations, so Dougherty asked her about times. When was the first time she saw Luke bleeding?

It was when she went into the bigger room, Linda said. "I saw it and I thought, oh boy, 'cause he's got a, you know, we gotta . . . we . . . something's gotta be done." That was in the morning.

"During the overnight hours, when they were getting hit with the cord and that kind of stuff, they weren't bleeding at that point?" asked Dougherty.

After looking muddled for a bit, Linda touched her finger to the tip of her nose and explained, "Well, Christopher had a bloody nose, but he gets a bloody nose all the time."

"Did that happen when you smacked him?" asked Grant, with a whisk of his hand, indicating a slap.

Her eyes popped, and her head froze. "Um . . ."

"Could it have happened when you smacked him?" he repeated.

"No. Maybe 'cause the kid has bloody noses constantly. He has bloody noses all the t—for no reason. No. No." Linda said she was a little bit frightened by the way everyone was acting around Luke and Chris.

The cell phone resting on her thigh began to ring, so she picked it up. For several minutes, investigators listened to a one-sided conversation. Linda moved her mouth from the phone to tell the investigators she'd learned that her "friend Joe" had been arrested. She explained to the person on the other end that she should probably hang up, because investigators were questioning her. Right after that, they heard, "Okay. Okay. Where do I get a lawyer?" After a little more conversation, Linda put down the phone and said, "Yes, I—I would like a, um, a lawyer."

"Is that what Traci told ya?" asked Grant.

"Um, no."

"Who was that you were talkin' to?"

"Uh, Pastor Tiffanie."

"Oh, that's what she said?"

"She said, 'You should request one.'"

"You guys probably shoulda got medical attention for those kids, too, huh?" said Grant.

"Did you guys think about calling the police?" added Dougherty.

"May, may I have a, a law—" In a delayed response to Dougherty's question, Linda nodded strongly. "Yes. Absolutely. Yes. Yes. Absolutely. Yes."

Dougherty grabbed the clipboard next to him and stood while saying, "Too bad any of you guys did what you did. It was, like, the most un-Christian thing I have ever heard of."

Grant, who had stepped out, now returned and said in a gruff voice, "Let me grab your phone."

"Do I need a lawyer?"

"Yeah, you're getting arrested," he shot back. "So let me have your phone."

"I'm being arrested?" she asked faintly.

"Yeah. Absolutely," said Grant, turning his back on her to walk out the door.

Dougherty, arms folded, issued a parting shot. "You're kiddin', right?"

Much later, Officer Hyatt came to run down questions on a form with Linda. He handcuffed her right hand to a restraint on the wall, and she began sobbing. Earlier, he'd interviewed Traci. But he wasn't there to drill Linda. He couldn't. She'd asked for an attorney. Still, she had a lot of questions, and he politely answered as best he could. Would she go to jail? Wear "prison clothes"? Be found guilty? She began pleading her case to Hyatt, who remained neutral.

"Anybody who's any part of that is now liable for that. You know?"

"I understand," Linda said, and started to unravel. "Yeah. Yeah." She began shaking her head from side to side and cried out, "And Lucas . . . ohhh." She put her free hand to her mouth and exclaimed, "Oh my God," and wailed, and lapsed into a meltdown.

"I know," said the officer. Horrible. Those poor kids, he said.

She cut him off, inconsolable, "I can't . . . I can't . . . They're good kids!" she cried, heaving, wiping her face with a tissue. After a while, struggling for air to speak, she apologized for losing control. "Sorry. I really am sorry," she choked.

"You're not makin' *me* feel bad," said Hyatt. "I'm glad *somebody's* showing some remorse around here for what happened."

After Linda was taken from the room, her son entered in handcuffs, an army-green T-shirt and khaki pants, gulping breaths. Left alone, he repeated, "I'm sorry. I'm sorry. Oh my God. So sorry." He prayed nonstop under his breath.

"What's your last name?" an officer asked Bruce, sent to collect his clothing.

Bruce continued writing for a pregnant pause before answering, "Leonard." They photographed him.

"Have a good night," said Bruce, and as the officers left the room, he went back to writing. He got up, walked around the room, and looked at some papers in the office. It was a labored walk, Bruce bent forward, shifting his weight from one foot to the other as he ambled, eventually back to the desk. "Oh God."

He got on his knees in front of the chair and prayed. When he was done, he took another piece of paper, ripped it in half, and began writing on it. He walked around the room again, and an officer came in and told him to stay seated unless he needed to use the bathroom. Bruce went back to his chair but only for a moment before getting up and walking some more. Investigator Kubat came in with a police officer and took Bruce for fingerprinting. Then, they brought him back to the room, where he sat alone. When they returned, Bruce asked, "What time is it?"

It was 1:15 A.M.

He fell asleep in the corner.

At 5:10 A.M., an officer entered. "The judge is in."

Bruce's condensed, handwritten statement said the whipping was intended to make Luke feel pain, realize some of the pain he had caused, and bring him to repentance. *He was sitting up, lying down, slept some, up again, laid down again, keeping an eye on him, then noticed no movement, did CPR, went to hospital, and he didn't make it.*

How many months ago it was that God spoke to me something that shocked me then. He said, "There's great wickedness in this place."

—Pastor Tiffanie Irwin
to the congregation on November 2, 2014

There were plenty of secrets in the Word of Life Building, and authorities were about to uncover them. Through the interviews, police learned several of the parties had been texting one another during the counseling session. That formed the basis for one of the search warrants.

"The building was so massive, they were communicating via text messaging, because one would be on the third floor, and one would be in the church, and it's too much work to walk all the way up the stairs to talk to somebody," Pietryka later said.

In the early-morning hours of October 13, police were given authority to seize the cell phones of some of the suspects and access text messages, call logs, and contact lists to identify coconspirators and accomplices. They searched Debi's white van and confiscated the suspects' clothes and shoes, photographed them in their underwear, and, at the end of their police interviews, put them in outfits that looked like hospital scrubs. Police also took blood and DNA evidence and photographed specific body parts, including Joe's and Sarah's hands. Even Chris stripped down and was photographed. The welts on his body were important evidence. But he would be going to the hospital while the rest of them went to jail.

At the same time, police made entry into the rear part of the Word of Life Building, which housed the big and small sanctuaries. They were authorized to confiscate the personal papers of anyone who may've been involved, and to look for firearms and ammunition and any item that might have been used as a weapon.

State Police crime scene technician Danielle Kendall was among those searching the building. She entered from the back parking lot through the entrance that parishioners used—double doors under a white peaked roof. The main sanctuary was right inside the door, a room about sixty feet long, or roughly the length of a bowling lane. A row of closets served to create a foyer, or half wall. On the other side of the wall, numerous chairs were stacked in the corner of the mostly empty sanctuary. In front of the stack was a single chair. At the foot of the chair was a heap of paper towels and two flattened polystyrene cups covered in blood, along with a rubber earplug. Patches of blood surrounded the chair on the carpet. To the right of the podium, Kendall saw large, plastic, folded-up sheeting. There were several rooms off the main sanctuary—a nursery, dining area, and smaller sanctuary.

Kendall entered the small sanctuary and observed the keyboard, drums, guitars, and the desk from which Tiffanie preached. The pastor's laptop was open on it. The rows of chairs had notebooks on them, left behind by the Leonards. Looking out from the pulpit of the small sanctuary, in the far right of the room was a bathroom and a storage closet. The investigator made her way to the closet filled with percussion instruments and speakers. There were cables and cords coiled and hung on the wall, in several rows. The fourth cord in the top row looked out of place. It wasn't coiled like the rest but draped sloppily. Kendall examined the cord and noticed that the prongs were bent. The cord was stripped and there were traces of blood on it. She had found the whipping instrument.

Police charged Bruce and Deborah Leonard with first-degree manslaughter. The judge set bail at $100,000. Joe, Sarah, Linda, and Dave pleaded not guilty to second-degree assault and were booked into jail. The judge set their bail at $50,000 apiece.

From his hospital bed, Chris gave police another statement: *Christopher stated that Pastor Tiffany was in charge of the meeting and she was the person who originally talked to him and Lucas. Christopher stated that Pastor Tiffany told them they had to confess what they did and that was the reason for the meeting. When questioned relative to Pastor Tiffany, Christopher stated that she was a good person. He also stated that she had the power of God and that you were suppose to fear God.*

On October 14, Police Chief Inserra addressed reporters in an Oneida County courtroom, alongside New York State Police major Francis Coots, Oneida County district attorney Scott McNamara, and Utica police chief Mark Williams. To the clacking of shutter releases and the snap of camera flashes, the chief announced the charges. The investigation was in the early stages, and more arrests and charges could follow. An autopsy by the Onondaga County medical examiner had determined that the victim had sustained blunt-force trauma to his torso and extremities, and that the combination of injuries and the duration of the assault contributed to his death. "The initial reports of a gunshot wound are unfounded."

DA McNamara stepped in front of the gaggle of reporters to clarify the murder-related charge. "Manslaughter is if you're trying to cause serious physical injury to somebody, trying to hurt them really bad, and that ultimately they die as a result of those injuries." Authorities were not alleging the parents intended to kill their son.

At a hearing in two days, a judge would listen to testimony and decide if there was enough evidence to support the charges.

Though any mention of sexual molestation was left out of the press conference, news broadcasts were reporting that sources said church members attacked the boys because they'd been caught molesting children. That ignited strong feelings on Main Street in Clayville.

"No, no, no, no, no." Frances shook her head vigorously, as she recalled the allegations years later. "They were not like that. I'm sorry. That was a ploy, as far as I'm concerned. Seriously. Nope, nope, nope, nope. Nada, nada, nada."

Brenda later spoke for both her and her husband when she said. "We don't believe for a minute the boys did that. If they did, we would be shocked. I don't believe it for a minute."

Neither did Olivia. "They weren't weirdos. They didn't do anything like that in front of me. They never even talked about touching a
girl, being around girls, having girlfriends—nothing of that sort. They
never tried to do anything to me. They were respectful boys."

Police were coming up with the same results after tracking down
the names of children given by the boys during the beatings. There
seemed to be no truth to the claims. And yet, when the allegations were
unearthed at trial, testimony would leave more questions than answers.

Friday's hearing brought news reporters from all over the world to
a small Utica courtroom. All six defendants were in court, including
Linda and Dave, who had been released on bail. But the only defendants on the hook that day were Bruce and Debi Leonard, who entered
the courtroom the same as they would church, with heads hung. While
the hearing went on, for nearly four hours, Bruce kept his eyes closed
and Debi sat slumped over the defendant desk. None of the defendants
showed emotion, except Debi, who lightly wept at times. The prosecution's treasured witness was Daniel Irwin. Reporters wrote like mad
in their notepads when Dan, chewing gum, said the beatings stopped
"because Luke was dead at that point."

Both Debi's and Bruce's attorneys brought out the accusations of
molestation.

The judge decided the evidence supported the manslaughter charges
against Bruce and Debi. They would be held without bail. Outside the
courtroom, McNamara made a public plea for any former members of
WLCC to come forward. "It's very important that we can fully understand what we're dealing with here."

Four days later, a hurting community held a vigil at St. Patrick's–
St. Anthony's Parish, the Catholic church on the other side of the
hedges of the Word of Life Building. Hundreds came. They prayed;
they sang. They lit up the darkness with burning candles, leaned on
one another, and wiped their tears. One person turned photos of Luke
and Chris into pins and wore them on his shirt. Many signed a banner

with messages like, *I love u boys God bless* and *Justice for Lucas*. Later, citizens lined the sidewalk in front of the Word of Life Building and sang "Amazing Grace." One light shone inside WLCC. The neighbors shouted that they wanted the church shut down. Someone posted a cardboard sign that read: *Knock it Down There Killers*. Someone else used a red pen to correct *There* to *They're*. Well-wishers started a makeshift memorial under a shade tree to the right of WLCC's locked gate, leaving balloons, crosses, and posters. One poster had a message for Chris: *GET WELL*.

The next day, October 21, Chris entered the courtroom, head bowed, accompanied by a woman from the Oneida County Child Protective Services, to testify against his sister. Sarah did not look at him, instead staring down at the defense table. A thick tuft of shaggy bangs rested on Chris's black-rimmed glasses, and he did not look up, even as he swore to tell the truth, the whole truth, and nothing but the truth.

Reporters inched forward, trying to hear Chris tell what happened. He testified that Tiffanie had called the counseling session "to talk about what we had done," but that he and his brother didn't want to share. The judge stopped Chris before he made any comments about molestation. When the hearing was over, the judge determined the assault charge against the mother of four would stick—for now. Sarah's situation was about to get much worse.

By this time, Joe Irwin had bailed out of jail and was not expected back in court until December. That, too, would change.

By October 21, Bureau of Alcohol, Tobacco, Firearms, and Explosives (ATF) agents had tracked ten purchases of handguns and rifles, including bolt-action and assault rifles, since 2011, to Traci, Joe, and Dan. None had a pistol permit. The sale of a Russian Saiga 7.62 AK variant semiautomatic rifle was traced to David Morey.

Separately, Kristel and Chris informed police of the recorded sermons and the surveillance cameras outside the building. Police thought it likely that the sermon in question was memorialized in some format, and they wanted that recording—and access to a potential treasure trove of other evidence. On October 26, the judge granted another search warrant, this time for a greater area of the church, including the Irwins' living quarters. They were allowed to search the attic crawl space, halls, storage areas, and more, and to look for all video and audio recordings and digital storage devices (computers/laptops, camcorders, hard drives, memory cards, cell phones, flash drives, etc.). The warrant also allowed police to search the persons of Linda, Dave, Tiffanie, and Traci for cell phones and digital storage devices. This second round of searches began on October 28 and took three days. When police entered the property, they passed through a metal gate that now had a handmade sign made of white poster board and black marker: *Church closed during our time of mourning*.

On the first search day, police assembled Traci, Tiffanie, and Dan in the church garage. As her mother was being searched, Tiffanie started complaining about feeling cold. She said she needed another jacket, and Dan offered her his coat. But before she put it on, Officer Hyatt combed through it. Satisfied the pockets were empty, he handed it to Tiffanie. When it came time to search Dan, Hyatt noticed Tiffanie was awfully restless, putting her hands in and out of two jackets: her original coat and the one Dan had given her. When Dan's search was done, Tiffanie tried to hand his coat back to him, but Hyatt intercepted it and asked a police sergeant to look through it.

The sergeant found a thumb drive that hadn't been there before. "Is this yours?" he asked Dan.

"No," said Dan, shaking his head emphatically. "It's Tiffanie's. Nothing on there is mine."

A team of police scoured the building. On the second floor, they saw a portable hyperbaric chamber. Made of fabric, it could be rolled up and stored or transported. They snapped a series of pictures. It was an unusual piece of equipment, worth noting.

In the room where Chris had stayed, authorities in blue latex gloves cut out stained sections of a mattress. They photographed one storage room that held dozens of computer towers and another stacked with items from floor to ceiling, capped off with chairs hanging precariously upside down at the tops of the stacks. Among the clutter: a folded table tennis game, children's push toys, a mini trampoline, cots, baseball bats, cross-country skis, and exercise machines. There was also a handmade double-headed battle-ax. There were piles of toy guns, many wrapped in duct tape.

One of the Irwin boys' bedrooms had numerous wires dangling from the ceiling like a field of snakes. The floor was a minefield of empty drink bottles and heaps of clothes. There was an empty bed frame with the mattress next to it, and boxes and clothes piled on top of the mattress. School desks covered with junk. Two grenades on a desk next to a computer monitor. One desk drawer made for pencils instead held throwing stars and a bowie knife. A deeper drawer was crammed with large, fixed-blade hunting knives, a switchblade, and brass knuckles.

On their way out the bedroom door, police snapped a picture of Bible verses written on the wall in black marker.

In the middle of one room was a bizarre structure that roughly resembled a shed, built of engineered wood and covered on the inside with empty foam egg cartons. Police guessed the Irwins had been trying to build a soundproof room.

Searchers saw a mass of playpens and bassinettes and incubators. From the master bedroom, they took several financial documents. And they discovered a cache of firearms—thirteen long guns and a black magazine. They found two empty rifle boxes and would later attempt to trace who bought the guns that belonged in them, only to come up empty. Authorities would learn that the Irwins had turned over thousands of rounds of ammunition to their attorney. They had expected such an arsenal. What they found in the basement, however, came as a complete surprise.

As searchers made their way through the building, they walked into a small storage room filled with cats. Inside the room was a steel trapdoor laid flat in the floor. They opened it and climbed down old wooden stairs. At the bottom of the stairs, their feet met loose dirt on a hard surface. The space was only four to five feet high, and they crouched to walk through it. This was the foundation of the gymnasium annex. Trash lined the sides—PVC pipes, plastic buckets, a broken toilet, a rusty old desk chair—and there was lighting strung around pipes that ran the length of the foundation. As police reached the end of the storage area, the floor turned to dirt, with bricks strewn haphazardly on top of it. The foundation to the right of them had a massive hole in it. Searchers dragged their knees as they made their way through the crawl space. On the other side was what looked like an alleyway. At the far end of it, there were cinder blocks stacked against the foundation, and a dirt berm between the blocks. Several shovels and a pickax were on the dirt, and searchers found three shotgun waddings.

Investigator Pietryka later described one of WLCC's best-kept secrets: "There are barriers down there, and what they did was actually cut holes in these walls, and there was a fifty- to seventy-five-yard shooting range down underground." They'd likely compromised the building's foundation to create it.

Authorities later discovered in Dan's writings his detailed visions of an apocalypse—Utica was going to burn down and everyone would go to the church to be saved. Dan's beliefs were repeated in audio recordings. The Irwins recorded even their casual dinner conversations. Their penchant for documentation would be their biggest downfall. By the same token, wading through it would prove a massive undertaking for law enforcement. In all, police seized more than seventy-eight items, mostly cell phones and computer equipment. Investigators began the daunting task of analyzing the digital evidence by sending it to the New York State Police Computer Crime Unit. They would use a special apparatus to duplicate the data while preserving the original devices, which would be sent back to New Hartford PD.

On October 29, police conducted yet another search, this one initiated by Bruce's brother Jason. His mother's van had been parked at the church since the crime, and Rick Wright had been offering to help Jason pick it up. That was unusual, Jason told police, because Rick didn't normally speak to him. Police searched the vehicle and found it contained the seat that had been removed from Debi's van to take Luke to the hospital. On the seat was blood.

BUILDING A CASE

As a teenager took his final breaths under the watch of a congregation at the Word of Life Christian Church, Investigator Dave Cady's hands were folded in prayer. At breakfast, he and his wife were sharing Bible readings before Cady left for work. It was something they'd done for years—give thanks and pray for safety. In his twenty-one-year law enforcement career, Cady had been fired upon and attacked, never knowing if that day he put on his uniform would be his last.

He started as a patrolman in the small village of Boonville and, two years later, transferred to the Oneida County Sheriff's Department, where he quickly earned a spot on the SWAT team. In 2000, Cady became an investigator assigned to the Criminal Investigations Division and, four years later, transferred to the Oneida County Drug Task Force. His specialty was electronics: body wires, video, etc. In 2010, Cady took a position at the Oneida County District Attorney's Office and continued his focus on digital gathering of evidence. The Word of Life case was in his wheelhouse.

Cady's belief in God predated his law enforcement career. He'd been baptized a Catholic and grew up attending church, but in his teens and early twenties, he'd lost touch with the Catholic Church. Cady's belief in God, however, was resolute, and he called upon his faith in 2009, when his father was stricken with dementia. Faced with his dad's steady decline, Cady realized a way the two could connect: the Bible and prayer. He relied on it to get his father through the illness, and then through the end of his life. In the wake of his father's death four years later, the investigator's faith only got stronger. On October 12, 2015, it faced a weighty challenge.

On the day of the news conference announcing the WLCC arrests, Cady phoned a former intern and told him, "Hurry up and come back, because we're gonna have a lot for you to do."

On the other end of the line was Anthony Sokolowski, a Utica College senior. He'd interned at the DA's office the previous summer and planned to return in the spring before heading off to law school. He'd listened to news reports of the beating death. That was the first he'd heard of the Word of Life Christian Church, though he had grown up fewer than ten miles away from it. Now the name was heard all over the world. This was going to be a big case, he realized, and he couldn't get a piece of it until January.

Cady wasted no time. He already had a couple of interns who were doing jail call intelligence, listening to conversations of defendants in a narcotics case. But when the Word of Life case got dropped in, everything else got shut down. He put them on listening to jail calls of suspects in Lucas Leonard's death.

Jayden was calling his sister frequently, in addition to visiting her sometimes several days in a row. She always asked about her kids and wanted to see them. They're "safe and resilient" her brother assured her. The other inmates were asking Sarah to do Bible study. They called her unit the "Prayer Block."

"That's just so cool to me," she told her brother.

The intern jotted down, *She's been working out. Can do pushups now. He tells her she's a good mother. She jokes about jail food.*

At one meal time, an inmate threw soup on Sarah. The interns learned she'd been reading a lot and painting portraits. She was also improving her basketball skills and working on swearing less often. Jayden had dinner with Grace and reported back to Sarah that Grace would be testifying for her, and though it made Grace nervous, she would do anything for Sarah.

The interns learned how Jayden labored over thoughts of Bruce in jail, accused of hurting his own sons. Bruce's motto, Jayden told

Sarah, was always "Don't touch anyone. I was a bad kid, and no one laid a hand on me, even though I deserved it."

Bruce was in his unit reading the Bible and getting along with everyone. The younger inmates reminded him of his son. One of the more dangerous inmates on his block seemed to have the biggest heart.

"Keep your head up, Bruce," he would encourage him. "You'll get through this."

Nightmares kept Bruce awake at night.

From her cell, Debi could hear Sarah sing. She found it soothing. She heard Sarah laugh on her way to court and sent her a note that it warmed her heart. When Debi talked to WLCC members over the phone, she seemed happy. She never mentioned Luke.

One call, in particular, would have a ripple effect. Debi told Jayden she had good news about her case but couldn't talk about it over the phone. Jayden cautioned her to make sure the good news was not at Sarah's expense.

The Leonards could not afford to post bail, but Joe and the Moreys were freed within days.

Cady was told what was coming in the way of evidence but didn't know how much to expect. The first package to arrive on his desk was a box of paper documents: financial papers, church member notebooks, and diaries. Before they even cracked open the diaries, the staff in the district attorney's office had an inkling of what they might find. DA Scott McNamara was on the front lines of the case, already weighing reports that the church might actually be a cult. As early as the day Luke's body wound up at the hospital, police had noticed Tiffanie's hold over the others. They noticed it when they questioned suspects. They wrote of it in depositions provided by former church members: *brainwashed.*

It was within the first week of Luke's death that McNamara was driving to work and heard a radio talk show host interviewing a national cult expert about the Word of Life crime. McNamara called the broadcaster and asked, "How did you find this guy?"

That cult expert was Rick Ross, and McNamara would make good use of him.

While other prosecutors might have been turned off by the formidable task of putting together a cult case against such a large number of defendants, McNamara was intrigued. A book about a cult was the reason he'd gone to law school. When McNamara was a high school senior, a friend was talking about *Helter Skelter*, prosecutor Vincent Bugliosi's recounting of the Manson Family murders. But McNamara didn't know anything about the book. Not wanting to sound ignorant, he bought it, read it, and found the prosecutor's job fascinating.

"I don't typically take a lot of cases," McNamara later said. "I took the case because of that, and I took the case because of the way Luke died. And a weird coincidence was that Luke and I shared the same birthdate."

McNamara was getting ready to present the case to a grand jury. He was seeking charges against all the Irwins. He would need to paint a picture of a cult and show the Irwins' consistent control over their flock and over events the night Luke was killed. He would call Ross as a witness, and the DA's office would pay Ross as a consultant to help them organize evidence as the case went forward.

Behind the scenes, an interesting sidebar was developing. McNamara had been checking the jail visitor logs to see who was on the guest list, trying to get a feel for the size of the cult. One name kept showing up on Bruce's list, and it was for a religious visit: Rich Dibble. McNamara would remember the name but not meet the face behind it for several months.

Father Richard Dibble was an Anglican priest who barely knew Bruce but felt compelled to provide him emotional support. Inmates were limited to two visitors each week, but an attorney or a member of the clergy could go anytime. Rich showed up at the jail as little more than a stranger to Bruce. Their children had attended the same homeschool co-op, but it was mostly for mothers and children. Rich had seen Bruce only a couple of times, once being when Debi had her heart attack and he brought the family a meal. But the men shared something bigger, a commonality of hopelessness and despair brought on by horrendous loss. Rich's son had died two years earlier in a tragic accident. Even surrounded by family and his faith community, it had been an impossibly painful time. Rich believed Bruce's situation to be even more dire given that his spiritual support system may have played a role in his son's death. He offered Bruce unconditional friendship.

Rich didn't pay much attention to news and current affairs but could not avoid the diners in his small town overtaken by reporters typing on their laptops. He made an effort to shield himself from their reports. He did not want to know more—not yet, and not from them.

"Something in me told me that whatever had happened, there'd be plenty of judgment for Bruce. He didn't need more from me," Rich later said. "And he needed somebody just to walk with him."

Their first visit, Bruce was his guarded self, though he seemed grateful to have a visitor. Rich made a commitment to see him as much as he could. During their visits, Bruce did not talk about the events of October 11 and 12, and Rich didn't push him. He let Bruce steer the conversation. A lot of times, the topic was WLCC. Bruce relayed his experiences as having all been positive, with one aberration—Luke's death. He was unable to perceive evil in the Word of Life. He could not put evil motives to the circumstances surrounding his son's death. As Bruce spoke of things that appeared to illustrate an inordinate amount of control by church leadership, Rich noticed that that level of control felt normal to Bruce. Later, Rich became aware that WLCC members were visiting Bruce and got the impression the Irwins were using members to send messages, retaining their control even from behind bars.

Through Bruce, Rich also became aware that there was another Leonard daughter, Kristel. At the same time, he learned that Bruce had figuratively sorted and placed Kristel in a box up on a shelf. Bruce's reluctance regarding his own daughter caused Rich to be leery of her as well.

From their initial discussion, Bruce's focus was on the welfare of his children. He was wary of the foster care system and also wanted his kids to continue their spiritual upbringing. After a time, Bruce asked Rich to petition for custody. It was at the family court hearing that Rich met Kristel.

"It seemed like her stories were made up to gain our trust as a banished person," he recalled. As the days, and the story unfolded, and the strangeness and complexity of the story emerged, Rich chose to believe no one.

As police combed through astronomical amounts of data, noticeably absent was the piece they sought the most: the recording of Luke's final counseling session. Acting on a tip that it was in the hands of Tiffanie's lawyer, Oneida County assistant public defender Kurt Schultz, the DA issued Schultz a subpoena to appear before the grand jury with all the Irwin property in his possession. Schultz fought the subpoena. At a hearing, he wouldn't admit to having any evidence at all.

"The argument," Schutlz told the judge, "would be that anything that may or may not be in my possession would be there as the result of information that I were to obtain through an attorney-client privilege. And then the other argument I would have is that some of the items that are mentioned in the subpoena, if they were, in fact, in my possession, would have private information on them for the individuals who possessed those pieces of property."

"Is the property, whatever property may be in your possession, has it been tampered with in any way since it came in your possession?" asked the judge.

"Since my possession, none whatsoever." Schultz went on to say, "It appears some of the property, someone attempted to destroy the property, which would be tampering with evidence. I would think that would be my only— My job is to secure the property."

The judge ruled that Schultz would not have to testify before the grand jury but would have to turn over the evidence. On October 29, Schultz gave police two cell phones, one laptop, one hard drive, one tablet, one thumb drive, one handwritten note containing passwords, the charred remains of a broken memory card, and two pieces of asphalt roofing material. Shultz told them that's how it was provided to him, with the asphalt. Someone had put the memory card in roofing shingles and set it on fire.

State Police could not extract any data from the broken card. They took pictures of it and sent the photos to the FBI, who determined the memory component was missing.

On November 24, an explosive development: Pastor Tiffanie Irwin was charged with murder, along with Word of Life members Traci, Joe, Bruce, Sarah, Linda, and Dave. The second-degree murder charge alleged the defendants caused Luke's death by showing a "depraved indifference" to human life, engaging in conduct so reckless that death was likely. Dan did not face that murder charge but was indicted on a lesser charge of manslaughter. The grand jury indicted all the defendants on a host of charges, including kidnapping, assault, and gang assault. They were all held without bail.

Debi's name was unmistakably absent from the list. She had already cut a deal. It was her grand jury testimony that helped seal the charges against the others. In exchange for her testimony, her manslaughter charge was reduced to two assault charges—one for Luke and one for Chris—and she agreed to plead guilty. For that, she would serve five years in prison. As part of her deal, Debi also agreed to testify at any of her codefendant's future trials, including her own daughter's.

Early on, McNamara knew he needed an insider to explain what had been going on. He was trying to determine who was the least culpable and who could help them the most. He brought in Debi for an interview, and she was cooperative. She told him how abusive the Irwins were to her, in particular. Because Tiffanie had never touched anyone, it would be difficult to secure an indictment. Debi's cooperation was critical. But when McNamara brought her in a second time, now to cut a deal, Debi acted like she held all the cards.

"I wanna get out today," she demanded, and asked to plead guilty to crimes that didn't even exist on the books.

"Let me explain something to you," McNamara said. "In my opinion, you're going to get indicted, and you're going to get prosecuted. You're not in a position where you're going to dictate to me what's going to happen."

If she agreed to cooperate, McNamara said he would sit down with her and her lawyer and come to a reasonable punishment, but, "You're not walking on this. You lost a son. If you want to help us bring to justice the people that were behind you losing your son, then we can work."

For her safety, Debi was moved to a different jail.

Back on Oneida Street, town officials were working to shut down the Word of Life Building. In December, they initiated a civil action and won a temporary restraining order in state supreme court that barred anyone from entering or operating out of the building. Court papers cited the beating as a violation of the town's public-nuisance code, noting that neighbors had become *extremely fearful of their physical well being*, and *The defendants have maintained an air of secrecy refusing to cooperate with Town officials and the Town Police with regard to access of their property*. The town cited an incident on November 26, when police and fire personnel were dispatched to the building for a possible structure fire. They alleged a female at the building would not identify herself, denied there was a fire, and refused to let them in to check.

"They're not going to get away with this," Traci told a WLCC member over the jail phone, calling it religious discrimination. "So they can fuck themselves, or they're going to pay me so much money their heads will spin."

Traci's mother and sisters, who she'd long ago cut out of her life, now rolled the dice and went to see her in jail. But Traci told a WLCC member to "get with" her family, because she hadn't talked to them in thirty years, and now they wanted to take her visit time. Traci wanted the slots reserved for her church family.

Someone from the church did, indeed, get with at least one member of Traci's family, approaching her at her place of employment and asking for commissary money: $80 a week to be split among all four Irwins in jail. The family member was told that Tiffanie had skin so sensitive she needed certain soap and this would help pay for it. The family declined.

The New Year was less than a month away, and the prosecution had a mountain of work in preparing for trial, not to mention the revolving door of pretrial hearings.

The remaining WLCC members—Rick Wright's family, Brooke Bowden, Kathy Morey, and an elderly female parishioner—filed a lawsuit against the town in response to them shutting down the church. The town ended up dropping its complaint.

Meanwhile, interns were still listening on the jail phone lines. Against judge's orders, Jayden was sneaking Grace on the phone to talk to Sarah. Bruce had signed a form allowing Grace to attend public school. There, she punched a boy who wouldn't leave her alone. Jayden was trying to get custody of his younger siblings and Sarah's kids. Sarah was trying to stay distracted and said she would grieve later.

On a phone call with her father, Kristel delivered astonishing news: she'd separated from her husband and was living in an apartment. An intern wrote, *She says the marriage was not based on love. it was an assignment. . . . She talks more about the marriage being an assignment by those who are no longer over her life.*

Linda's family told her Naomi had stopped by to visit them. The intern noted: *Linda says be careful because [Naomi] is trouble.*

Bruce signed up for an art and poetry contest in the jail. He won third place and got $30 toward commissary. *BL says he cried a lot this morning, and that it felt as bad as it did at the beginning.*

Dave and Dan were hanging out together in jail, playing cards. Dave was described as sounding depressed. *DM said someone tried to hang themselves today.*

SF says she is feeling better, more grounded than last week. [Jayden] is in Chicago, but he wants to go home. They tell each other jokes & laugh together . . . SF asks if its normal that her ankles hurt from working out. [Jayden] tells her to land on her toes. SF says she is getting jacked. They say "I love you."

The other inmates gave Traci the nickname Church Lady. She was using a WLCC loyalist as a messenger to go to each of her family members and tell them to turn down any plea offers.

"Everyone said no plea," the member relayed.

On January 11, Tiffanie turned down a plea offer from the district attorney's office that would've had her pleading guilty to the top charge of second-degree murder and sentenced to at least eighteen years in prison. One by one, her codefendants said no to the same offer.

Intern Anthony Sokolowski arrived in Investigator Dave Cady's office in January, ready to roll up his sleeves. He was assigned to listen to the defendants' recorded jail calls for anything that could point the prosecution in the right direction or help their case. But these people weren't giving much away.

"The way they talked on the phone, they were almost computerized," Sokolowski later said. The men appeared conditioned to say certain things; trained and programmed to act a certain way. "It's not so much what they were saying, it's what they were not saying. They were having conversations like someone was looking over their shoulder." David Morey was the only one who consistently used the phone. "He would have a twenty-minute conversation where he never said more than seven words to anybody. He was very robotic. He would talk to his father, talk to his sister, and all he would say is, 'Okay . . . okay . . . okay.' Never got excited. Never got sad. Never had an emotion, really."

Sokolowski went to Cady's office with a recording and played it for him. "Dave, I don't understand why those people are talking like they have strings on them."

Cady listened to the segment. Phone calls of criminals were nothing new to him. They weren't the most sophisticated speakers, but they at least followed social norms in communication. Most of the WLCC folks could not even maintain a back-and-forth dialogue. Inexplicably, Sarah was loquacious in comparison.

Dave appointed Sokolowski as a liaison to the DA and had him bring his observations to McNamara.

"They're not saying much," Sokolowski told the DA, "but you can tell they're not necessarily normal in their conversation patterns."

Though he'd just come on board, even to Sokolowski, it was very obvious, very early, that many of these defendants were under some-one's control. It wasn't until Cady's team got videos of the church ser-vices and read through the personal notebooks that a picture unfolded of how and what the Irwins were doing to their disciples. Sokolowski learned that everyone who wasn't Tiffanie Irwin, or one of her confi-dants, was not allowed to speak out of tune. Otherwise, they would have to deal with Tiffanie.

There came a time when the legality of listening to jail calls was challenged in court, and because of that, Cady pulled the interns from eavesdropping duty. But he had plenty of other work for them. The State Police had sent him a hard drive containing more than three hun-dred hours of videos of WLCC services and counseling sessions, mate-rial extracted from the digital evidence collected during the search. Their task was to watch every second of it.

The DA's office provided Cady with large paper sheets detailing a time line of the church, and Cady used them to create a banner that ran across the ceiling of his office. It started at the door and wrapped around the entire room. If they were looking at video from a partic-ular day, they could check the time line to see what was happening that day. They also had huge sheets of poster board, and the interns put photos of the defendants on them, creating a hierarchy chart—a who's who of WLCC. His team was trying to establish how Tiffanie was controlling her followers. It didn't take long for them to learn that she was painting herself as a prophet with a direct line to God. The prosecution would need to get a jury to understand that these people participated in the beatings under her supervision.

The first video that Sokolowski watched was an earlier counseling session with Luke, in which Tiffanie tried to get him to ask her to pray for the healing of his knee. Sokolowski found the conversation demoralizing. "It was meant to just absolutely obliterate any sort of confidence or masculinity within him," he later recalled. "It was essentially to make him feel like he was nothing in front of her, to where he had to earn her respect back."

Digital evidence was rolling in, in the form of hundreds of thousands of text messages, photos, emails, and audio recordings from the defendants' cell phones, tablets, and computers. Computer forensics specialists at the crime lab took each cell phone and put it in a two-foot-high glass box to prevent someone from wiping the data remotely. The box blocked the signals from cell towers. Police then put the phone in airplane mode and worked on it. With a special software program, they were able to extract even deleted material. But they could take only what was authorized by the search warrant. The data was filtered to specific time spans, and to keywords like "Sarah." On Debi's phone alone, they extracted more than forty thousand text messages and more than thirty thousand iMessages. McNamara had never had a case produce so much evidence.

Cady decided to run his operation as a police investigation, with his office as a command post. He was given more than a half-dozen interns, and they would develop leads. Some would watch videos, some would listen to audio, and others would read diaries and text messages. That was when it became more intimate—and crazy, really.

Sokolowski took his role seriously, devoting much more time to the project than his required daily schedule at the office. It became all-consuming. Every day, for a solid ten hours, he was involved in the nooks and crannies of these individuals' lives. After walking out the door of the DA's office, he would immerse himself in his notes to see if they needed to switch directions or watch certain videos again.

"Because on first glance, something that doesn't seem like a big deal—something as simple as a side-eye look from Tiffanie—can be an indirect message to somebody," he later said. Everyone at the church was in tune with her emotions and trying to please her, because as far as they were concerned, she was their ticket to heaven. She controlled every aspect of their lives, and not just in church.

But Grace—things were different with her. It appeared to Sokolowski that Tiffanie was protecting her because she was a girl, even grooming her to become a version of the self-proclaimed prophet. Kristel later regarded Tiffanie's and Traci's actions as molding Grace for the ultimate control. "[Grace] was treated exactly the way that I was treated at that age, being courted, if you will, by the Irwins, encouraged in her spiritual growth, told that she was doing a great job, really being drawn in to be a part. And I believe to a fifteen-year-old girl who has no other connection, and that intimacy with super spiritual grown-ups, there's really nothing that can shake that connection."

The church sermon videos were in twenty-minute segments, and each morning, Cady's team would gather in his office and talk about what kinds of activities were going on at the church. Inevitably, some of the college students would make comments equating this kind of behavior with Christians in general. Cady cringed. The comments played in his head like a skipping vinyl record: "Well, see, that's what happens. That's the way these religious wackos are"; "See, there is no God. God wouldn't let this happen."

There didn't seem to be a believer among them. Just two years earlier, Cady's belief in God had pulled him from a pit of despair, and now, his God was being trashed. He wanted to stand up and say, "No. You've got this wrong," but in a government office, he had to be careful. Government and religion were not to be mixed, under normal circumstances. How could he work in a public office while at the same time showing these young people that what Tiffanie Irwin preached was not representative of Christian beliefs? He looked to his faith for an answer.

Before leaving for work one morning, Cady sat at the table and prayed with his wife over coffee. "Lord, work with me on this. Help me find out how I can show people your goodness. How I can show that this is not you." He felt a deep need to right a wrong in the Leonard case and made a promise to God to give justice to those left behind. He would iron out Tiffanie's misshapen biblical meanings and bring back grace to God's words.

Cady saw that Tiffanie's sermons were aberrant, and he needed to draw that distinction for the interns. When they were sitting in the morning meetings and talking about Tiffanie's interpretation of a particular verse, Cady would look up the verse on the computer.

"Look, guys. This is what Christians believe." He'd read it aloud. Cady's Christianity helped the team understand that Tiffanie was molding these passages to fit her agenda. It was one of the ways she manipulated members.

Cady's eye was also drawn to something else in the videos. A singer and songwriter, he noticed the costly instruments—high-end guitars, keyboards, drums. The young men seemed to be playing different guitars every time. There were the search warrant photos of the hyperbaric chamber, the expensive firearms collection, and the tens of thousands of dollars that Traci had been spending on dogs. A motive of money began to unfold. If Luke left the church, his family could follow. Church membership had already dropped significantly, and fewer members meant less money for the Irwins. The DA's office estimated the Irwins were collecting about $100,000 a year in tithes and offerings. Some members were even handing over their work bonuses and tax refunds.

But was the church a cult? Cady and his interns created a file they named *WOL Greatest Hits* to showcase some of the more significant sermons. The DA's office gave the video segments to their cult expert, Rick Ross, to demonstrate Tiffanie's approach. Ross guided them in putting together a reference sheet that listed important videos, text messages, diary entries, and other evidence, to illustrate Tiffanie's control. They labeled it *Tiffanie Compilation*, and it was more than sixty pages long. The DA planned to use the information in cross-examining Tiffanie at trial. Ross advised them to organize the entries under seven headings: *Control of Movement, Control of Language, Control of Fear/Fear Manipulation, Control by Humiliation, Control of Finances, Control of Interpersonal Relationships*, and *Threats of and/or Acts of Physical Harm*. Each entry was in chronological order, as a clear picture had emerged: over time, Tiffanie had become more unhinged.

"It was a phenomenal job," Cady said later, "and we just got it done."

Rich continued to visit Bruce, and though he was not successful in getting custody of Bruce's children, he did come to know Kristel. It soon became apparent that she was the levelheaded one.

Bruce was experiencing a partial enlightenment. Like his son Luke's, Bruce's brain was always turning.

"His questioning began when he contemplated the biblical requirement that in a court proceeding, the truth is established by a minimum of two witnesses in agreement on something," Rich later explained. "But he was tracing things back in his mind, things the Irwins had asserted, which seemed to him like they were supported by multiple people. He was thinking and realizing that the people who supported it had gained their support for it from the Irwins. So there was really only one source."

This was a revelation to Bruce: he may have believed things to be true that were not.

As Bruce, Rich, and Kristel began to drop their guards, a relationship developed among them. "Bruce shared all sorts of things about trying to figure out what had happened," Rich later recounted. "And there was an intense resistance inside of him to question the leadership. It was noticeable, but I didn't understand it. And there was a constant referral to times in the past when he felt an unquestioned anointing on the church, or on Jerry and Tiffanie. He had all these high mountaintop experiences that really cemented his belief in them, and his mind popped back to those often, when questions came up about them."

This was a tough hurdle to clear. One night, Rich did an online search for cults, trying to get a handle on what was happening and how to help. He emailed a cult expert, and the person called him. Based on their conversation, everything finally made sense.

Rich read up on the subject and learned techniques for trying to get Bruce to come to his own breakthrough. He'd done right by taking a sideline approach. Cult leaders, he learned, plant a psychological trigger that causes the follower to shut out anyone who criticizes the group. Rejecting that critic is like a reflex. One way to circumvent that mechanism is to find a nonthreatening way to discuss another group the person recognizes as a cult, because he doesn't believe his own group is one. Rich also learned to never to make any direct statements but to ask questions. Last, he enlisted Kristel to assemble a support group of past members.

March brought a significant development in the courtroom. Sarah's attorney moved to dismiss the kidnapping charges against her client, and in response, the district attorney agreed. He also agreed to dismiss the kidnapping charges against Bruce. He had come to believe the Leonards, even Sarah, had been held against their will. "How can you be holding someone against their will when, in essence, I think you're being held against your will?" McNamara later explained. "The only people that were keeping anybody against their will was the Irwins."

At this time, investigators were also getting deep into the phone content they'd extracted. On Tiffanie's phone, they found an eyebrow-raising text sent the afternoon of October 12: *SD cards and paraphernalia away...yes.*

They discovered Joe's internet searches on October 12 for *sprained wrist*. On Dave's phone were searches for *surviving prison*, and visits to internet articles including *Eight Tips on Surviving Prison for the Newly Incarcerated, Top 10 Tips for Surviving in Prison (That Your Homie Didn't Tell You), How to Survive in Federal Prison (with pictures)—WikiHow,* and *8 Tips for an Easier Prison Stay.*

In the backup of one phone, police found alarming audio recordings. In a folder titled *voice memos*, there were thirty-nine recorded counseling sessions between Tiffanie and Seth Wright, making up fifty-eight hours of audio. At least one of those recordings had the distinct sounds of an individual striking Seth. There were also photos of the back of a young man's neck with what appeared to be red welts. Police more than once tried to interview Seth and other members of his family, but in their report, indicated *The Wrights have refused to cooperate with law enforcement.* Regardless, the information was sent to the DA's office for possible grand jury review.

As the pages of the calendar turned, attorneys for each defendant filed court papers asking for relief on various matters. Tiffanie's lawyer even asked that she be released from jail on her own recognizance; basically, freed without having to pay bail. It was denied.

Sokolowski was astounded by Tiffanie's courtroom demeanor. "She was the only person I've ever seen walk into a courtroom facing a murder charge and think 'I am so above this,'" he later said. "She walked in. She would look at the cameras. She'd look around. Flash a little half grin. And she relished the spotlight because she knew she was the center of attention, and she had that in her church. Now, she has it in a courtroom."

The others were still very broken; always nervous, always unsure of what to say. They were still acting their roles: heads down, no eye contact, low mumbles. Folks in the gallery felt an inclination to yell, "Speak up!"

There were motions to dismiss the grand jury indictment, suppress physical evidence, throw out oral and written statements made to police, and change the location of the trial. Defense lawyers argued the extensive news coverage made it impossible for their clients to get a fair and impartial jury. There were also motions to hold separate trials for each defendant. McNamara agreed with that, partly. He wanted to split the group in two, with Bruce and Sarah together in one trial, and the other six in another. He felt trying the four together would help a jury better understand each defendant's role and Tiffanie's leadership. He also surmised if they were tried separately, the other defendants would testify for Tiffanie. Oneida County court judge Michael Dwyer agreed with the prosecution on most every point, including the groupings of who would be tried together.

The motions were fairly standard, though one was unusual. Tiffanie's lawyer filed a motion asking the judge to bar any counseling session recordings from being presented at trial, claiming it violated priest-penitent privilege, also called clergy privilege. The prosecution argued that the privilege was for the parishioner, not the pastor, that the privilege did not exist if statements were made in the presence of a third party, and that "communication or threats made during the course of physical abuse are not entitled to be cloaked in the privilege."

Once again, Judge Dwyer sided with the prosecution.

Investigator Pietryka was learning just how crafty these people were. After Luke's death, Tiffanie had started communicating with WLCC members by a shared email account to prevent her messages from being sent to other devices. They would use the same username and password to log on to an email account and save messages as drafts, but never send them.

"Very smart," Pietryka later said. "We saw that technique being used by narcotic traffickers." And he discovered they'd been using a confidential email service that had users share a secret code to view an email. The service encrypted emails, and then permanently deleted them after they were read.

Shifty as the Irwins were, they could not get ahead of police. Pietryka captured the IP addresses involved in the confidential email service and eventually traced subscriber information for the users of those addresses. That's how authorities learned another WLCC member was present the night of the crime: Brooke Bowden. Through this confidential email account, Tiffanie had Brooke tell her what she remembered from that night. Brooke had not been in the counseling session. She had stayed with Kathy and the children all night. Brooke's parents confirmed that Linda had driven their daughter home the following morning.

There was another piece of digital data from the evidence collection that sparked attention. Luke sent this text to Tiffanie on July 10, 2014: *I have molested [Ada] twice. When we used to have prayer, afterwards I would get up on top of the van at home and expose myself to cars passing by.*

Startling as that discovery was, police were in store for another. Investigator Pietryka was reviewing the contents of Dan's cell phone and one discussion thread jumped out at him. It was a text dispute about dogs, between Traci and a woman named Beverly Visser. The dispute referenced Beverly keeping Traci's secrets. The same texts were on Traci's phone, including this foreboding message from Beverly: *you have gone over to the darkness.* Beverly had been trying to collect $27,000 for the dogs that Traci had bought, a bill that Traci disputed.

Pietryka called Beverly. In Indiana, she'd seen the news reports of Luke's death. She'd jumped out of her seat, pointed to the TV, and exclaimed, "I've been there!" Now, an investigator was calling her, but she wasn't sure why. When he asked her about the disagreement with

Traci, he could not have guessed the tale he was about to hear. Beverly told him the story of meeting Traci through the dog breeding business, and how Traci had taken Jerry to Indiana for treatment, bringing the hyperbaric chamber with her.

The hyperbaric chamber? Authorities had found the device during their search. Now this woman was telling them Traci had taken it to Indiana. But there was more. Beverly told the investigator of Jerry's death, transporting the body across state lines for resurrection, Traci's three-hour police interview—and that Jerry may have died in the hyperbaric chamber.

Traci had stayed in Indiana for a little while after Jerry's death, and then said goodbye to Beverly. It was two weeks later that, according to Beverly, she got a disturbing phone call from Traci.

"She told me that Jerry didn't die in bed, that he died in the hyperbaric chamber," Beverly later alleged. "And I said, 'What do you mean?' and she said, 'I woke up and the alarm had gone off on the hyperbaric chamber.'"

The one that Traci had purchased was called Flexi-Lite, a top-of-the-line unit manufactured by Newtowne Hyperbarics from about 2000 to 2012, the most expensive on the market. Newtowne's managing director, Marie Foster, later identified the model, for the purposes of this book, through search warrant photos. The unit is designed for solo use of an able-bodied person. Made of ballistic-grade nylon that's coated on either side with a medical-grade urethane, the individual would climb inside and secure the outer bag with eight straps and steel buckles, and then close the inner bag with an airtight zipper. An incapacitated person would not be able to get himself in or out of the chamber.

Foster said there were much lower-priced models available at the time this one was manufactured, but this unit could be modified by purchasing different valves overseas. "Most people purchase these types of chambers specifically to use them at higher pressures," said

Foster. The Flexi-Lite was built to reach a maximum pressure of four psi (pounds per square inch), but the modified valves would more than double that.

An air compressor continuously pumps fresh air through the chamber, while old air is exhausted through relief valves. Foster noted an oxygen concentrator in the search warrant photos. She said a concentrator would be used to pump oxygen into a mask that the user is wearing.

This chamber was not manufactured with an alarm, said Foster, but the oxygen concentrators usually had them, to alert that something was wrong, such as a power outage. "If the power went out, or there was a lack of oxygen to the patient in this chamber, he could asphyxiate." The alarm could also point to a problem with the exhaust valves, which could mean excessive buildup of carbon dioxide inside the chamber, leading to respiratory distress and, ultimately, death.

Pietryka wanted answers. He interviewed Beverly over the phone, and among his notes: *When [Beverly] asked Tracie what had happened, Tracie told her that they put Jerry inside the hyperbaric chamber overnight and when they awoke the next morning, they found him dead.* Pietryka contacted the captain of the Mishawaka Police Department and asked for the case report on Jerry's death investigation, and some other documents, including the coroner's report. Although no autopsy had been performed, the certifying physician had written Jerry's immediate cause of death to be myocardial infarction—a heart attack. Stroke was listed as a contributing condition. The manner of death: natural.

The Mishawaka police captain assigned an investigator with the St. Joseph County Metro Homicide Unit to record an interview with Beverly, who repeated the peculiar tale. In the end, authorities could not prove negligence in Jerry's death. There was not enough evidence, and there was no body to exhume, because Jerry had been cremated.

Pietryka sent the interview and related reports to DA McNamara for any potential value at trial.

I've always felt, and I still believe, and I'll believe till the day I die—Luke wanted out. He just didn't know how to get out. Because when you're nineteen, and you live at home, and you've never been in the outside world, you don't have any means to support yourself, how do you walk away? . . . We deal with that same situation every day when you talk about domestic violence. People stay because they have no other choice, at least in their own mind. . . . . What could Luke do? Where's Luke gonna go? Where's Luke gonna live? He knows nothing else except for the church and its preachings. And he doesn't trust the outside world. He's been taught not to.

— ONEIDA COUNTY DISTRICT ATTORNEY SCOTT MCNAMARA

Sarah and Bruce would go on trial first, scheduled for the end of June 2016. McNamara brought in Debi for pretrial prep and was blown away by her first words: "I don't remember anything."

"Don't play games with me, Debi," said McNamara.

But Debi didn't quit the act. Her outright hostility lasted all of five minutes before the DA had had enough.

He stood up and said, "Forget it. I'm not playing your game, Debi," and walked out the door. Then he thought about it. Should he push the issue, or let it go? Testifying was part of the deal she'd made, but she was also a mom whose testimony could convict her own child. "I just made the decision it wasn't going to be worth it, and I wasn't really sure I wanted to do that," McNamara later explained. "I'm a prosecutor, but I'm also a human that has feelings. And I just didn't think that forcing her to do that was the right thing to do."

He decided he would instead call Grace to the stand. But that presented its own problems. Grace would not talk to men. McNamara would have to pull Assistant DA Laurie Lisi off a major murder case to question Grace during trial. Lisi's background as a former sex crimes prosecutor would be helpful.

The week that Bruce and Sarah were to be tried together, there was a sudden shift. In the eleventh hour, Bruce and his lawyer met in the jury room with McNamara and the judge. Bruce was considering accepting a deal that would have him plead guilty to the assault charges, with the promise that every other charge, including murder, would be dropped. The DA wanted him to serve fifteen or sixteen years in prison.

As the parties tossed around a possible sentence, Bruce looked at the DA and asked, "Why fifteen years?"

"I wish I had an answer for you," said McNamara. "I wish I knew what the right number was. Let me tell you something: this is a very unique case. Usually you—people like you, the father of the victim—are coming to me and asking me to make sure I get the most, or get a certain sentence. I don't have that in this case. Luke's dead, and all the people that should be on his side are defendants in this case. I picked that number because I think it's the appropriate number. But there is no magic formula to this. We do this every day, and I wish I could tell you. I wish I could say that I'm giving you a year for every five times you hit him with a cord."

"I just wanted to know how you calculate it," said Bruce.

He decided to take the offer, but just as he was getting ready to plead guilty, Bruce told the DA, "I'm not going to testify against the Irwins."

That was part of the agreement. In exchange for dropping the other charges, Bruce would testify for the prosecution. McNamara reminded Bruce of the deal he'd just made.

"I'll tell the truth," said Bruce, "but I'm not testifying 'against' anybody."

In what's called a plea colloquy, a question-answer session that's required before a judge accepts a guilty plea, Judge Dwyer questioned Bruce on the details of the crime. Just two minutes in, Bruce, who was standing in front of the judge's bench, nearly collapsed and had to be helped into a chair.

McNamara questioned Bruce, too, this time with Bruce in his seat at the defendant's desk. "Did you ever think that night that maybe Luke was saying certain things because he wanted to hurt you people, because you were hurting him physically, and the only way he could hurt you was with his tongue?"

Bruce sighed, and the words came slowly. "I . . . I don't know, sir."

"Is that possible?"

"You . . . you're asking me to speculate?"

"No, I'm asking you if it's possible. You knew your son."

Bruce started and stopped, his words inaudible, and then broke down sobbing. First were choking sounds, then silence, then loud heaving. His body visibly trembled before he managed to say, "I don't know, sir." He tried to say more, and then flung his head back, wheezing and sobbing. He turned down his attorney's offer of a cup of water and struggled to regain control of his emotions.

"Was there a biblical reason for the utilization of a whipping?" asked McNamara.

"The only thing I had vaguely in—" He shook his head and found the right words before starting again. "The only thing that was vaguely in my head at that point was that 'blows that hurt drive off evil.'"

The boys could not have left if they wanted to, McNamara said, because Joe and the others wouldn't have let them. After much consideration, all Bruce would say was that they couldn't leave because they had all gone to church in the same vehicle.

"Well, once Lucas collapsed and was on the ground, obviously *he* couldn't go," said McNamara.

"You don't know," said Bruce, cross but breathless.

"I know I don't. That's why—"

Loud sobs cut off the DA's words, and Bruce hollered, "Oh!" before crying and moaning. He took several deep breaths. "You don't know what it is to lose a child. You don't know what it is . . . to . . . to have anything at all to do with it." He finished by adding a curt "sir" and then began loudly crying again, guttural.

"Bruce, if you could say something to Lucas right now, what would you say?"

He wailed, "He's gone! How can I say it to him?"

"If you could, would you say you were sorry?"

"If I could . . ." He answered in broken by sobs. "Yes . . . Yes. Yes."

After Bruce's guilty plea, there was another development: Sarah opted out of a jury trial. In what's called a "bench trial," Judge Dwyer, alone, would decide her fate.

Sarah Ferguson's murder trial began on June 23, with Rebecca Wittman as her defense attorney and Scott McNamara and his first assistant DA, Michael Coluzza, for the prosecution. McNamara started from scratch in his opening statement, detailing the cast of characters and the layout of the Word of Life Building. The church, he said, was not your mainstream church.

"One of the more unique things of the church is that Pastor Tiffanie claims she speaks directly to God, and he speaks to her." And the list of sins was more expansive, including witchcraft and arrogance. Rebellion, lust, and molestation were common themes, and, "The evidence will show that certain terms used by this group have a much broader definition than what is commonly understood." He detailed, in summary, the events of October 11 and 12, 2015, "which can only be viewed, in hindsight, as a modern-day witch trial."

Sarah's defense attorney did not make an opening statement.

Testimony began the following day. The first witness was New Hartford police sergeant Justin Gehringer.

Members of the news media were in the front row with their cameras in the way. The judge stopped proceedings briefly. "I'm trying to be as accommodating as possible for the media," he said. "You're going to have to move to the right so the other spectators in court can actually see what's going on." Dwyer instructed some to stay down, others to move, a bit of musical chairs. "Could I ask those three people in front, that you've already been moved once, could you go . . ." They stood and waited for direction. "Go to the first row back. There. Security would appreciate that. Okay, please proceed, Mr. McNamara."

Sergeant Gehringer was the evidence technician who took photos at the hospital, including photos of Luke's body and the white van. He also executed the search warrant on Bruce Leonard just before midnight on October 12, and then went to help search the big sanctuary on October 13. In his testimony, he introduced evidence of the whipping instrument—the computer power cord with the broken metal prongs and stripped outer sheath.

The prosecution called eighteen witnesses over five days. At the top of the second day of testimony, Christopher took the stand wearing a crisp, black-and-red collared shirt. He was now eighteen years old years old and living with a foster family. After some basic questions, McNamara zeroed in on Tiffanie's role at WLCC.

"As part of being a member of the church, were you required to submit to the authority of Pastor Tiffanie?"

"Yes," answered Chris, head up and looking straight at McNamara. He said that prior to Tiffanie, he was required to submit to her father, Pastor Jerry.

Chris answered questions about the night of October 11, when Tiffanie told everyone to leave, except for the Leonard family. A lot of his answers were "I don't remember." But he recalled Joe Irwin punching him in the gut. It hurt, he said. And he recalled Joe going over to Luke and asking him the same questions Chris had refused to answer. "When Joe Irwin came back over to me, and I wasn't saying anything still, he told—my dad told Joe Irwin to hit me again."

"And did Joe Irwin hit you again?" asked McNamara.

"He either hit me or kicked me. I'm not sure which." He next remembered Linda punching him in the nose. He mostly remembered being whipped but wasn't certain who had whipped him first. There was no mistaking who hit him the most with the cord: "Sarah."

"Now can you tell the court—did there ever come a time that some people moved your brother Lucas?"

"Yes."

"Who moved him?"

"Joe Irwin and David Morey."

"Why did they move him? Or what did they do?"

"They moved him onto the tarp."

"Do you know why they moved him onto the tarp?"

"I think so he wouldn't bleed onto the carpet."

Did anyone give his brother water? Try to help him? Give him medical attention? Ice for his genitals?

They did not, said Chris.

McNamara took Chris back to the start of the incident. "Were you and Luke being asked to repent your sins, or were you just being questioned about them?"

"At first, we were being questioned, and then to repent."

"During the course of the counseling session, did you admit to things that you didn't do?"

"Yes."

"And why did you admit to things you didn't do?"

"Because I wanted them to stop."

Chris sat stiffly and looked intently at the DA as he questioned him. He did not fidget or look away, or turn his head aside as though thinking. He answered succinctly and his lips barely moved.

"Did you admit to things that you did do?" asked McNamara.

"Yes."

"Did you hear Luke admit to things that you knew he had done?"

"I don't know."

"Did you ever hear him admit to things that you never saw him do?"

"Yes."

The boys were getting hit within minutes of the counseling session starting, he testified, and the whipping began quite soon, too.

"How would you describe your relationship with Lucas?" asked McNamara. "Was he your friend?"

"Yes."

"Was he your best friend?"

"Yes."

Chris thought about running away that evening but didn't think he would make it out of the church. "I . . . I . . . I think I would've been stopped." He didn't believe Joe would've let him leave, and the gate and doors to the church were typically locked.

Chris talked about Luke visiting Kristel's church. "I asked him not to go." He said he thought they should be going to only one church.

"Was that something you thought, or something you were taught, or—"

"Both."

McNamara asked Chris who, in his family, was closest to Pastor Tiffanie, and Chris said it was his father, because he was always texting her.

The DA moved on to Sarah. "How would you describe your relationship with her prior to when this took place?"

"Tense."

"Had you had problems with her?"

"Yes."

During cross-examination, Sarah's attorney, Rebecca Wittman, got into this further. She asked why Grace had moved in with Sarah.

"I'm pretty sure because Sarah needed help with her kids," he said.

"Okay. You're pretty sure of that?"

"Yes."

"Within the household, when Grace moved upstairs, had anyone talked about her moving upstairs because she was being abused downstairs?"

"I think so."

"And do you know who talked about that?"

"I don't remember."

"And do you know whether that fact had been discussed in the church?"

"I believe so."

"Okay. And was that perhaps one of the factors that was causing what you would call it to be a tense relationship with Sarah?"

"I believe so. Yes."

"At some point, did you know about a peephole in the bathroom?"

"Yes."

"Who made that peephole?"

"I don't know."

Eventually, Wittman asked, "And that was a peephole that could be used to look into the bathroom and see people when they were either showering or using the bathroom. Correct?"

"Yes."

"And do you know whether Luke had used that?"

McNamara objected.

"Overruled," called the judge. "If he knows, he can answer."

Chris answered, "I don't know."

Wittman asked, "Do you know whether you had used that?"

"Yes."

After further questioning, Wittman said, "You told Mr. McNamara that during the events at the church, that you admitted to things you didn't do. Correct?"

"Yes."

"And do you remember what things you admitted to that you had not actually done?"

"I did not put my penis in my niece and nephews."

"You told Mr. McNamara that you also admitted to things that you did do. Correct?"

"Yes."

"And what things did you admit to that you had actually done?"

"I touched them inappropriately."

Sokolowski, sitting in the courtroom, was stunned. He thought, *There's finally fire to all that smoke.* And he wasn't alone. It made for sensational news copy. All the reporters' heads lowered simultaneously as they began hurriedly taking notes.

But McNamara was privy to information that others weren't. By the way Wittman asked the questions, and based on Chris's definitions, he wasn't sure that Chris was admitting to molesting anybody. Early in the case, McNamara had asked Chris if he'd ever done anything sexual to Sarah's children. Because of Chris's definitions of molestation, McNamara had been very specific.

"I said, 'Did you ever put your finger inside of the vagina of your nieces?' And he said no. I said, 'Did you ever put your finger inside of the anus of your nieces or nephews?' And he said no. So I asked him very specific questions. What he said was, 'Well, we used to have to change their diapers.'" McNamara later explained, "I think when he changed her diaper, he probably looked to see what a vagina looks like."

All of Sarah's children who were verbal and who had been interviewed by sex crime and pediatric experts said they had never been touched in or near their privates, except by a doctor or their mother.

Still on the witness stand, Chris testified it was at the start of the counseling session that he admitted to inappropriate touching but only fabricated graphic detail when the group insisted he tell more.

"Was there also either yourself or Luke admitting to having abused the baby in her crib the night before?" asked Wittman.

"Yes."

"And was that an admission made by yourself, or Luke, or both of you?"

"I don't remember."

"And did one of you say that you held—" She looked down at her notes and restarted. "That a hand was held over her mouth so that she wouldn't make any noise?"

"Yes."

"And that there was blood."

"Yes."

The church group was directing most of the questions to Luke, said Chris, and when Luke answered, sometimes graphically detailing sexual abuse, his demeanor was "just saying it."

"Had you ever seen a voodoo doll?" asked Wittman.

"I think I remember vaguely seeing a voodoo doll. Yes."

"Would that have been at your house?"

"I think so. Yes."

On redirect, McNamara asked a few follow-up questions. He wanted to know why Chris admitted to doing things he hadn't done.

"Because I wanted them to stop."

"And did you think that if you said certain things, that they would stop whipping you?"

"Yes."

"Did they ultimately stop whipping you when you said those things?"

"No."

He asked about the drive to the hospital, when Joe asked if he was okay. "And you told Miss Wittman on cross-examination, you told him that you were okay?"

"Yes. I just nodded and said, 'Yes.'"

"And, in fact, that wasn't true, was it?"

"No."

"You were in a lot of pain. Correct?"

"Yes."

The judge asked questions, too. He tried to get Chris to pinpoint the number of times his father had hit him. Chris estimated it was about thirty. His father had asked him to turn so that his back was to him, but because of the way he was swinging the cord, it was wrapping around and hitting Chris in the chest. He remembered that Joe held him down one of the times he fell.

"Did you want to stop going to that church?" asked the judge.

"Sort of," said Chris. "Yes."

The following day, Grace was the first witness. She wore a black T-shirt, and her curly brown hair had been cut to shoulder-length. She was now sixteen and living in a foster home. On the news, her face would be blurred, because she objected to having it broadcast. The judge made it clear to the media: "If you want to do the blue dot, you want to do the wavy lines—whatever you want to do, but no one can violate this directive."

Assistant DA Lisi asked Grace why she'd moved into the attic in 2014.

"To keep me safe." Lucas had watched her take a shower, she said.

"And did you catch him watching you in the shower?"

"No." Grace twisted back and forth in her movable seat as she answered questions. She was slouched forward and sometimes straightened her shoulders. She would cock her head to the side, or occasionally smack her lips while thinking.

"How did you know about that, Grace?"

"He told me."

"Did he tell anyone else?"

"He told my pastor."

That was when Tiffanie told Sarah to move Grace upstairs. Her parents didn't know the reason behind it, but Grace told the court it was to protect her from her two brothers. As an added layer of safety, she and Sarah put locks on the doors—padlocks on the outside, padlocks on the inside. One door was not only locked but blocked with furniture.

"Can you tell me, Grace, what do you think of when you hear the term 'sexual abuse'?" Lisi asked.

"When someone touches you on your private areas when you do not want to be touched."

"So inappropriate touching?"

"Yes."

"And can you tell the court, Grace, have you ever been the victim of sexual abuse?"

"Yes."

"And can you tell me, Grace, when was the first time that you remember being the victim of sexual abuse?"

"I think I was four or five."

"And do you remember who the person was that touched you inappropriately?"

She believed it was Lucas.

"So when you were four or five, Grace, how old would Lucas have been?"

"Um, nine or ten."

"Okay. Is Lucas the only person that's ever touched you inappropriately?"

"No."

"Did someone else touch you inappropriately, Grace?"

"Yes."

"And who was that?"

"Christopher."

It started around the same time, she said. Christopher would've been seven or eight.

"And was this a onetime incident with Christopher and a onetime incident with Lucas, Grace?"

"No."

"Was there contact between his hand—this is Lucas, okay—was there ever contact between Lucas's hand and your breast?"

"Yes."

"Between Lucas's hand and your buttocks?"

"Yes."

"Between Lucas's hand and your vagina?"

"Yes."

"Was there ever contact between Lucas's penis and your vagina?"

"Yes."

There was no penetration, Grace testified. And she said Christopher's contact was the same.

"And, Grace, can you estimate for the court how long that went on for, between Lucas and yourself, and Christopher and yourself?"

"Till I was thirteen." That was when she told her pastor about it. It wasn't until 2014, the shower incident, that she told Sarah something had happened but wouldn't go into detail. Grace then recalled for the judge the night of the bloody beatings and how the questioning started. Christopher wouldn't give complete answers, said Grace, and she was getting very frustrated.

"And you didn't think he was telling the truth," said Lisi. "Correct?"

"He was barely answering."

"Okay. So did you do anything at some point, Grace?"

"I punched him in the back." It was Grace who'd thrown the first punch.

Joe backed her up. "He said, 'You have three seconds to answer,'" she testified. And then he punched Christopher in the stomach. He punched Luke in the stomach and kicked him in the gut, sending Luke doubling over.

"Is there a time period that is being talked about in terms of when Lucas and when Christopher are supposed to have abused Sarah's children?" asked Lisi.

"We were asking them how they had done it. Like, how they had gotten access to the kids."

"Okay. And why were you asking that question, Grace?"

"So we could ensure that it wouldn't happen again."

"Okay. And were you also—correct me if I'm wrong—a little perplexed as to how they could be having access to the kids?"

"Yes."

"All right. And why was that, Grace?"

"'Cause it wasn't very likely. That me and Sarah were with them pretty much twenty-four-seven." And there were locks on the doors. And the window was pretty high. It was unlikely anyone could've climbed through it.

Grace testified that Linda Morey introduced the power cord, but she recalled Linda placing it in her mother's hands first. Then Sarah took it from her father. Grace testified that she left to go to the nursery to pray that her brothers would tell the truth about molesting their nieces and nephews, "because if they would tell the truth, they would not have gotten beaten."

"Were they ever actually caught in the attic, Grace?"

"No, but sometimes, like, if me and Sarah and the kids would go to the store, we would come back and the house, like . . . things were not where they were. One of Sarah's paintings, the canvas was ripped as if somebody used a knife on it."

Lisi asked Grace about helping take care of the children when she lived in the attic. "And did there come a time when that became maybe a little bit of an issue?"

Grace was uncomfortable changing diapers, she acknowledged. "I knew that when people are molested, there's a good chance they molest others, and I didn't want that to happen." She told Tiffanie, Traci, and Sarah about it, and they told her not to change diapers anymore.

During cross-examination, Wittman pinned down the boys' conditions on the night of the crime. They were talking and standing on their own. Grace didn't think either of them needed medical attention.

The judge asked the witness some questions. Grace had said her parents were made aware of her sexual abuse during the counseling session. Judge Dwyer asked, "So before the whip was used, your mother and father both knew of the allegations that you had made against your brothers?"

"They're not allegations," Grace firmly replied. "They are fact. And yes."

Though there were four witnesses that day, it was Grace's testimony that made headlines, like this one from Syracuse.com: *Sister Says Brothers Touched Her, Watched Her.*

Leo Sullivan was among those who testified for the prosecution when court resumed the next day. The director of trauma at St.

Elizabeth hospital said he was called to the emergency room for a trauma patient on October 13, 2015. It was Chris, who was tender virtually everywhere they touched him. His face was swollen, especially his nose, also his chest, genitals, and thighs. His back was severely swollen and black and blue, and there were areas of broken skin. During the time he was in the hospital, Chris had lost three to four units of blood through internal bleeding.

"Can you describe what that's a photograph of?" asked Assistant DA Michael Coluzza, showing a picture of Chris's knee on an overhead projector that was also on the computer screen in front of the witness.

"There is a curved scar," answered Sullivan. "This is a fairly typical injury. It's actually a textbook injury always seen in child-abuse classes, where a cable is bent and it's used to whip a person."

"So you've seen this before in your practice?"

"Many times."

The doctor testified that Chris suffered kidney damage, having lost about 50 percent of kidney function.

"He also had air outside his lung, and that's a very serious problem." Air was under the skin. It went up around his airways into his esophagus. "If that air was just a little bit more and tracked up to his brain, he could have brain damage."

Chris's significant breakdown of muscle tissue called for an aggressive schedule of IV fluid and a weeklong hospital stay. The first two days were spent in the intensive care unit, where he was watched very closely—one nurse for every two patients—and monitored every few minutes. "If he had air in his epidural space, and he had any evidence of neurologic compromise, he might suddenly be brought to the operating room to let the air out of his skull if it was pressing on his brain."

The doctor testified he'd seen the type of muscle breakdown that Chris was experiencing in individuals with a massive crush injury, such as someone who'd been pinned under a car for hours. And

Chris's kidney damage was so severe that it created air under the skin, something that could only happen from a significant amount of blunt trauma.

"Doctor, I'd like to ask you a hypothetical question," said Coluzza. "Professional heavyweight boxers endure multiple extraordinarily hard punches to their faces and bodies during an ordinary boxing match. Is that right?"

"That's correct."

"Okay. Therefore, wouldn't boxers, people in that profession, sustain similar injuries and kidney failure like you saw in Christopher, and the bruising that you saw in Christopher during the ordinary course of their sport?"

"No. A boxing match is only ten rounds. They really . . . they're only beat up for ten rounds. It would take quite a bit—hypothetically, I guess if they went 110 rounds, it might happen."

Had he not been found, merely drinking water would not have saved Christopher, Sullivan testified. "His kidneys would have shut down. I would estimate in five to ten days, he would've expired."

Lead Investigator Brad Pietryka was called next to the stand. He testified to the many defendant interviews conducted the first night and attempts to retrieve a recording of the counseling session turned deadly. And there was one final question the defense did not like.

"As a police officer, are you a mandated reporter when it comes to child sexual abuse?" McNamara asked him.

"Yes, I am."

"And based upon the totality of this investigation, did you make any reports regarding sexual molestation?"

"No, we did not."

Wittman objected to the relevance.

"Sustained," said the judge. "I said to both sides, allegations don't mean anything to me. If something hasn't been proven here in court, I'm not going to consider it here as evidence. So I understand what you're trying to do, but I just don't think that it's going to be needed."

Wittman argued against hearing testimony from the prosecution's next witness, who physically examined five of the six children who came out of the Word of Life Building that fateful night. "The issue of whether these children were sexually abused," said Wittman, "is not the subject of the indictment, and I would argue that the testimony is collateral to the issues at trial here."

That argument was overruled, and Coluzza called Susan Blatt to the stand. Blatt was a New Hartford pediatrician who had special training in examining children who may have been abused physically or sexually. She also worked for a child advocacy center. Over the previous fifteen or sixteen years, the center had called her to do examinations as needed, specifically on sexual abuse victims. Blatt would start with a comprehensive physical exam, checking the child's overall condition, but she would also look for signs of oral trauma or bruising, two common indicators of sexual abuse. She also checked the genitals.

"Well, for girls it's a little less intrusive than it is for a grown-up woman. We don't use a speculum. We don't go into the vagina with an instrument, but we're really looking at the outside of the vagina and the opening. We're looking at the hymen to see if there's been any damage."

She also looked for injuries that could indicate past sexual abuse, like scarring around the anus.

On October 13, 2015, early in the morning, Blatt was called to perform six of these examinations. The children had all been interviewed by police and social workers.

Coluzza asked about each child, beginning with Grace. Blatt testified that Grace was cooperative with the exam and answered any questions. She had no signs of injury or illness.

"As part of that overall examination," asked Coluzza, "did you find any signs of oral trauma upon Grace?"

"No."

"And, Doctor, what would the significance—what would be the significance in an examination of this nature about oral trauma?"

"Well, sometimes sexual abuse involves penetration of a penis into the mouth, and so, theoretically, there could be damage to the teeth, or—"

"You found no such evidence?"

"No."

"Doctor, as part of your examination, did you also do a genital examination upon Grace?"

"Yes."

"And did you also do an anal examination of Grace?"

"Yes."

"And can you tell us: did you find any evidence of bruising or trauma?"

"Everything was normal."

"Did you inspect her hymen?"

"Yes."

"And how did that present?"

"It was normal."

"It was intact?"

"Yes. Intact."

"And you also examined her anus, I take it?"

"Yes."

"Doctor, did you find anything remarkable there?"

"No."

"And what would you be looking for, specifically, in that portion of the examination?"

"Looking, again, for damage to the hymen from penetration by a penis."

"Doctor, did you find any physical manifestations, any physical signs of sexual abuse?"

"No."

"Did you find any physical evidence that she had been subjected to sexual intercourse?"

"No."

"Doctor, did you find any evidence of nonsexual abuse, ordinary physical injuries?"

"Not with Grace. No."

But if the sexual abuse had consisted of touching, there would be no signs, Blatt testified, unless the touching was very rough. The doctor had also tested Grace for HIV, pregnancy, and sexually transmitted diseases. All were negative. Ezekiel, too, was cooperative and showed no obvious signs of sexual abuse.

"Did you find any evidence of nonsexual physical abuse? Any physical injuries upon his body?" asked Coluzza.

"Not on Ezekiel."

Gabriel, who was seven years old, also consented to a physical exam. Like the others, he showed no signs of sexual abuse. "As to your overall examination, did you find any evidence of recent injury?"

"He had some bruises on the back of his upper legs, and it was hard for us to tell what might have caused them, but it was more that we—that's not the area you expect to see bruising in a seven-year-old boy. So upper legs in the back."

"Where do you— As a pediatrician, have you treated children for accidental injuries a number of times?"

"Yes. And we know patterns that are normal. Most children bruise the front of their legs, their lower legs, and their knees in just routinely playing."

"And these injuries were in another area?"

"Yeah. Upper thighs in back."

"Did you attempt to do a genital examination of Ada?"

"We discussed it with her. We didn't attempt, and she said she refused." The standard exam turned up no signs of sexual abuse.

Both Noah, age three, and Ivy, age two, were thoroughly checked and came up negative for signs of sexual abuse. On cross-examination, Wittman said, "Doctor, for each of the individuals that you've just testified about, you prepared a report, and in that report, you had an impression about whether there had, in fact, been sexual abuse. Correct?"

"Right."

"And it was essentially the same impression for all of the children?"

"Yes."

"And that impression included the fact that, although there were no signs of abuse, abuse could not be ruled out?"

"Correct." Many types of abuse, she testified, do not leave any signs.

It was late on October 12 that police walked Grace, Ezekiel, and Sarah's four little ones to the Willowvale fire station after getting them out of the Word of Life Building. In the conference room, an officer gave them soda and made them french fries, chicken fingers, and hot dogs. Each of the four youngest was given a stuffed animal, that they clutched and played with as they talked endlessly about God and Jesus. Oneida County Child Protective Services caseworker Alecia O'Keefe* arrived just before 1:00 A.M.

Ezekiel didn't know what year he was born. Grace didn't know his birth year, either, but told the caseworker he was twelve. None of the children knew the correct spelling of Ferguson. None had been immunized.

Linda Morey was at the firehouse and, before leaving, told Grace to make sure no one talked. Grace clamped down and told the caseworker, "We want a lawyer. We're not going to speak to you, or anyone else."

The caseworker walked Ada to the bathroom, because her mom wasn't there to take her. Grace walked in behind them and stood until they were done. Grace then asked O'Keefe if the children could go home with her. O'Keefe explained that Grace could not take the children because she was a child herself. Then Grace asked if they could all go home with Linda. They couldn't. They were in the custody of the Oneida County Department of Social Services.

Grace turned to the children and told them they would "be touched very badly," and that bad things happen in foster care.

Ada and Gabriel started talking about Aunt Kristel. She didn't go to their church anymore, they said, because she no longer believed in Jesus.

"Do you still see Aunt Kristel?" asked the caseworker.

"No." They both shook their heads.

Grace quickly changed the subject and told the kids not to talk to anyone about "family business." She became utterly frantic when O'Keefe got Ada and Gabriel ready to leave and yelled, "If anything happens to them, someone is gonna be in big trouble!"

The children were shaken. While in the car, on the way to a foster home, they asked if they were going to be hurt. O'Keefe told them they would be safe. Gabriel said everyone at his home had been hurt. "Bad things happen at my home."

"Stop talking," Ada admonished. "Remember what Grace told us."

"Did Grace tell you to lie?" asked O'Keefe.

They both said, "Yes." Grace had taught them to lie, said Ada, and told them to lie to anyone who talked to them about their home. "Grace must've forgotten how bad it is to lie, and how mad Jesus Christ would be."

O'Keefe brought the kids to the foster home and walked them inside. On the way in, they asked about the pumpkins and Halloween decorations. O'Keefe told them about the holiday of Halloween. Ada asked if the caseworker would tuck her into bed. O'Keefe put her to bed and reminded both children to "always tell the truth."

After a night's rest, police and child advocates interviewed and examined all the children. Ivy was found to have what appeared to be two circular marks that looked like cigarette burns on her left leg. Ada said her mother would discipline her with a paint stick. Sarah would make her pull down her pants and then hit her on the buttocks and thighs. It would hurt to sit down after the spankings, Ada said. There was also a paint stick at the church that her mother used. Ada had fresh bruises on the back of her thigh, a location consistent with her account.

Ezekiel was asked about discipline at home and said he would get yelled at, grounded, or spanked. He would get hit on the backs of his thighs with paint stirrers or hard plastic spoons but said it didn't hurt much, and never caused injury or bruising.

Ezekiel said that on the night of the counseling session, he'd heard Luke admit to "inappropriately touching" him. Police questioned him about it. The investigator noted in his report: *[Ezekiel] was interviewed regarding his own experience with Lucas and Christopher. He advised that he had found out that Lucas and Christopher had been abusing him, he stated that his sister Sarah had told him this.*

Could he remember what happened? Well, they did use to slam him on the sofa "for fun and games," he said. And they picked on him for being short. One time, Luke pinned him on the couch and tickled him. Sometimes, his brothers smacked and flicked him. The investigator asked if they'd ever flicked his penis.

After thinking hard, Ezekiel said, "I don't think so." After more thought, he added that there had been one time, he was maybe eight years old, when he was sitting on the couch and Luke poked him with a stick in the privates.

Grace, when interviewed, was adamant her brothers had sexually abused her. Chris, when interviewed, acknowledged inappropriate contact with her. But was it sexual abuse? McNamara likened it to a child's normal sexual exploration by playing house or doctor. Authorities had recovered a text from Grace to Tiffanie, dated July 21, 2014.

It said Grace was compelled by the pastor's sermon to confess to the whole church everything she had done, if Tiffanie believed that's what God wanted. This was the confession she was prepared to make: *When i was little i let Luke and Chris touch me for money.*

Debi had told McNamara she once caught the kids showing their privates to each other and scolded them. Finding out the differences between boys and girls, McNamara later pointed out, is a normal part of development, but these children were denied that, because they were cut off from the rest of the world.

"I don't think it's all that uncommon. Here, the boys were so isolated they can't play doctor with the little girl next door. They're gonna play doctor or house with their sister."

What about that text from Luke to Tiffanie confessing to molesting Ada and exposing himself to passing cars?

"I don't believe he did it," McNamara said. Luke and Grace were in two different places emotionally. The Word of Life teachings were deeply entrenched in Grace, while Luke had checked out a year before the incident. McNamara believed Luke had been coming up with outrageous statements as a snub to those controlling him.

Right after Dr. Blatt's testimony, Bruce Leonard walked to the witness stand in his orange jail garb. He had a much different look, with his clean-shaven face, hair cut short, and black-rimmed eyeglasses.

Bruce talked about leaving the church with Luke to take care of the neighbor's dog before the counseling session. McNamara wanted to know if he notified the pastor that he was going to leave.

Bruce's drawn-out way of speaking hadn't changed. There were a lot of pauses in every answer. "Let her know that we had something to do because normally, normally we would have been just simply there."

"Okay. And could you have just left without notifying her?"

"Well, we wouldn't have, because that would be just like taking off without . . ."

"And that church service, once you're there, are you supposed to get permission from Pastor Tiffanie to leave, or notify her? How does that work?"

"Well, it's . . . it would be normal just to— Well, what we did is let her know ahead of time that, hey, we had this chore we needed to leave to go take care of, so . . ."

"When you're at church, do you have to get permission, or is it appropriate to get permission to leave before you leave?"

"Well, yeah. Courtesy."

McNamara asked about the questions Tiffanie was posing to the boys. "Were some of the questions being asked about what Lucas had done to his brother Ezekiel?"

"At that—okay, I don't think so on that."

"Well, let me ask you that: did Pastor Tiffanie ask if Luke had been mean to Ezekiel? Not sexually abuse him."

"I think I'd say yes on that."

"But it was molestation as it applied to Grace?"

"I think so."

"And at that point in time, when Pastor Tiffanie was talking about that, did you have any knowledge that, in the past, there had been inappropriate contact between Lucas, Christopher, and Grace?"

"I had some suspicions. Wonders. But I did not have clear, for-sure knowledge."

"And what were those wonders? Did you wonder if the kids had engaged in playing doctor and house and those kinds of things kids play?"

"I . . . I did not have specific . . . I wondered. Not as . . ."

"Had you ever caught Lucas, Christopher, and Grace in a situation where you thought they were engaging in inappropriate physical contact?"

"No."

"Had you ever been told by your wife, Debi, that she had caught them engaged in inappropriate contact?"

"No."

The DA got around to asking about the night in question. "Now at some point, does this counseling session turn into a whipping or a flogging of your sons?"

"Yes."

"Can you tell us how that started?"

"Okay. Someone passed a cord to me."

"And what did you do when that cord was passed to you?"

"I whipped Luke, and I also whipped Christopher." About twenty times, said Bruce, and never in the groin.

"Why were you whipping the boys?"

"To— So they would understand the hurt that they caused. Just for discipline. For punishment." And to try to get them to repent their sins. Nodding his head shamefully, Bruce added, "I realize it was wrong."

"Is there a biblical verse that has some relevance to the whipping?"

"Yeah. 'Blows that hurt drive off evil.'" He was trying to rid the boys of evil, but more so, it was a reaction to what they had already said.

"In hindsight," asked McNamara, "would you agree that it was an overreaction?"

Bruce nodded and then looked up at McNamara and said, "Yes, sir," before crying, shaking, and squeezing his eyes shut. He testified about Luke and Chris falling, Sarah screaming at them to get off the floor, and Joe and Dave yanking them up.

"What were you doing when they were being whipped by Sarah?" asked the DA.

"I was letting it happen."

"What was your wife doing?"

"She was crying."

Bruce said the boys were not free to leave. "The— Well, because we were essentially committed to getting it resolved."

Why couldn't Bruce just go home? Take the kids with him.

"Well, we couldn't. We couldn't just go home, you know. This is too—too big. Too crazy. Too . . . Didn't know what we would be— what to do at home, you know, how to . . ."

"Did you need Pastor Tiffanie to make the decisions?"

"To, no . . . no, to counsel what to do."

"Did you need her for that?"

"In . . . in this situation that we were in, like, altogether . . ." Bruce shrugged and acknowledged, "Yeah. We needed . . . 'cause it all . . . it all started with, you know, got some issues to get resolved."

"With her calling a meeting?"

"Yeah. And so, and then we go home and what to do? That was . . . so, yes. We could have gone home, but we couldn't . . . but go home and do what?"

Wittman objected when McNamara asked if Bruce's sons were taught to submit to the authority of the pastor of the Word of Life.

Bruce was allowed to answer. "Okay."

"Is that a yes?" asked McNamara.

"Yes."

"Is Pastor Tiffanie a prophet?"

"She often hears from God."

Robert Stoppacher was the forensic pathologist who performed the autopsy on Luke. He testified that Luke "had a three-quarter-inch laceration, or a tear of the shaft of the penis, and that went completely through the skin to the tissue beneath the skin." It was a tear the length of a penny at the end of his penis. "Lucas was an otherwise healthy nineteen-year-old, and there was no natural disease that was identified on the internal examination." There was extensive bruising and bleeding that went deep below the skin into the fat layer, and in some cases, into the muscle below the fat, about an inch and a half deep.

And what about the cancer that Tiffanie had prophesized? There were no signs of the disease. A toxicology report also showed no signs of drugs or alcohol in Luke's system, but did turn up a potentially fatal level of salt. Luke's blood loss had brought on dehydration, which can cause sodium levels to rise. And it didn't appear that Luke had been offered any liquids. Stoppacher explained that high concentrations of sodium in the body's cells cause the cells to shrink, which is particularly harmful in the brain.

"What kind of signs would you see in somebody that has a high sodium level, if it was affecting their brain?" asked McNamara.

"Most commonly, as the brain cells lose their normal function, the person exhibits signs that they're neurologically not intact, or not normal." Confusion, muddled thinking, he explained. They might become lethargic, difficult to arouse, or even unconscious. There might be twitching or seizures.

"In your opinion, could Luke's life have been saved after he was beaten, if he was administered any type of first aid?"

"In my opinion, yes."

"In particular, let's talk about his penis. Could his penis have, the bleeding of his penis been treated without the need of an operation?"

"Well, I think the basic first aid, and wrapping it, and stopping the bleeding would have gone a long way. Yes."

"So putting pressure on the wound, the things that normal people—people like myself that don't have a medical degree, you know, you just put pressure on it and apply pressure?"

"Correct."

"What about the dehydration? Had he been provided water, more than just one little cup of it, would that have helped his condition?"

"Well, certainly . . . it certainly would've made the chances of survival greater."

"Had he been taken to the hospital so that he could've been given IV—would that have saved his life or made it so that it wasn't fatal?"

"In my opinion, yes."

Before ending for the day, the defense called Deborah Leonard, the first of their two witnesses. She was wearing the jail-issued jumpsuit with a white T-shirt underneath, dark brown moles sprinkled all over her neck and chest. Her hair was completely gray and hung past the middle of her back. An unsightly mole the size of a quarter was prominent on her left cheek, next to her ear. Age pulled down her mouth at the corners.

Debi testified that Sarah hit each of the boys "a couple times" and that the whipping lasted "a short time."

McNamara was dumbstruck. She'd told him initially that she was petrified by the violence and afraid she would be whipped if she intervened. And there was a piece of her story he'd never before heard. Debi was now claiming that after Sarah left, Luke walked out of the small sanctuary with "two other guys," possibly Joe and Dave, and she heard metal slamming, and yelling. She said she believed they may have taken him to a locker room, implying the men slammed Luke up against lockers. McNamara had been onsite and, though there was a locker room, he didn't think Debi would've been able to hear anything from there.

Debi testified that she didn't see Luke again until seven o'clock the next morning, "and he was standing, and he was—appeared to be tired, but fine." She didn't see Joe punch Luke in the stomach, only heard Linda tell Chris to take his earrings out and saw Dave hold one of the boys up against the wall. She had no idea who brought the power cord.

When it came time for cross-examination, McNamara was ready. He showed her a picture. "Debi, I want you to take a look at that and tell me if you recognize who that person is."

"Could he identify the exhibit?" asked Wittman.

"Sure," said McNamara. "It's People's Exhibit Number Thirty-Six."

"Lucas," answered Debi.

"Who is that?" he asked again.

"Lucas."

"And does it look like Lucas only got hit a couple times? Is that your testimony? A couple times?"

"No, it doesn't."

"How about People's Exhibit Number Thirty-Eight?"

"No."

"It looks like he got hit more than a couple times. Correct?"

"Yes."

"I want to show you what's been marked as People's Exhibit Number Eighty-Four, and take a look at that. Do you recognize that to be your son Christopher's back?"

"Yes."

"And you would agree that there's a little bit more than a couple hits there? Correct?"

"Yes."

"Would it surprise you to know that your husband testified that he hit your son someplace between twenty and thirty times in the back?"

"Yes, it would surprise me."

"I want you to take a look at that. Do you recognize that to be the leg of somebody? This is People's Exhibit Eighty-Six. Do you recognize that to be an injury to a knee?"

"Yes."

"And you've actually seen this one before, People's Exhibit Number Eighty-Seven, haven't you? As a matter of fact, why don't you tell the court what you said to me when you saw that picture of your son."

Wittman objected to the form of the question, so McNamara reworded it. "When you first saw that picture, did you say to me—"

"Objection."

"—'Will Christopher ever be able to have children?'"

"Pardon me?" asked the judge.

Wittman shook her head.

McNamara repeated, "Did you ask me if Christopher would ever be able to have children?"

anyone else have anything that they'd like to bring up?' and I said, 'I actually have something, and I would like to bring up the peephole.' So I asked the boys about the peephole. I said, 'Do you know anything about a peephole in the bathroom?' to which Christopher said that he did. And I said, 'What is it for?' and he said that it was to watch the—to watch the family members taking showers. And I said, 'What do you mean? Who were you watching take showers?' He said that he was watching Mother, which is my mom. And Dad. He watched me and Grace. And I said, 'Did you watch my children taking baths?' and he said that he had. So I composed myself. I was like, okay. I was sitting there like this . . . I'm like, all right, all right, okay. I can do this. And I said, 'Um . . . have you ever—have you ever touched my children?'"

She paused and swallowed hard.

"And there was no response. I said, 'Excuse me. I said, have you ever touched my children?'" Her voice cracked. She licked her lips. "And there was still no response." She leaned forward and continued, just shy of yelling. "I said, 'Excuse me, please.'" Her lips curled, showing teeth. "I said, have you ever touched my children?" She rested against the seatback with her arms across her chest and enunciated each word. "To which there was then a response. A positive response. He said yes, he had. Okay. All right."

Sarah tilted her head, closed her eyes, took several deep breaths, and looked angrily toward the floor, awaiting the next question. She testified Luke made several admissions. From the witness stand, she answered in graduating intensity, "They went into detail as to what they did, as I was asking, 'What do you mean you rubbed your cock on them?' 'What do you mean you rubbed your penis on my children while you're masturbating?' 'What do you mean you took them to a room and touched them, made them take off their fucking clothes?'" She flung back her arms and, with hands outstretched, voice shaking, said, "I'm sorry," pushed back her hair, wrapped herself tightly in her blazer, crossed her arms again, and exhaled deeply. In a subdued voice, she continued. "I said, 'What do you mean?' And they went into further detail. And further detail. And further detail." Like placing a lid on a boiling pot, Sarah's voice dropped to a forced flat tone. "I took a cord, and I proceeded to use it on the genitalia of my brothers." She said she stopped when she thought Lucas peed his pants.

Sarah talked about leaving, wrapping her head in a blanket, and falling asleep. Someone brought her a drink, which woke her. "And it was suggested to me to go check on Ada at this point." Ada's genitals were red and swollen, she said. "It could've been from, you know, I don't know where it was from. It could've been, you know, previously I was thinking, before this situation, because she would come to me and say, 'Mom,' she would come to me and say, 'Mom, my pee hurts.' 'Mom, my pee hurts.' So I would check on her. At that point, I had no idea why her privates would hurt. But I would check on her, and it just looked like maybe she had possibly rubbed too hard, you know, wiped too hard, or something like that. And on one occasion she had what looked to be a marker, like, all over her privates. And I just, I thought, okay, this is, this is really strange. 'Ada, how did there become marker on your privates? What's happening?' And she wouldn't answer me. She just—she just, she wasn't going to tell me. So I was like, okay, all right, well, that's something to keep in mind."

After checking on Ada the night of the beatings, Sarah went back to the dining area, curled up, and fell asleep. She told of waking to someone screaming for her parents to go to the big sanctuary. "There is one other, one other tidbit that I'd like to bring out. As I'm running up the ramp, through that hallway, um, I would like to say that Traci Irwin, who was not present at all that night, came rushing past. 'Where is he? What happened?' She went down. I just wanted to bring that fact out. She was not present the whole night."

Coluzza objected, calling it hearsay. Before the judge could respond, Sarah interjected, "That wasn't hearsay. I saw that. I was there."

"Sustained," said the judge.

Sarah said she had no idea why police were outside the building. She'd seen Chris walking around. "He looked to be okay." He would have some swelling, for sure, she thought. "But other than that, I just—it just wasn't even—I just wasn't mentally in that state to even think about it."

Wittman showed her a picture of Luke's jeans, and Sarah said they did not look like that when she last saw him.

It was time for Michael Coluzza to cross-examine Sarah, but he was only a few questions in when she interrupted him. Coluzza told her, "It's not a time you can make whatever statements you want. Just answer the questions."

Coluzza went over Sarah's history with WLCC. "And can you tell me, during that period of time, did the subject of tithing to the church come up?"

"That's been a thing from the very beginning," she said, cocksure. "Have you read the Bible, sir?"

"Miss Ferguson," the judge reprimanded, "just answer the questions."

Yes, she said. She liked to tithe.

"And did that become a point of contention in your marriage to Andrew Ferguson?" asked Coluzza.

"Money, in general, was a contention with Andrew Ferguson. I was not allowed more than twenty dollars a week, sir. Would you like to continue on this topic?"

"Sure," said Coluzza. He asked if tithing had been one of the factors that led to her separation. She denied it. Coluzza pointed out that after Sarah left her husband, the Irwins took her in, along with her two children. "After your marriage ended, you were the custodial parent for those children. Correct?"

"That's correct. I had gotten full and complete, total custody, because he chose not to show up at the visits when—I'm sorry, I'm a little bitter about this—but for their birthdays."

"Miss Ferguson. Please," Coluzza admonished. "If you can limit your answers."

"I'll try. I'm sorry. It's been eight and a half months, and I haven't been able to speak."

"Miss Ferguson, I'm not here to litigate your divorce."

Sarah said she didn't know the rules of testimony, and the judge informed her, in plain language: "Listen to the question, and answer the question."

Sarah admitted she was able to experience the world beyond the church and denied that her brothers were sheltered. "They played outside. They had many friends in the neighborhood. They were part of [the homeschool] group, and they did extracurricular activities. They definitely experienced the world up until that point."

"Not to the extent that you had?" Coluzza asked.

"Actually, age-wise, they experienced more than I had, age-wise. I'm telling you the truth."

She admitted to becoming suspicious of her brothers while living in the attic and said that during that time, she was in constant communication with Traci and Tiffanie. Traci, she said, was like her mom.

Coluzza read several texts and emails aloud, including ones that expressed feelings of anger toward her parents, and then this: "*Luke has been acting weird in general lately. Pretty much accosting Chris the other day. He came up behind Chris and was like, hugging him from behind, like, in a gross manner. Like a joke. But it wasn't funny at all. I didn't get it at first, embarrassingly, but finally, I told Luke to leave him alone. I should have just rebuked the devil.*"

"Mhm," Sarah uttered.

Coluzza continued reading. "*I may have, actually, now that I'm thinking about it. It was just really gross. Luke calls it popping Chris's personal space bubble. I call it gross. And molestation, actually, now that I think about it.* Did you write that?"

"Yes, I definitely did."

"And you wrote that to the Irwins, to Traci."

"Yes, um . . ."

"And essentially, you're describing Lucas grabbing Christopher from behind in a joking manner."

"He was essentially humping him from behind, sir."

"And you described that as sexual molestation?"

"As I stated, he was humping his brother from behind, and Christopher's expression was not enjoying it. Yes."

"But you reported it to your church as molestation. Correct?"

"Yes."

"Do you understand that brothers—"

"Hump each other?"

"—tease each other, wrestle with each other, and sometimes do gross things when they're doing that?"

"When you find out, sir, you have a peephole in the bathroom—"

"That's not an answer to my question. The question is: do you understand that brothers sometimes kid around in rough ways and sometimes kid around in gross ways?"

"Yes, but this is not a normal situation, sir, as you have brought out."

"And this was done in your presence?"

"Yes, it was. And I—"

"And you referred—you reported it to your church as molestation. Is that correct?"

Sarah looked at the computer screen in front of her and began reading the text verbatim. "I said, *And molestation, actually, now that I think about it. I'm sorry that I didn't text you about that right away.*" She looked up at Coluzza. "Because they wanted to be updated on what was happening as far as the molestation."

"They wanted to be updated," he said. "Correct?"

"They wanted to be sure it was not a thing."

"They wanted regular reports. Correct?"

"It wasn't so much like that, sir."

"All right. Message 580, please," said Coluzza.

As someone brought up a different text on the screen, Sarah made use of the void by adding, "Keeping children safe."

"Ma'am, please. You're not responding to a question that's been asked." Coluzza continued. "Question 580—excuse me, message 580. Is that another one of your text messages to Traci?"

"Yes."

"All right. And that message was sent on December second of 2014. Correct?"

"That's correct."

"And in that message, you say, *Luke was acting super, super weird, very slinky like. When I rebuked the devil, he left the room.*"

"Mhm."

Coluzza continued reading. "*And then when he went past me, he went like, way out and around me. I mean, like, in a weird, awkward way. And then, right before they left, he darted upstairs and I was hit with this fear. Like, a flight fear. I thought he was going to come back downstairs with his knives, so I quickly and quietly darted to the front stairs to avoid him, and when I got there, I like, stopped and realized what the heck I was doing. So I rebuked the devil and deliberated which way to go and, lo and behold, he came out of momma's room to go down the stairs that way. With his Bible. It's so stupid. If he were really planning to harm me, I would've just been right in harm's way by giving into fear.*"

Coluzza turned from the screen to the defendant. "Did you write that?"

"I sure did."

"Did you write further, a little bit later in this message: *So Grace and I came back upstairs, and I scooted up to check on the kids to make sure they were OK?*" He leaned toward the monitor. "You have—" He paused before continuing. "*[Noah] was asleep and [Ivy] was content in her highchair, so I went downstairs to cast cowering demons from the boys' room, and Grace was casting them out of daddy's office. When she got done, she came to the boys' room with me, and we consecrated it to Jesus and commanded all sexual perversion and immorality, and started listing demons and casting them out and forbidding them to return."* He again turned to Sarah. "Did you write all of that?"

"Yep. That was a thing. So can I answer that question?"

"You've answered the question. Yes. Let me ask a follow-up question."

"I'm sorry." Sarah flagged the judge. "Sir? Your Honor? Can I just talk to you for a second?"

The judge nodded. "Do you have to use the bathroom?"

"No, I just want to answer his questions."

"Okay," said the judge, "you just have to listen to the question that is asked and answer that question. If your attorney has a follow-up, she will have an opportunity to ask you more questions later on."

"Okay."

The judge reiterated, "Just listen to his questions and try to answer that question."

"I got you. All right. Carry on, sir. I'm sorry."

Out of Sarah's view, Coluzza turned his head and raised his eyebrows, and then continued. "Ma'am, you and Grace performed some sort of exorcism of devil spirits out of the boys' room on that date?"

"Thank you for asking that question. So here's the thing. I misunderstood and I, yeah, I kind of went overboard. Yes, I totally did, and it's something that I find really humorous now that I think about it. But it was not—reading it sounds asinine, as it kind of was slightly. But, so . . ."

"Why did you think there were cowering demons in your brothers' room?"

"Um. Hm . . . Why did I think there were cowering demons in

my brothers' room? I'm a very spiritual person, okay, and I believe strongly in the spirit world. I believe in angels and demons. I've actually seen manifestations. It's a thing. It's scientific. It is a thing. And so, based on the question that you asked me, I'm answering this question with the best ability I have. Please just bear with me. Please be patient with me. This is the first. I've never been in this situation before, and I don't mean to be overbearing or rude. I'm just trying to answer the question."

"Miss Ferguson, I'll let you continue," said Coluzza. "Go ahead and explain yourself, please."

"Thank you. So based on that, based on my personal experience, and I do believe in spirit—in the spirit realm, and I just happened to go slightly overboard. That's all. And now it's, 'Hi, world! Here is my very embarrassing moment.' Thank you for that."

"This is something that you reported to—"

"It was something that I told them."

"—your church. Correct?"

"It wasn't a report. I was communicating with my—she was kind of like a Sarah godmother. She's kind of like a woman who took me in. And that's an embarrassing moment. That happens."

"Miss Ferguson, you believe in demons. Correct?"

"I believe in angels and demons. Yes, I do. I believe in the spirit world. So if you—do you watch *Oprah*?"

"You believe that demons can occupy space in our world?"

"I do."

"Do you believe demons can occupy people in our world?"

"Um, I believe honestly—this is a fun conversation for me, so, cool. I believe that human beings are able to invite certain spirits. I believe that you can invite evil spirits, or you can invite good spirits. So, yes. Actually, I do believe that."

"And Pastor Tiffanie, in fact, teaches this kind of belief in her church. Doesn't she?"

"Tiffanie definitely supports spiritually."

"And it's not uncommon for her to talk about demons taking control and being responsible for people's answers to certain questions. Isn't that true?"

"No, that's not really true."

"No, that's not true?" Coluzza repeated.

"Not necessarily. No. Maybe I don't understand your question."

"Do you believe that sometimes people's actions or words are the result of a demon taking control of their thoughts?"

"In essence. I mean, that is definitely—it can be a thing, because if you invite such a spirit, you then can be, in essence—I mean, have you watched—?"

"Don't ask me a question." Coluzza's words had bite.

"I'm sorry. Okay." She threw up her hands. "Learning process. I'm sorry."

"Miss Ferguson, were you trying to cast out some demons from your brothers' rooms at that time, and Grace's room?"

"Yes. When, mhm." She leaned forward and squinted. "It says, *So I went downstairs to cast cowering demons from the boys' room.*" She lifted her head. "And yes, that is a thing."

"Okay, and, in fact, you also talk about molestation. Don't you? Molestation takes the work of a demon that takes possession of somebody?"

"Why else would somebody molest someone? I mean, for real. I don't understand."

"So is a demon at the helm when you saw Lucas grab Christopher from behind? Is that your belief?"

"Not necessarily. I'm not saying— I wouldn't go that far. It's just—"

"It's probably two brothers horsing around and one of them got a little inappropriate, as opposed to a demon controlling them?"

"In this situation—I'm not sure where you're going as far as the spirituality of it, but in this situation, when you have extenuating circumstances, I definitely would err on the side of caution. So that's why the need for the text message."

"At least as of December 2, 2014, that's about ten months before Lucas died," noted Coluzza, "you're exorcising demons out of his room?"

"I was exercising extreme caution."

The prosecutor moved to a different message that Sarah sent to Traci: "*I bind you spirit of slumber and sleepiness! And it just clicked, like, yeah! That's a demon! So we took authority over that garbage, too. Then, we headed to Grace's room, and we took authority over sexual sin, sexual perversion, molestation, masturbation, fear, worry and anxiety, and every nasty feeling of nostalgia, or any other draw towards sin.* Did you say those things?"

"It's right there. Totally did."

"Okay, so Grace's room got an exorcism of sorts, too. Didn't it?"

"That's where she had said that a lot of the molestation happened to her. And she felt comfortable doing that. Yes."

"And you went there to cast out the demons?"

"This is around the same time frame. Yes."

"And these would be demons that possessed your brothers, who were the perpetrators of these acts on Grace?"

"No, I'm not going to say that. I'm just saying that why else would somebody—I just said this. We just covered this. It's a matter of me going super overboard, possibly, maybe, in this situation, and I was making myself better, making Grace feel better. And, in addition to that, I do believe in demons and angels, and I'm not the only one. So please don't make me feel that I'm less than a human being for believing in spirituality."

"Miss Ferguson, what you just said, maybe you went a little over-board in this message or last message, is that what happens to you emotionally? Do you go overboard when the subject of molestation comes up?"

"No, not—no, not necessarily."

"Did you say, at the bottom of the message, please, *During this time, I took authority over the devil, but before I even realized what I was saying, I was saying—take authority of the spirit of sexual sin and abuse. I realized like, mid saying, it what I was saying, but by then it was too late to stop saying it. That's when Chris grabbed his Bible and started reading, and Luke left the room, and like, I could see him getting angry?* Did you say that?"

She affirmed.

Coluzza asked the defendant if she was getting angry with her brothers. Sarah corrected the word to "frustrated."

"I wanted them to be better, honestly," she continued. "If you want—if you want the truth. I wanted them to be better, and I was very thankful that—the reason that I wrote, *that's when Chris grabbed his Bible and started reading* is because I was very happy because it appeared that they were possibly getting better. And that is the truth. So, no, I was not more and more angry. I was frustrated."

"On February 6, 2015, did you write, *Luke started hanging all over Chris again while I was doing laundry, so I spoke up and told him it wasn't appropriate to do, so get off of him. Give him space. I was glad to be able to stand up for Chris this time. I could tell he appreciated it?* Did you write that?"

"Yes, I did."

"In that case, it upset you to see Luke, once again, hanging on Chris?"

"Are you kidding me? Yes."

"He wasn't humping him at this point?"

"I didn't write it previously in the other one, and I'm just telling you what I recollect, so possibly he was. I cannot tell you for a fact."

And there was a message she'd sent a few minutes after that one. Coluzza read it. "*It was so angering to see! I followed Chris privately and told him not to let Luke do that to him. I told him to stand up*

*for himself. He thanked me. And it's going to be a short night down
there. Already Luke has silently grabbed [Noah] and started feeding
him. I got him back. After seeing Luke do that to Chris again, there's
no way I'm going to let him get away with that."*

Sarah enthusiastically admitted to writing that one, too.

"And is it fair to say you're angry at, and highly distrustful of your
brother Luke by this point?"

"Absolutely. Because of what I had seen and what Grace alluded
to."

"So, you're not going to let Luke anywhere near your children. Is
that right?"

"That's correct."

"Is it fair to say then, that during this period of time in the house,
you're not letting those kids out of your sight?"

"We weren't at that house. We were at my brother's house. But
yes."

"Because you're concerned with your children's safety. Correct?"

"That's correct."

"So, you're either with your children at all times, or Grace is. Is that
fair to say?"

"Um, hm. Yes. That's correct."

"You're closely guarding your children at this point. Would that be
fair to say?"

"I care very much about my children. Yes."

"Okay. Let's go to the next message."

"Sounds like a plan."

It was from January 20, 2015. "Are you describing Luke shooting
paper balls at Ezekiel?" asked Coluzza.

"If you would like to get into this subject, Luke used to regularly
take pellet guns and shoot Ezekiel. He would take anything—he broke
Ezekiel's collarbone. Would you like to continue on this one?"

"I want to talk about this message."

"Okay, sir."

"So going to message 889, did you write, *Probably right either there, or in the next room over. That stuff happens so often he can't possibly miss it. The most he does is, 'Luke, stop it!' Luke laughs it off as a joke, continues, and it just goes around and around. It's retarded?*"

"Yes, I did."

"And what he's doing is essentially putting pieces of paper or paper wads into a BB gun and shooting it at his brother?"

"Um, I actually don't see that in that text message, but that—"

"Is that what's going on?"

"I don't remember, sir. But I do know what regularly did happen was pellet guns being shot. Yeah. Have you ever been hit with a wad of paper? It hurts wicked bad."

Coluzza asked her to look at message 890.

"It says, *I mean, he's the one that told me that Luke shot him in the back, and he was laughing about it like it was the greatest fun in the world.*" Sarah read that part aloud, before stopping. "Which is, I would like to add, is what happens when you're abused. You tend to have this weird relationship with your aggressor. It is actually a thing."

Coluzza refocused her. "You wrote, *That's how it usually goes, unless he gets mad about it, and then he throws a fit, which is when Daddy gets involved.*"

"Yes."

He continued reading. "*Like I said, he may even add for [Zeke] to stay away from him, which doesn't happen either, because [Zeke] goes right back for more. It's all twisted. The whole thing.*"

"Yes, which is why, like, in relationships, if you have an abusive, say, husband, you don't usually—there's a part of it that is—"

"You're not responding to my question. Okay?"

"I am responding to your question."

"You're describing something that's twisted, where Zeke himself is laughing and going back for more."

"Yes."

"Miss Ferguson, is it possible for brothers, teenage and younger brothers, to physically wrestle around, or play around, or even fight with each other and have that not be sin?"

"Where did sin come from? I'm sorry, what?" She dramatically snapped her head to the side. "What just happened there?"

The judge jumped in. "Can you answer the question?"

Sarah asked to hear it again. Coluzza repeated, "Is it possible for young brothers to wrestle around, roughhouse, maybe even fight, and have it not be—let me change the word—'molestation'?"

"Yeah, that's not even talked about there. That was about Ezekiel being abused in a different way by his brothers."

"So you regarded that as abuse?"

"You don't?"

"I'm asking you."

"I do."

"Okay. And you reported that to your church. Correct?"

"It was not a report."

"To Traci?"

"I communicated to a woman who is like my mother, because it was bothering me."

Lucas, the prosecutor pointed out, was at the center of it all. Coluzza read a message that Sarah had written about her son Gabriel putting her in a bad spot by asking to sit on Luke's lap. He read another about Sarah becoming suspicious that Luke was getting into the attic. "Did you write the following? *We just got home. A couple times I've had suspicions that Luke is coming up when we're not here. I'm pretty sure he's now leaving calling cards to let us know.* Did you write that?"

"Yes, I did."

He read a message about Sarah not wanting Luke riding in the car with her to the store, and followed it up with, "You don't like your brother very much at this point. Do you?"

"I adore my brother. Thank you very much for insinuating such things."

Another message: "*I had the best time in praying, praise and worship. There was such resistance at first, but I kept focusing on Jesus, and focusing on Jesus, and focusing on Jesus some more. I'm saying the demons that try to rule downstairs were being so stirred up, the cats started acting crazy, and things were banging around for a minute, lol. I don't even know what it was, but I was looking at my Jesus. And then, at a point, I knew the devil was really, really mad at me. I saw, while my eyes were closed, off to my left, a demon that looked like Luke when he's acting out that demon possessed angry*— Excuse me."

Coluzza lost his place, but Sarah finished for him. "—*he's acting out that demon possessed angry thing he gets, just like staring at me with a stance of fury.* Yes, I wrote that."

"The brother that you adore, Luke, appeared to you in the form of a demon?" asked Coluzza.

"No, Luke did not appear to me."

"The demon appeared in his form. Correct?"

"That's correct."

"Okay, so what you told us a little while ago, that you were being silly on those— When you exorcized the room, you're talking about it again seven months later. Correct?"

This was totally different, she said. Before, she was "going crazy."

Coluzza continued. "And on April 25, 2015, did you state the following on that date? *My mom and Luke went to the Stanley tonight to watch Ann's daughter, actually, who is dancing in some kind of recital. She's about ten or eleven. I think my emotions have been kind of been pricked a little bit just realizing all that my mom and dad make sure that these kids do. I mean, it sounds like they're constantly doing something fun, or that I would have definitely liked to have done when I was younger. I don't mean to sound like a baby. It just makes me feel bad if I think about it, because a lot of stuff I asked to do when I was little, begged even, and the things I did do, they pulled me out of, like dance, which I love.* Do you remember writing that to the Irwins?"

"Yes. I definitely remember writing that to Traci."

"And there's a little bit of jealousy going on that they're giving this kind of attention to Luke?"

"It was more jealousy—um, it was—okay, so here's the thing: When I was younger, to answer your question, when I was younger, I wasn't allowed to go past the two houses right out front, whereas the boys and Grace and Zeke were all allowed to run all over Clayville. I really enjoyed dance. I enjoyed music and such as that, and I wasn't allowed to do things like that, whereas the four kids get to do—they got to do all kinds of stuff like that."

Coluzza had Sarah admit that her children rarely left her sight, and if they did, it was only for a few minutes.

The line of questioning moved on to the events of October 11. Coluzza asked why Lucas had said he wanted to leave the church.

Sarah responded, "I honestly don't remember. It was something to the effect of—he wanted to leave so that he can molest little girls and not get in trouble for it. He was very . . . we have actually similar personalities as far as outspokenness." She stopped and then quickly added, "I do apologize for any outspokenness, PS."

Luke's attitude was disrespectful, hardened, she said, and he and Chris had laid out an elaborate plot to kill their parents.

"The question comes up: When would they have had the opportunity to do all of these sexual acts they're referring to? Correct?" asked Coluzza.

"Their answer, and the answer, is they used a crowbar to open my door and to get into my apartment when I was asleep and Grace was asleep, and they proceeded to cover my children's mouth with their hands, and they proceeded to rub their penises all over my children's body and tell them, sir, that if they told anyone, they would murder them. That is actually the answer to your question," she said through gritted teeth.

"So, as I understand it, then, they're relaying this elaborate story of prying your padlocked door open at night?"

"Sometimes, we would forget to padlock the inside, because it had appeared that things were getting better downstairs."

"But they were admitting, these two boys were admitting at night when you're asleep, padlocked, to prying open a door?"

"That's correct."

"Without waking you up. Correct?"

"That's correct."

"Without waking Grace up. Correct?"

"That's correct."

"Without the four children waking up. Correct?"

"No, not necessarily correct on that one," she answered flippantly.

"And two boys somehow silently and swiftly covered the mouths of four children and molested them there on the spot?"

"Maybe it was just one at a time, as they said. Maybe they would discuss it previous, as they said that night. They discussed exactly how they would do it, sir."

"And they would molest your children, and then leave. Correct? After warning them of the consequences of disclosing to you."

"Hey, it worked for Grace and Ezekiel."

"They would leave?" he repeated.

"Yes."

"And they would eliminate all evidence that they ever forcibly entered your apartment. Correct?"

"No, not correct. But I just don't know because . . . yeah."

"And all of this was done as both you and Grace slept without stirring?"

"I am, unfortunately, a very hard sleeper, sir."

"Multiple times they admitted to?"

"This is the truth. That is what they admitted to." And their admissions, said Sarah, made her angry.

"Who introduced the whip?" asked Coluzza.

That was the start of when Sarah's mind got murky. She couldn't remember anything that happened that night, except holding a cord she described as being six feet long, striking her brothers' genitals, and falling asleep with a blanket over her head. She remembered checking Ada, though, and Coluzza asked why that child was the only one she checked, when the boys had admitted to molesting all four.

"Because they went into the most detail as to what they had done to Ada. They said they penetrated her. They said they went into my daughter. That is why I checked Ada."

Coluzza asked if she'd listened to Dr. Blatt's testimony that Ada was the only child who would not agree to a physical exam. "And it's just a coincidence that the one child you chose to check is the child that you knew from two days ago that Dr. Blatt couldn't examine genitally. Isn't that correct?"

"Yes. That's correct, which bothers me intensely, actually."

"You specifically recall running into Traci, and where, and under what circumstances you ran into Traci after the beatings. Correct?"

"That's correct."

"As a matter of fact, you went out of your way to share with the court that she wasn't involved at all. Correct?"

"That is correct."

"Okay."

"To my recollection." She nodded heartily. "Good point. Good point."

The prosecutor's last question was, "Do you believe what your brothers received was just punishment?"

"Absolutely not."

On Tuesday, each side got a final chance to argue their case to the judge, beginning with Rebecca Wittman.

"Sarah Ferguson," she said, "is not blameless in what happened to her brothers on October 11, 2015." Her client admitted to whipping them, but, "The question is not so much what did she do. The actual question is how responsible is she for what she did or didn't do."

Every person who testified they were present the night of the incident said they had no idea a counseling session was going to be called. Wittman said the DA's questions about the church and how it operated, text messages leading up the incident, and whether people believed Tiffanie was a prophet were irrelevant.

"However, the collateral question that came up during this trial was whether Sarah's children, or other children, were abused by Christopher and Lucas. Although it is collateral, the DA has attempted to prove that it did not occur. The issue of whether Sarah's children were abused is only relevant as to what Sarah Ferguson thought or believed on October 11. . . . Christopher testified that it did occur." Wittman read back portions of his testimony.

"Grace Leonard testified that it occurred for years. The peephole existed, and it was used. It is against that backdrop of information, as opposed to the backdrop of being under Tiffanie Irwin's spell, that the boys' comments on [October 11] were heard by Sarah. . . . Grace Leonard, sexual abuse victim, threw the first punch." Others got involved—two, three hours? And then, it stopped, Wittman said. Sarah left the room thinking the boys were in pain, but not that they needed medical attention. "The fact that their unclothed bodies reveal lots of bruising and a laceration does not translate to—that

Sarah should be charged with knowing, recognizing, and appreciating their true medical situation as their kidneys were becoming compromised, or their sodium levels were rising many hours after she had left the room.

"Does Sarah Ferguson leave them in a snowbank with stab wounds she has inflicted? Does she toss them into the lake after they've been beaten and ignore their cries and tell lies about where they are? Does she beat an infant over a period of days and throw the infant on the floor? No. She leaves apparently okay—appeared to be in no imminent danger—brothers in the care of their parents. . . ."

There was plenty of evidence, the defense lawyer pointed out, to contradict the DA's claims that Sarah should have known they needed medical attention. While clothed, the only apparent injuries were to their hands. Sarah perceived the blood on Lucas's pants to be urine. Everyone else present that night testified they believed the boys were in pain but no imminent danger. And Debi testified that at 6:30 A.M., Luke was walking around.

"Grace sees Luke on the tarp and thinks he's faking." Wittman pointed out that Chris told Joe he was okay and even helped move scaffolding. "Later, at the church, Sarah sees Chris eating, and he appears tired, much like herself . . .

"Perhaps most importantly," said Wittman, "when they are escorted from the church, no law enforcement personnel hustles Christopher into an ambulance." He was driven, with Sarah, to various police stations and questioned and photographed before being taken to the hospital. "A big deal was made out of the fact that Sarah had a few hours of first aid training many years ago, when she was a flight attendant, to suggest that she should've administered first aid and called 911. There is a whole SWAT team of officers waiting outside the church on October 12. No one says, 'Get that man in an ambulance.'" There was no way to know how he looked twelve hours earlier, and there were no obvious, outward signs of life-threatening injuries, she argued. "If

"I did," answered Debi.

During her testimony, McNamara handed Debi the long computer power cord and asked her to illustrate for the court how she held the cord and used it. Later, at her sentencing, Debi would relay this scene and make disturbing allegations about it.

Sarah testified last, the next morning. She came dressed in a conservative black blazer over a black-and-gray patterned shirt, wearing eyeglasses with thick black frames and her hair in a bun. Sarah began by detailing her background—where she'd lived and gone to school, her family makeup. Did she consider Bruce her father?

"Um, he's the one that wiped off my knees when I would fall down and generally take care of me. Yes." And she talked about Grace moving into the attic. "It had been brought to my attention that some sexual misconduct had happened between her and the boys. And I was not going to allow that to continue. So I found her sleeping in the living room, and I was like, no, come on, you're coming with me, and I brought her up to my apartment, and there she stayed."

Sarah focused intently on her defense attorney's questions and provided answers calmly. It was through Pastor Tiffanie that she learned Grace had been molested. Grace had confessed it to the pastor. And Tiffanie wouldn't provide details. Sarah would have to hear them from Grace, when she was ready. But that time never came.

"She would just say, you know, things were really bad. She would say, 'I do have my virginity, but that's about all I have.'"

Aside from all the locks on the doors, they also boarded one up. As for church?

"It was just an overall awesome experience. It wasn't—there was no creepiness involved or whatever, you know, people want to misconstrue it as."

She tensed on the witness stand, crossing her arms when Wittman began a series of questions about the whipping, and the peephole.

"Tiffanie was talking about something to them, and she's like, 'Does

Christopher was at risk of dying in five to ten days, how could Sarah have perceived that Lucas, who received similar injuries, might die twelve hours later?"

Could Luke's death have been caused by other injuries inflicted upon him after Sarah left? That was something the judge should consider, said Wittman. He would also have to determine not just the defendant's level of culpability, but how her mental state contributed to events. The lawyer contended her client was not guilty of murder, but of the lesser charge of criminally negligent homicide.

Then it was McNamara's turn. "Your Honor, the conduct of the defendant in this case, how she killed her brother Lucas, is perhaps more morally reprehensible than had she intentionally killed him." She left him to die painfully and slowly, over twelve hours. It was her overall actions, "the wanton cruelty, the brutality and the callousness" that night that showed depraved indifference, he argued, which was the element necessary for the second-degree murder conviction. The top prosecutor rehashed the time line of the counseling session and talked of the boys' admissions, including raping Sarah's two daughters. He drew attention to the fact that Sarah, Grace, and the children lived in a heavily fortified apartment and said it was common sense to expect to hear cries of pain and visible signs of serious injury if such abuse were to have occurred.

McNamara talked about the forensic evidence that showed Lucas was bleeding profusely. "The blood soaked his pant legs, and finally traveled all the way down Lucas's leg to his heel. The upper portion of Lucas's sock was saturated with blood. In addition, the blood entered Lucas's left sneaker."

For the defendant to claim she didn't know Lucas was bleeding "defied logic."

"After Lucas collapsed some time after seven o'clock, he was not provided medical attention, nor was there any testimony that would suggest that anybody—anybody—any of his captors, any of his tormenters, any of his assaulters provided him any comfort. With any care. With any first aid. With water that his body so desperately needed."

Sarah put a blanket over her head, drank an energy drink, and went back to bed. When she awoke, "she went and checked on, not the welfare of all four of her children, but I submit to you, in an interesting twist, she only checked one. Happened to be the one that wouldn't consent to a physical examination the next day. . . . She interestingly doesn't check on her two-year-old. All of that testimony totally contradicts Bruce, and I believe Deborah's testimony that someone was asked to check on the children, and someone came back and reported that they were fine."

A lot was learned from Sarah's emails and text messages, said the DA, "because they provided available insight to how she felt about her brothers and, unfortunately, the manipulation of the Irwins to divide families, and to create mistrust among loved ones." The texts, he said, conveyed her jealousy of, and hatred toward, Christopher and Lucas, her anger toward her parents, and her belief her brothers were plotting to do evil things. "Simply put: she couldn't stand them."

The only people who could've helped Luke that night were the people who hurt him, said McNamara. "The last fifteen hours of Lucas Leonard's life was spent in a place, a place he was taught to believe was a house of God. But in reality, from approximately nine o'clock on October 11, 9:00 P.M., until approximately noon on October 12, 3354 Oneida Street was anything but a house of God. It was a venue for a witch trial and a flogging that's unrivaled in Oneida County history, a torture chamber for two young men that had been whipped more than seventy-six times."

That concluded what had been a lengthy trial. Not wanting to prolong it further, Judge Dwyer rendered his verdict that very afternoon: Sarah Ferguson was guilty of two counts of first-degree gang assault, two counts of assault, and one count of first-degree manslaughter.

She was not guilty of second-degree murder. In the end, though Judge Dwyer "did not believe very much of her testimony," he did believe that Sarah truly had not recognized the risk of death to Luke and that there was no proof anyone present had known the risk. This ruling gave attorneys on both sides a peek into what they could expect at the trials of the remaining defendants.

When you allow your children to play with human beings like they're toys—that's a problem.

—DA Scott McNamara
on Traci Irwin, December 5, 2016

Rich Dibble made his presence known to Scott McNamara in the late summer of 2016. The DA was willing to set up a meeting with Rich in his office with himself and other top officials. Rich wanted to share what he'd learned about cults, and about Bruce. He asked McNamara if he could help bring a deprogrammer to jail to work with Bruce. The DA said he would do what he could.

After that meeting, Rich added another person to his visit list: Scott McNamara. He established a relationship with the DA, partly to feel him out. He wanted to learn if McNamara was trustworthy. Rich ended up finding an ally in the very person Bruce viewed as an enemy.

"It seemed more important to him to really get at the bottom of things than to just do things that seemed successful so he could get votes the next time he ran," Rich later said. "He struck me as having some incredible integrity."

While the idea of a deprogrammer was a good one, an apparent problem was realized: once Bruce's mind was freed, he would have to deal with the awareness that he had taken part in killing his child. Bruce was already deeply grieving, and with mental health care in jail—and then prison—seriously lacking, Rich and Kristel were concerned that Bruce could harm himself. They decided to sideline deprogramming. But it ended up happening on its own, to an extent. Bruce selected a book from the jail library that happened to be about a cult, and he was able to recognize and label the group as such. Rich had not pushed the topic before, to avoid driving Bruce away, but this was his chance to segue into a thoughtful discussion about cult groups. That got Bruce's wheels turning.

"He began to accept the idea that things may've been orchestrated," Rich recounted.

Rich had one lingering concern: Bruce still saw the district attorney as the bad guy. Irwin loyalists had vilified McNamara, which caused Bruce to outright reject every piece of information that came from the DA's office. Often this created unnecessary hurdles and didn't help foster Bruce's understanding or healing.

On September 1, Sarah was sentenced. Behind the scenes, the judge read letters of support from seven people, all but two of them from Rick Wright's family. Rick's wife and all four adult children sent letters, and most included the same words: "honest," "integrity," "responsible." Themes were also repeated, such as her submission to authority: *Sarah is very respectful of authority. I can't remember a time when she disrespected someone in authority.* Just about every Wright letter alluded to Sarah's method of disciplining her children, for example: *Several times I've witnessed her simply and lovingly instruct her children when they misbehaved.* Another repeated theme was Sarah's love of Jesus: *Sarah takes her faith in god seriously and it has a noticeable positive effect on the way she acts.*

A relative of Sarah's wrote the judge, alleging she'd lived as a battered woman in a previous relationship, and that under the scars, Sarah was kind and gentle. Grace also wrote a heartfelt note about Sarah taking on the role of mother to her, explaining that when she'd first moved into the attic, she'd been *a disrespectful kid who had no idea how to treat people correctly.* Much of the time, Grace would be up very late studying for a test, she wrote, and Sarah would stay up with her to keep her company, often until at least four o'clock in the morning. Grace wrote that a scholastic diagnostic test showed that at age fifteen, she was performing educationally at a twelfth-grade level, something she attributed to Sarah's influence. She would've stayed at a fifth-grade level, she wrote, if it weren't for her sister. She added that if it weren't for Sarah, *I am also positive that I would be dead, either by my hand or the hand of my brother Lucas*. Grace wanted the judge to know that her sister was one of the most caring women she had ever known, and that Sarah's favorite color was turquoise. She did not like bugs. She loved Mediterranean food. Hers was a nerdy, bohemian sense of style. She loved music and played guitar and drums. Her favorite artists were Johnny Cash, Elvis Presley, and Keith Green. She cried watching cartoons.

McNamara was first to speak at the sentencing. He called it "the most malicious, brutal, and callous beating" he'd seen in his twenty-four years as a prosecutor. Sarah held herself up as a religious person, he told the judge, yet broke one of the Ten Commandments. "She's putting up a picture about precious moments and showing her children. You know what, Your Honor? There's a certain amount of hypocrisy to that." McNamara asked the judge to sentence Sarah to no less than twenty-five years in prison to send a message: "Vigilante justice has no place in our society."

Wittman next addressed the court, saying Sarah Ferguson's world was her children. And whether the things Lucas and Christopher said in the counseling session were true, they were given in excruciating detail. Now, two of her children were brought to see her for one hour every other week; the other two had not seen her in person for an entire year. Wittman asked the judge to display "humanity and compassion" in deciding a fair sentence.

Sarah took the opportunity to address the court as well. She was not in street clothes, as she had been during trial. Instead, she wore her county-issued jail uniform. In a short, eloquent plea, she said, "Regardless of what popular belief may be, or what the probation report says, I do truly love my brothers. I did not intend"—her voice cracked, and she began to cry—"or purposefully inflict—knowingly—serious physical damage. I was not aware. I just—I snapped. My brain just could not—" She threw back her head, inhaled deeply and stepped back from the podium. After composing herself, she continued softly, "I could not handle any more. And I truly—I truly am sorry for causing them pain. I really am sorry!" Her last word was clipped by a piercing cry. Sarah stepped from the microphone, put her hands to her mouth, and wailed. "My God!"

Judge Dwyer wanted to keep his comments brief, as many more defendants were facing trial in the same case. He did not want to influence future trials. "At any point," he said, "anyone could've stopped this." That no one did, was inconceivable to him. Nothing, said the judge, was going to change the bottom line: "You killed your brother." And with that, he sentenced her to twenty years in prison for manslaughter, twenty for the assault of Lucas, twenty for the gang assault of Lucas, five years in prison for assaulting Christohper, and five years for the gang assault. The sentences related to Lucas would be served at the same time, and the sentences for the crimes against Christopher would be served at the same time, making Sarah's entire sentence twenty-five years in prison.

Sarah's moment of contrition seemed to last for just that—a moment. As deputies led her from the courtroom, she looked left and scanned four people sitting next to each other: Kristel, Kristel's uncle, her cousin, and Helen Lehrer. Then Sarah's eyes went back and settled on Kristel, locked in a stern glare. She kept that chilly stare and scowl as she glided through the exit door.

Sarah's sentencing outcome sparked an avalanche of plea agreements. On October 7, Traci and her son Dan accepted deals that would have them each serve two years in jail for unlawful imprisonment, a felony. Traci told the judge she accepted the offer because a jury would likely believe "lies" against her. Both Traci and her son took what's called an Alford plea, in which the defendant maintains innocence but agrees there's a likelihood the evidence would lead to a conviction. As for the remaining defendants, the prosecution made another plea offer with a catch—all four would have to accept the offer, or all of them would go to trial. Two weeks later, the remaining defendants accepted plea deals.

Tiffanie took an Alford plea to first-degree manslaughter and second-degree assault. She agreed to serve twelve years in prison on the top charge, and five years on the assault, to be served concurrently.

Linda and David Morey pleaded guilty to two counts of second-degree assault and would be sentenced to five years in prison on each charge, also to run concurrently.

Joseph Irwin pleaded guilty to first-degree gang assault and second-degree assault, but it was a challenge getting there. In court, before pleading guilty, he continued to argue his innocence. "I didn't cause the damage, but I was there for when it happened."

"Acting as an accomplice, you did hold Lucas Leonard up at times, and you demanded that he stay in place so that the others could whip him?" asked the judge.

"No, I didn't. I didn't. No."

The judge had McNamara outline the evidence against Joe. "Throughout the night, he was in charge of arranging who was going to watch the boys so that they wouldn't leave," said McNamara, "and made sure the rest of the family stayed on the compound known as the Word of Life Church."

The judge added, "I have also heard plea allocutions of both Bruce Leonard and Deborah Leonard, and both of those individuals told me that as they were inflicting physical injury . . . that you were actually making sure that the boys stayed in place, and when they fell to the ground because of injury, that you had them stand back up so that more whipping could be inflicted."

"No, I did not," Joe insisted. Only after a bit of wrangling did he admit to physical contact. But he claimed he hit each boy just a single time: Chris in the stomach and Luke in the shoulder.

"So you tell me what else you did while the whipping was taking place," said the judge.

"I left the room." He was hardly there. He didn't see much of anything. He didn't make them stand.

"Mr. Joseph Irwin," said the judge, "can you look me in the eye and tell me that is the absolute truth—"

"Yes. I promise."

"—that you were not there while those two young men were being whipped?"

The DA stepped in and continued to outline Joe's role, which the prosecution would present at a trial. Joe forced the boys to stand for hours, said McNamara, a common form of punishment at WLCC.

After a time, the judge stopped proceedings to announce he could not accept a guilty plea unless Joe admitted his role.

The accusations and denials continued back and forth. McNamara stepped in again. "We would have significant evidence to show that this defendant, over the course of the years, engaged in conduct directed at not only Christopher Leonard, Lucas Leonard, but also Seth Morey and Cal—excuse me—Seth Wright and Cal Wright, including a brutal beating of Seth Wright, where it was very clear that these men were being taught, throughout the course of these years, that Joseph Irwin was clearly a force that was not to be crossed."

From the spectator seats, Linda Morey's daughter, Kathy, cried out, "He's lying!"

"And that he—"

"Liar!"

"And that he trained these two young men to comply."

Deputies led Kathy out of the courtroom.

"There will be testimony," McNamara continued, "that he would stand at the back door when people arrived to church, as a guard."

"I was greeting them," said Joe.

"That he would be the person that would open the door and lock it."

"I was a door greeter. That's what I said. I hated it, but I was a door greeter."

He took the long route, but Joe finally said the one word that would put him away: "guilty." He would serve eight years on the gang assault and five years on the assault, to run at the same time.

McNamara later reflected on Kathy's courtroom outburst. "Near the end, it was very weird, because Kathy Morey and the two Wright kids were almost like Charles Manson's disciples in the sense that they weren't involved in the case but were making their presence known outside the courtroom by being very disruptive. They almost became like groupies. They were obviously under Tiffanie's spell. They were always in the courtroom. They were always making snide remarks. One time, I was actually being interviewed by the media and Seth Wright was behind me making faces at me."

On December 5, 2016, the judge sentenced a shackled fifty-year-old Traci Irwin to two years in jail. Behind the shield of her Alford plea, she repeatedly maintained she had no knowledge of events that tragic evening. During an impassioned pitch to the judge, she whipped off her eyeglasses, leaned forward, and said, "But you're wrong." Traci emphasized, "I had no knowledge. . . . If I had five minutes to redo something, I would choose five minutes right there to save Luke."

Before the judge sentenced her to the agreed-upon two years in jail, he, too, wanted to make a point: "There was no one in that building that didn't know what was going on."

Daniel went before the judge eleven days later. He stood with chains around his waist, hands resting on thighs, handcuffed at the wrists. Kristel delivered remarks before his sentencing, standing at a podium to the side. She was poised and spoke in the style of her family—slow and deliberate. Daniel's actions, she said, showed utter disregard for human life. His attitude throughout this entire ordeal had been "mocking" and "scoffing."

Dan shifted his weight back and forth nervously.

"Something is dreadfully wrong," Kristel said, "when a young man who holds a clergy position in church decides to do nothing while he observes appalling violence had been committed and two people are suffering terribly. . . ."

He watched her intensely.

"Daniel showed more care and concern for a carpet than for my brothers."

His eyes filled with tears.

"He sat guarding the beaten one, guarding the one bleeding to death—because in some deranged way, he decided that is how a church demonstrates the love of God." Dan's punishment, she told the judge, was too light.

Dan declined to speak, but his lawyer called him a reluctant participant that night. He reminded the judge that it was Dan who carried Luke's body to the van. The judge acknowledged the defendant's display of remorse.

Siblings Joseph and Tiffanie were sentenced three days later. Kristel again spoke, but her words to Joe did not have the impact they'd had on his brother. She recalled for the courtroom how Joe had told her she needed to give the church a large sum of money, on the heels of Tiffanie's threat that God would bring harm to the loved one of the person who didn't comply. A threat of this nature anywhere else, Kristel pointed out, would be considered blackmail or extortion. "Because of the authoritarian nature of the mind control practiced at the Word of Life, I did not recognize the manipulation until after Luke's death. . . . I adored him," she said of her brother. "He was my buddy. He is now my hero. The name Lucas means light. Lucas Benjamin's lionhearted bravery enabled him to allow his vessel, his jar of clay, to be smashed, revealing brilliant, inextinguishable light, which shone as a bolt of lightning to expose the darkness that was lurking at Word of Life. I will continue to ensure that the thunder of Luke's lightning will roll." She called on members of the justice and mental health systems to become educated on mind control. "It is a real issue with potentially destructive outcomes. . . . It is a matter of public health and safety that individuals be guaranteed the right to freedom of the mind."

Asked if he wanted to speak, Joe said, "Yeah. I do."

He began, "Kristel, I forgive you. You'll never know how sorry I am about Luke, and you'll never know how sorry I feel for Christopher, because you don't have any idea what it's like to lose a brother. But I lost a brother that day to the worse circumstances you could imagine. You left of your own will. Nobody said anything to you, but you decided to do this."

In her remarks, Kristel had referenced the bowie knife strapped to Joe's leg during church, but he now said it wasn't real. "I don't see how you could begrudge a twelve-year-old wearing his new toy knife in church amongst who I thought were friends. I don't understand how you could hate me for holding the door for you every Sunday, but I'm sorry I didn't smile. I'll try to change that later on. I'm sorry I'm so big. I'm sorry I intimidated you. You could've mentioned that before. Maybe I could've shrunk. Maybe I could've changed my genetics. I dunno." His sentences were broken by breathless gasps. His voice trembling, he turned his attention to the judge. "But I guess, Dwyer, I forgive you." He turned to the DA. "McNamara, I forgive you. . . . I had to endure months with a father of Luke in jail, watching him, emotionless. Emotionless. Hate me for nothing. I tried to help him, and he would just . . . he would just bite my head off. I understand he was in a lot of pain, but he never cried." Joe, though, cried every night, he said.

"Okay," said the judge, ready to move forward with sentencing.

"I mean that," Joe interrupted. "And I forgive you." He turned to go eye to eye with McNamara. "I forgive you McNamara, Kristel . . ." His eyes searched the room for Kristel, but because she was seated directly behind him, he didn't see her. "Wherever she is, I forgive you. I mean it. I am not just saying it for the cameras. I really mean it."

Joe was walked back to the defense table as his sister approached the bench for sentencing.

Tiffanie's lawyer spoke briefly, stating his client's role in the tragedy was merely to be present. Then Tiffanie had thoughts to share.

In her staccato performance voice, chin up, an air of confidence that reached a level of self-admiration, Tiffanie spoke of "unexpected" and "shocking" events the night of October 11. She spewed indictments of those involved in her court case: McNamara violated the gag order, the judge did nothing in response, and Tiffanie was refused fairness. She provided a copy of a prepared statement to Judge Dwyer, and then read it aloud in court. She labeled Judge Dwyer's behavior "offensive." Going back to the night of Luke's death, Tiffanie said, "I was incapable of reacting to what happened before my eyes."

"Just let me interrupt you," said the judge. "You were incapable of reacting to what you were seeing over how many hours? Is that what you just said? You were incapable of reacting? Do you want to explain that to me, or do you just want to let that go?"

"I figure that the paper that you've been provided explains that for me."

"And so, you have this built-in excuse for the rest of your life that you were incapable of helping two young men," said Dwyer. "Go ahead."

"I have wanted a trial from the start, so that the truth could come out," she continued, with a precise "t" that reverberated in the courtroom. She asserted she had been forced into a plea so that her friends and brother could accept their offers. Now that the others had entered their pleas, she wanted to take hers back. "I want a trial with a fair jury and a fair judge. I ask you to step aside."

Without responding to her request, the judge said, "Mr. McNamara, I didn't give you an opportunity to be heard. Do you wish to be heard?"

McNamara commented on Tiffanie's role in the church. "As with any good leader of an authoritarian group, she didn't need to give the order. It was implied." People "like her" get others to do their bidding. "And we've seen that historically with people like Charles Manson, Jim Jones, hence the statement 'Drink the Kool-Aid.'"

The judge addressed Joe first. Though Kristel had read Joe's face as crocodile tears and recoiled at his words, Judge Dwyer received them as heartfelt, going so far as to say Joe had shown the most remorse of any of the defendants. "And I'm sure that Lucas Leonard's sister appreciates your comments." But "someone had to step up and say, 'This cannot go on any longer.'" And because of Joe's size, people were looking at him to do it, said Dwyer. "I'm sorry that you lost your friend."

Joe was led from the courtroom, and the judge moved on to Tiffanie. She had been told when she took the plea that it would be final, he said. "Your only complaint is that the issue—or, the offer made by Mr. McNamara was contingent on all of the remaining defendants accepting it, or his telling all of them that they had to go to trial if each defendant didn't accept it? Is that the only basis that you're asking to withdraw your plea of guilty?"

"Actually, I shared more just a few minutes ago," she answered curtly.

"Okay, then—"

"Would you like me to read it again?"

He did not, he told her. But that didn't stop Tiffanie from presenting more complaints. She said the grand jury testimony of Rick Ross was so prejudicial the judge should've thrown out the indictments. "Instead, you stated—"

"And you base that on how many years of legal training?"

Following some debate, Judge Dwyer indicated that Tiffanie had no legal grounds to withdraw her plea.

The ruling did not come without final commentary from Tiffanie. "You have not been a fair judge."

Mother and son Linda and Dave Morey were sentenced on January

9, 2017. Linda still had that lively step as she pranced to the defendant's designated spot in front of the judge's bench, a semblance of a smile on her face. Her skunk-like hair in a long ponytail, she appeared diminutive next to her attorney. Linda was animated when she apologized, not to the victim's family but to her own. "I cannot express in words how sorry I am that I had any involvement that night." She called it a horrible tragedy. "Almost every day I ask myself why did this happen? What could I have done to stop it? I apologize to my wonderful husband, my parents, my daughter, and all of my family. I am truly so sorry. My heart aches. My heart is broken. My life will never be the same ever."

His client had no idea that when she gave Bruce the cord, this would end in death, said defense attorney Anthony LaFache. "She was upstairs with Traci when she got a text something terrible had happened. . . . She spent the next couple hours with Christopher. They made some food and talked."

Before handing down the five-year sentence, Judge Dwyer said he believed Linda's remorse to be genuine. He wished she "would've had some foresight when introducing the cord."

Dave's sentencing went fast. He was wordless.

There were two people left to be sentenced: husband and wife, Bruce and Debi. They were up in about month. But something interesting happened in that time. Bruce was constantly turning to Scripture to help him figure things out. He'd read a parable about a rebellious seer named Balaam and his talking ass. Balaam was riding the donkey on a journey God did not want him to take, so God sent an angel to block Balaam's path. The donkey veered off path to avoid the angel, which Balaam could not see. Balaam kept beating the donkey to get him back on the path. The donkey miraculously spoke to ask what he did to deserve being beaten. As Balaam argued with the donkey, the angel made his presence known.

During a visit with Rich Dibble, Bruce relayed this parable and his revelation about it: God had spoken to Balaam through a dumb ass—the initials "DA." Bruce took it as a sign he should listen to the district attorney. Rich had been hoping for such a breakthrough to get Bruce to see that McNamara was not a bad guy.

Rich went to the DA. "I was wondering if you could do me a favor. Could you talk to Bruce?"

"Yeah," said McNamara. "Why?"

"Bruce had a vision that he should listen to what you say. Could you just talk to him?"

Bruce hobbled into the DA's office, escorted by two female deputies and carrying a thick stack of papers. "Where's my lawyer?"

"Your lawyer's not here," said McNamara. "I'm not talking to you about the case. I don't wanna talk to you about the case at all, so we don't need a lawyer." McNamara wasn't exactly sure *what* they would talk about. Rich had not given any clues. "I just wanted to talk. I wanted to see how you're doing."

Bruce was standoffish. "Well, I'm doing fine."

"I'm just worried about you," McNamara said. "I'm a dad. You're a dad. I'm just worried. Are you doing okay?"

Bruce softened. "I cry every single day. I tried so hard to raise my family so that something like this would never happen." He was alluding to what he understood to be the molestation of his daughter Grace. He spoke of the way his family name had been tarnished and his life put under the microscope on the world stage.

The two chatted simply. But the whole time, McNamara's brain was searching for an answer to one question: What am I supposed to say?

"We just talked," he later recounted, "and I told him, 'I hope you outlive your sentence. I hope you see the outside of a prison someday.'"

Bruce looked at him blankly, probably confused as to why the man putting him behind bars was also wishing for his release.

They talked for about an hour. With not much left to say, and plenty of moments of awkward silence, the DA got up to walk Bruce out, and as they were nearing the door, put his hand on Bruce's back. "You're a good man." Bruce stopped and turned to him, as McNamara added, "You just did a bad thing."

It seems not only did Bruce need to hear those words, but McNamara needed to hear himself saying them. It got the DA thinking—*maybe I should come down a little more on the sentence.* By this time, it was clear to McNamara that everything Bruce had done was because of his worship of Tiffanie.

"He was so brainwashed," he emphasized. "And even though he pled guilty, I continued to look at stuff in the case, and it just bothered me a lot on how brainwashed he was, and how he was being punished for Luke going to church with Kristel. Tiffanie really put a lot of pressure on Bruce to get his family under control. He was sending her the hours that he would read the Bible, and I don't even know how he found time to sleep."

It was February 6, 2017, the day of Bruce's sentencing. As the day progressed, McNamara could not shake one thought—"I don't think he needs to get as much time as we agreed." That's what he told the judge and Bruce's lawyer in chambers. "I'm good with ten on him."

Bruce's and Debi's court appearances were on the same day. Debi went first, and she read from a statement she'd written. She apologized to Ezekiel, Sarah, and Grace. And to Chris and Luke, she said, "I have not hurt you physically, but I said some pretty horrible things to you both that I know hurt your hearts." She apologized next to Jayden, to her grandchildren, and finally "to my church family. I apologize for bringing you all into this. I love you all very much, and I ask your forgiveness."

To Bruce, she said, "We should have done much better." She then claimed the DA lied to her from the start. Then, she said she had a lot of questions. If Christopher had been so close to death, how could he have performed CPR and walked handcuffed to the police station?

"And why weren't the photos that I was shown in the court the same photos of what I was shown in McNamara's office? I never saw those photos before." The cord placed in her hand in the courtroom, she said, was not the one that was used the night of the crime. They had hit the boys with a percolator coffee cord.

"You promised me Chris." She told the DA, "You said, and I quote, 'Don't you want to see Chris? He's out of the hospital now. Don't you want to see him, and hug him, and kiss him, and tell him you love him? I can make that happen.'"

She had not seen Chris.

"You changed my plea on me as well." She had pleaded guilty in exchange for two years in prison, she maintained, not five. She characterized her representation as a "hack job," and lastly, took aim at her stepdaughter. "Kristel, I love you, but you never accepted my family or my marriage to your dad, and you never accepted my children. You're exploiting the death of my son for your own gain, and I find that repulsive."

In her seat, Helen by her side for support, Kristel shuddered. This tragedy had produced only losses.

Debi's momentum moved her to say that Kristel had no relationship with Luke. "You hardly recognized our existence when you saw them at church. Bravo on your performance, though. I'm sure you will get paid handsomely for them."

When Debi was done speaking, McNamara stood and told the judge he wanted to clear the record. "The things that I—she just quoted me as saying, I can assure you I've never said." He told the judge there were two assistants with him the day he talked to Debi, who could back up that he'd actually said he'd be willing to look into whether Chris wanted to see her. "Unfortunately, when I went to Chris, he did not want to see his mother."

"Mrs. Leonard," said the judge, "it just amazes me that you can spend the first half of your statement apologizing to everyone, and then the brainwashing takes over once again." He considered that she may have been mistaken about the amount of time she would serve. But the five-year sentence, he said, was clear to everyone on the date she pleaded guilty. And with two final words, Debi's case file was closed: "All set."

Bruce entered the courtroom with a manila folder in his hands, wearing a waist-length jean jacket over his jail jumpsuit and a stern look.

This was the part of the sentencing where the defense attorney would normally rally friends and family of the defendant to speak on the defendant's behalf. Instead, in a move that's almost unheard of, it was the DA who'd personally reached out to ask people to speak for Bruce. First, McNamara handed the judge a thick letter from a nationally known cult expert—not Rick Ross—who wanted to provide information for the court to consider in its sentencing. Then, the judge called up three individuals, one at a time.

Rich Dibble read a statement that detailed his visits with Bruce in the jail, and how the visits had started with his desire to help walk Bruce through the grief of having lost a son. The lack of privacy magnified Bruce's pain. "Bruce once described the media sensation as if being trapped in a spiderweb where he can be viewed from every angle and spoken of without his approval or input."

Rich suggested Bruce was suffering from shock and deep depression, and asked the court to provide him grief counseling. "At Joe Irwin's sentencing, he claimed that all this time in jail, Bruce Leonard never cried over the death of his son. It would be inaccurate to hold this picture and all it implies to be true. I know for a fact that Bruce Leonard loves his children, and that he has cried over all of them."

The judge asked Rich how often he saw Bruce in jail. It had been once a week for one year, and twice a week in the months leading up to sentencing.

"Have you ever been up to see Deborah Leonard?" asked Dwyer.

"I have once."

"Just once?"

Rich nodded.

"Okay. You were present in the courtroom when she—"

"Just now?"

"—voiced her opinion—"

"Yes."

"—and tried to blame a number of other people for her situation? I've seen tremendous change in Mr. Leonard, and I would say that, in large part, it's probably due to your counseling sessions with him, and I do appreciate that."

Debi's brother Jeff spoke next, not for his sister but for Bruce. Also reading from a prepared statement, Jeff talked about Bruce working for years in Jeff's landscaping business. He was an excellent employee who Jeff trusted fully to take over in his absence. "He did not often show much initiative on his own, however, seeming to prefer being told what to do rather than making decisions on his own. . . . Bruce was definitely a follower. This is not a derogatory term. Leadership can be quite difficult. Hard decisions sometimes need to be made, and many times quick decisions without all of the desired information. It has not been my experience that Bruce can make those quick kinds of decisions."

Jeff talked about his twenty-one years as a member of the WLCC cult. "Yes, I am calling it a cult. By every definition, this was a mind-control cult. Practically everything we did, every decision we made, had to go through the leadership, or there would be reprisals. We allowed the Irwins to virtually become the God of our lives." By serving the Irwins, they were serving God. Whatever the Irwins said was like gospel, and not to be questioned.

"My wife and I came to see that what Tiffanie Irwin and the others were telling us personally was nonsense." Jeff felt he could understand how Bruce was feeling that night—conflicted. "But how can you speak out against your pastor? He would've been trying to put all the pieces together while this was happening, some of it just too quickly. He would have been looking for someone to make a decision to do something." Bruce, he said, was not a monster or a murderer but a victim of circumstance.

The judge asked if he'd tried to encourage Bruce and Debi to leave the church when he was on his way out.

"It was difficult," said Jeff, "because of the lack of contact that we could have with him."

"What do you mean by that—lack of contact?"

"The lack of contact, well, basically because when anybody would leave, you'd be shunned by the remaining members. They wouldn't talk to you . . . and even today, my brother's family, I have no contact with them, and they live right next door to me. It's just—they are just—it's what was done when we were there. I did it to others when I was a part of the group."

The judge was curious to know what had made Jeff and his family leave. The Irwins, said Jeff, were starting to target his children. There were making accusations against them "similar to other things that you've heard during this case." His children were accused of molesting younger children in the church. He'd had enough.

Finally, Kristel got her chance to show the world the face of her father—the real man outside the control of the Word of Life. She presented a slideshow showing Bruce with the smiles no one saw on the news broadcasts. "When I was little, one of my favorite things to do was wrestle with my dad."

He showed her how to take care of the runts of the litter born on the family farm. "He guided me in nursing injured wildlife I'd find on the side of the road. He taught me to tend the living treasures I decided to collect. We built terrariums and cared for plants. We built habitats and cared for critters."

Losing her brother under such horrific circumstances was difficult beyond words, Kristel said later. Speaking at her father's sentencing was a close second. She told the court, "My deep love for him will never end."

"I think from everything you've heard today," said McNamara, "Bruce Leonard is a good man who, on October 11 and 12, did a bad thing."

It was Bruce's defense attorney, David Longeretta, who admitted to having the greatest amount of inner conflict involving his client. He almost didn't take the case. "I could not get my head or my arms around how a religious family could be involved in such a tragic and horrific act." But the attorney drove to jail and met the man, and that one visit was all it took for him to decide to represent Bruce. "Bruce was a very kind, loving, compassionate, concerned parent, husband, and person."

"Mr. Leonard," said Judge Dwyer, "a lot of good things have been said about you this morning. It reminds me of a funeral when someone is giving a eulogy."

"For what it's worth," said Bruce, "it kind of felt that way, too."

"Do you understand the difference of who you were when you were a member of that church, and who you are at this point in your life?"

"Well . . . more . . . I'm still a man with deep sorrow. Regrets."

"If I put you back in that situation today, would you be able to stop things?"

"Oh yeah," he said, speaking painfully slowly. "Oh yeah. Yes."

"Well, that shows you have learned from this journey that you've taken so far."

"Your Honor, you don't know how much I would— No . . . like no way would that *ever* happen again."

It was Bruce's opportunity to speak on his own behalf. He read from a piece of lined paper, a statement in his own handwriting. "I'm deeply, terribly sorry for my part . . . it doesn't matter if the things said were true or not. We did wrong. . . . Every day triggers a memory, and you go numb so you can function. It just hurts that bad. . . . My family is in fragments, separated by court order, bars, pain, and anger. . . . They haven't been able to mourn as a family."

There was no funeral, no memorial service.

"To know that your personal action and nonaction contributed to the death of your child is anguish I can't describe." The whipping, said Bruce, was wrong. "It was assault. And no one had the sense to say, 'This is assault. We can't do this.' And afterward, not realizing Luke was really seriously injured, we sat around talking about what to do until it was too late for medical attention to help. It seems obvious now, but it wasn't then."

The judge addressed Bruce and his supporters, the field of reporters, and onlookers in the gallery. "The only way you can do this job, day in and day out, is you have to do what you think is right. I know what I have to do, and I am going to do what I think is right."

Judge Dwyer handed down the reduced sentence. Bruce would serve ten years in prison. Shaving off those years could mean the difference between the Leonard patriarch seeing freedom again or dying behind bars.

In October 2017, members of the Leonard family bought a memorial bench, made possible by community donations. It was installed in the town of Paris park overlooking the swimming pools that Luke had so enjoyed. The bench was inscribed with his name and a quote from Antoine de Saint-Exupéry: "I know but one freedom, and that is the freedom of the mind." Made of recycled plastic, Luke's bench is impervious to any bugs that try to chip away at it. It is durable—strong. It cannot be worn down.

As with every defendant in the WLCC case, I offered Bruce Leonard the opportunity to share his thoughts for this book. True to character, it took him a while to decide. Ten months after reaching out to Bruce, I got a fourteen-page letter that took him one month to write, carefully choosing his words. His reluctance to respond was partly due to what he considered unfair media coverage of the crime.

None of us were professional criminals, quite the contrary. Yet the media made us out to be such, or worse.

He wrote that he suffered some harassment because of it.

It was trauma on top of personal tragedy of Luke's death.

But dealing with the fallout from media reports, he said, was nothing compared to the death of his son.

Losing a child is deeper, more profound, painful than any other family member. . . . I think about my family often but Luke is the one I think about every day. The death of a child is hard by itself, but add in my personal actions contributed to his death, regardless of how they got prompted. That's personal guilt and anger against self. Now add in this happened with other people "contributing" and these people are family/and or church where you've been a part for 20+ years. Thats another whole level. My overwhelming emotion was and still is grief over his death. Everything else is kind of piled on top of that. I'm a grieving parent. Yet at the same time I'm sitting in jail as a perpetrator so its like somehow I'm on both sides, suspended, on public display.

When I opened Bruce's letter, the length of sentences caught my eye. When I read them, it stood out that they were thoughtfully and creatively constructed. Over the course of writing the book, through watching WLCC videos, I had witnessed a man sit before Tiffanie, a woman decades his junior, and stammer, unable to put together coherent sentences. Through watching police interrogation tapes, and reading police statements, I saw similar responses. Bruce's comments were always boiled down to hesitant and disjointed thoughts. Courtroom transcripts also reflected this, but at each subsequent court appearance, his speech was less constrained. Bruce's communication was evolving along with his level of awareness.

And then I received this letter. Away from WLCC, Bruce found his words.

He expressed a mixture of emotions: sorrow, anger, confusion, depression, pain.

I (we) had about 5 major life crises events in one day—death in family, arrested, loss of job, home, status and more. We lost Luke but we lost our other children too and they became orphans in a way.

Unable to get adequate mental health care in jail (and then prison), said Bruce, *I wanted to go numb but I couldn't. By God's mercy I was able to cry and cry for months, gradually got to skip a day, then 2 or 3 days. I still cry, but usually catch it at a sniffle before the trigger gets pulled fully. I think I'm better but it still hurts. Like a lost limb and puncture wounds, scabbed over, mostly numb, learn to get around, then something bangs into it or it gets picked at by yourself or someone else then it hurts again.*

Bruce said others had asked for his side of the story. *It's a bunch of strangers looking to profit from a tragedy, that has the trigger CULT word attached to it.* He was also hesitant to respond because he didn't want his contribution to this book to be seen as an endorsement, since he hadn't read it.

Most important, offering his reflections meant Bruce had to confront a topic that was still very painful.

I am only part way processing—the "How the H___ did this happen?! In a church?!" question.

What I write to you is a compilation of personal experience thats been picked over in little bits. When I've tried to do this before I mentally abort.

Bruce continues to wrestle with the question of whether WLCC was a cult.

Three years ago I would've said "no way." Our pastor takes great pains to be scriptural, to preach it as God wrote it, backed up with word origin studies and cross-reference, encouraged to read the Word for ourselves.

He has come to realize that Scripture can be interpreted to support differing views, even by just emphasizing one part over another. Bruce talked of how WLCC leadership accentuated a position of being able to hear from God and frequently reminded members of their rebellious attitudes and the belief that God doesn't listen to sinners.

These things together add up to be a voluntary relinquishment of autonomy to (submission/obedience/confidence) in the church leadership. So without meaning to, I (we) allowed a man (or woman) to become "as God."

He believes the leadership being the God authority is the root of most, if not all, of what went wrong. *Coupled with an insecurity in self as far as questioning, and glossing over hesitations in a kind of pretend faith, wanting to do the right thing and having trust in leadership as good Godly people, who would do no wrong.*

Bruce attempted to answer the "why."

A young man died who shouldn't have died, in a "church" setting, by the hands of family and friends. The allegations/statements of molestation were emotionally overwhelming, hot button anger, and more, pressure and daze together. Not a good climate for rational thinking. Neither did we act in Christian fashion & just pray. With hindsight re: Oct 11, 2015, I can identify perhaps 5 junctures, something done or not done, by as many people, where the outcome would have been different. So why didn't we catch the junctions? Besides the emotional pressure of that day in particular, theres the thinking pat-terns previously established in each of us by prior events which tend to set the response for today. (habit). You might also use the word programming, or conditioned. We all get conditioned by life but the real question is did I (we) get purposely conditioned at WOL?, to submit to authority, to believe that the pastor/elders are hearing from God, that we are rebellious, etc . . . I believe we did.

None of it was obvious coercion, he said, but evolved gradually. *I can't imagine this happening 20 yrs ago, or even 10.* Looking back, he now recognizes that the Irwins made unfounded allegations against those who left WLCC, accusing them of having their own agendas, or of sinning. *I can't verify their veracity but at the time I gave credibility to the allegations without further proof.*

Bruce said he stayed with WLCC because he believed it offered more good than bad. *Ironic point—controlling your thoughts. Neg-ative (anxious) thoughts make a person depressed but a good word makes it glad (good report, nice greeting, a laugh). I'm saying ironic because it's a coping I first learned in the church (WOL).*

. . . . Part of my coping now is from things learned then even though I'm also here in prison because of WOL.

. . . . I don't know what stage of "processing" any of my co-defendants are at. I know if they've experienced even ½ of what I've felt its a wringer and I would be quite surprised if you did hear back from any.

I did not hear back from any.

I would describe myself as functional/depressed new normal.

Bruce expressed a variety of reasons for speaking out: *an OK report from my family, your reporter background, writing helps me process my grief, and perhaps something I've written will help someone.*

. . . . I hope something positive comes of it. I fear more negative publicity, especially for my children, from being portrayed as reli-gious, evil, weird cult.

And while Bruce has come to acknowledge undue influence, he said, *What I don't know is whether there was a purposeful orchestration of plan extending backwards for years to control us. Then if whether the control was sinister (for their benefit) or benevolent (in the sense of parent toward child).*

Bruce came up with his own warning signs of potential spiritual abuse:

- *Don't let a person become "as God" to you. It can happen gradually, without realizing its happening.*
- *Pay attention if your Scriptural church really revolves around a single personality with a prophetic anointing.*
- Disciple disfellowship/shunning: *People are social right from the start—if we don't get our "social" it messes with our well being and is a potent control technique.*
- *Length of Sunday service—open ended, hours long—kept going as long as God was inspiring or God said stop.* Bruce didn't feel free to ask for time off from the work crew, or leave a service early, *to do something secular—or social, like visit my un-Godly relatives.* Such action would meet Jerry's or Tiffanie's sharp disapproval.
- *Controlled interactions—even not on discipline—we discouraged from just social chit chat. I now believe that was wrong.*
- Arranged marriage: *[Kristel's and Helen's] marriages went kerplunk, failed. Makes you wonder how well Pastor heard from God.* Bruce said he doesn't believe his marriage to Debi was arranged. *We're still married—25 years. Don't know if we'll come out of this together but theres a hope.*
- Controlled education: *To send our kids to public school was a definite no no. (as Godly parents how could you even think about letting your kid go to a bullying, secular, perverted setting?) Well—we got kicked out of the church school.*

— *Bad mouthing former members—Leadership saying they left cause they were rebellious.*

— Coerced holiness: *In the time between Pastor Jerry Irwin dying and then his daughter Tiffanie taking the reins it seemed like there was a tightening, enforcing of holiness and seemed like everyone was getting called out for perversion, which I think is probably the one area most of us fail in thought if not in deed. God calls us, looks for response from us. He does not normally do a coerced threat—Do this or else! Tiffanie did some Do this or else!*

— Public openness: *Maybe 10-12 years ago we had a sign out front, church name, hours of service. The sign got taken down—I forget why—but it never got put back up. Pastor said God would bring the people that He (God) wanted there and God was well able to do so. Furthermore, Pastor said God said the increase in people would come when we were ready. Looking back I think that was a withdrawl rather than an outreach.*

— *End justifies the means—not if you're doing things Jesus style. Jesus never beat the devil out of anyone. The closest he came was drive the money changers out of the temple but they were free to flee. No one was specifically assaulted. Jesus kept the law. In our case at WOL if Luke had not died we would have gone home with 2 assaulted boys, and that would somehow have been OK. That's really scary. I mean scary in the sense of it would have been a "church sanctioned" crime, bad precedent, very bad. The potential ripples from that are also scary to think about. One could argue that Jesus was also a lawbreaker but the difference is that he broke man made laws that were at odds with God's law, but no violence, no vigilante action.*

— *Prophetic words with a threat of calamity—real example: "God is speaking to someone here to give a sum of money. If you're not obedient in this you leave (or open) the door for something bad,*

even life threatening, to happen to a member of your family."
My daughter and husband left the church without giving the
10,000 mentioned. Then Oct 11, 2015 happened. Looks like
fulfilled prophecy. Wow, that word was right on. Leadership
can now take credit for accurate word—They "heard" from
God, thus reinforcing that God speaks to them/through them.
It also sets up the person who didn't obey (in this case giving
the money) as the fall guy to blame for this calamity. It's a line
of crap—but nevertheless you can use scripture to prove it.

— Leadership prayers are better (more anointed, powerful)—really? . . .
It is scriptural to go to the priest or elders [for prayers], but
when the elders make a point their prayers carry more weight
than general congregation, or when certain persons are left out
of the prayer request chain because they would weaken the
effort—watch out!

— Pastoral succession: *In WOL the pastorship was simply passed from*
father to daughter, like passing along the family business. . . .
There was no pastoral selection process. Also the governing
administration of WOL was almost wholly one family (Irwins),
under the direction of the pastor.

— Single source of information. *Looking with hindsight, I realize*
I believed negative things about current and ex-members,
including family members, from the single source of Pastor—
hearing from God, which I regarded as a reliable, trustworthy
source. That led to suspicion, separation without additional
proof, and without hearing their side. I think there may have
been some degree of gaslighting too. You hear an accusation
from a reliable source and part of you moves to believe it
without additional proof.

Bruce wanted to emphasize that it's important to investigate any conflictions among your emotions, instincts, and reasoning.

I think all the points I listed had something that didn't sit quite right at the time, but it was on the edge of my mind, more in the feelings, not big enough to challenge, got pushed down or inside via "It's scriptural, they're hearing from God, or emotions are very changeable/therefore unreliable."

He may even have been reluctant to pursue those feelings, he said, because he was afraid of the answer.

Emotions have a valid voice and theres a reason underlying each which should be integrated into conscious thinking and action. I greatly regret not listening to my emotions/troubling to really investigate to get to the bottom of them. Might have avoided some current pain and shame for many.

Traci and Daniel Irwin were released from Oneida County Correctional Facility on March 24, 2017, having earned credit for time served.

Deborah Leonard's earliest release date is January 18, 2020. Linda and David could be released as soon as February 29, 2020. Joseph's conditional release is September 26, 2022. Bruce's is May 2, 2024. Tiffanie's soonest release is March 2, 2026, and Sarah's is March 8, 2037. Deborah, Sarah, and Tiffanie are housed together at Bedford Hills Correctional Facility.

In early 2019, Scott McNamara announced he will run for reelection to Oneida County District Attorney.

Brad Pietryka retired from the New Hartford Police Department after the Word of Life case concluded. It was the only thing he worked on in the year leading up to his retirement. He then took a part-time job as an investigator with the Oneida County DA's office.

Inspired by this tragedy to testify about the word of God, Dave Cady began writing and singing contemporary Christian songs. He has since performed onstage at a Christian music concert and produced Christian music CDs.

Anthony Sokolowski graduated from Albany Law School in 2019.

As of this writing, Rich Dibble continues to visit Bruce in prison once a month.

Lainey's Army, the animal group that rescued the Leonard pets, had them treated for various health issues, including Lyme disease and parasites. They were able to find homes for all of them.

Kristel Leonard and Helen Lehrer combined their families and married on February 17, 2018. Kristel said she suffers emotional trauma from her ordeal, including recurring nightmares in which she's trying to escape the Irwins. And the guilt is overwhelming, as she described to this author in an email: *Maybe if I had given the money, things would have worked out better. Maybe Luke wouldn't have died. Maybe neither of the boys would have been beaten. These are tough demons to fight.*

Maybe, she wrote, she should've reached out to Luke after he visited her church. She wondered if his death was her fault. After all, he was following her path out of WLCC. She never lost hope that her family would be freed.

I truly believed God would bring them out... and I guess he did... but I know that our individual perceptions of God vary widely. There was a sermon done [at Kristel's new church] on Psalm 66, and some of those who had come out of WLCC decided that God had us there for a time to suffer, and he had some purpose in it. At the time, I felt there was some validity, some comfort in thinking that way. Now though, I see my time in WLCC as time when I was a victim of abuse, a tool in the Irwins' hand to cause hurt to those I loved. I can't say that God didn't answer my prayers and the prayers of the others, in getting my family out, but the way it happened has left me questioning everything I thought I believed. I still want to believe, but I don't know what to believe.

ACKNOWLEDGMENTS

There were nine defendants in this case, and heaps of evidence. Multiple plea deals left most of the evidence buried. Had I known from the onset how complex this story was, and how deep it went, I would not have taken it on. But at every turn, I found myself astounded at how everything fell into place, as though the universe wanted this story told. Most of the individuals who helped with this story expressed they did so out of sincere desire to right a wrong. At the center of it was, and always will be, a young man whose wings never got off the ground.

Some individuals provided more assistance than others, but every contribution was valuable.

Spend a short time with Kristel Leonard and you'll find she is impressively bright. Learn her story, and you'll respect her fortitude. Write a book about her family, and you'll witness her patience, as long as it means getting to the truth. As I proofread the manuscript, I sometimes emailed her every day to make sure particular details were accurate, and she never complained. Her wife, Helen (Lehrer) Leonard was willing to participate, and I thank her, too, for the time and effort she put into this. I am glad they found each other. I'm also grateful that in this short life, I've gotten to meet these truly amazing people.

District Attorney Scott McNamara was my first point of contact on the law enforcement side. I'd had a lousy day in Utica, when nothing had gone as planned, so I attempted an unscheduled visit with McNamara, who was MIA. That mission failed, I sat in a courtroom watching Judge Michael Dwyer so I could get a feel for his presence. In walked McNamara, who unwittingly sat beside me. I passed him a note that read: *I've been looking for you.* Instead of having me arrested for being generally creepy (he had no idea who I was, or what I was talking about), he agreed to follow this stranger into the hallway and listen to what I had to say. That started a months-long relationship with several people in the DA's office.

Scott McNamara, Dave Cady, Brad Pietryka, and Anthony Sokolowski went above and beyond (cliché, but so true) in helping me with whatever I needed to tell this story correctly and in full. Each one selflessly spent an extraordinary amount of time interviewing with me. The label of "patience" also fits these individuals, who never once left an email or phone call unanswered; and there were many, as I found my way through the maze of the Word of Life Christian Church.

I made several trips to Chadwicks and Clayville, and the folks who lived there made me feel invited. They are good people in special communities. Thank you to everyone who talked with me, sat with me, and welcomed me into their homes. There were many others who interviewed with me over the phone, after I'd left the area, and I'm grateful to each one of them. Thank you to Utica radio station WIBX for their assistance.

My sister, Lori Ashline, was by my side from the start of this project, continually encouraging me, and I treasure her endless support.

Thank you to my family and friends who cheered me through this journey. I am afraid that if I list each one, I will mistakenly omit someone, and it's not worth it to disappoint anyone. You are all special to me.

My literary agent, Lane Heymont, is an incredible, dedicated agent, who has every quality any writer could hope for in an agent. I am grateful he gambled on me as a new author. I am also thankful to Pegasus Books and my editor, Katie McGuire, for taking on this debut author and sharing my enthusiasm about the project.

Michael Benson, who has authored dozens of true crime books, is a great role model and a genuinely nice person. When I wanted to write a nonfiction book but was roadblocked by questions, he took the time to work through the answers with me. For each question I couldn't find an answer to, he kept repeating the words that got me to page one: "Write it anyway."

Thank you to the person who was the single greatest motivator to me writing a book: VA. If I had never learned that VA told someone I wasn't capable of writing a book, I never would've worked so hard and pressed through so many self-doubts to complete and publish a book. There is no greater motivator than to be told you can't.

International Cultic Studies Association (ICSA) offers support to former members of cultic groups and to families of those involved in cultic groups and high-control environments.

SOURCE MATERIAL

The information in this book comes from author-conducted interviews; police interviews; audio and video recordings of WLCC events, sermons, and counseling sessions; defendant and witness text messages, emails, and digital and paper journal entries; court transcripts; documents obtained through the Oneida County Clerk's office; documents obtained by police during the course of their investigation; and more.

Some quoted material in the book is not dated. That material may not appear in chronological order in the book. I sometimes combined material to help convey an accurate impression of what went on in the cult during a certain time period, though the events may not have occurred all in the same day or on successive days. I only employed this where such events were not relevant to the time line.

Members' physical descriptions are based on interviews, photographs, and videos. The description of Luke's room and the Leonard attic came from photographs extracted from Sarah's phone during the investigation. Descriptions of the inside and outside of the Word of Life Building came from police photographs and personal visual observations.

Characterizations of an individual's thoughts and feelings were taken from that person's own writings, or from interviews.

Many scenes were largely built from defendants' recall of events through their own writings. Tiffanie's and Sarah's writings were so detailed that they not only included their deepest feelings but illustrations of their surroundings, down to what individuals were saying and where they were sitting or standing.

Many scenes from the Leonard home at the time Sarah lived with them are taken from trial transcripts and Sarah's recollections of events documented in her texts and emails that were seized during the search warrant.

The trial scenes are from trial transcripts, interviews, and police reports.

I built the scene of Luke's fatal counseling session from a combination of witness statements, court testimony, and other records, like Brooke Bowden's recollection, detailed in an email to Tiffanie. I imagined some nonessential details to create a more visual picture for the reader. For instance, it is proven that Chris had such a serious nose bleed that his blood had splattered on his clothing, the wall, and the floor. It is reasonable to conclude that, at some point, it dripped into his mouth. I wrote of individuals moving in their chairs or turning their heads when there was not necessarily reference to those minor details. As far as punches or kicks thrown, where and who they hit, and the number of strikes, those details were taken from a variety of sources, including witness depositions and court testimony. Details involving facial expressions, thoughts, phrases, actions, and locations of individuals came mostly from court testimony, text messages, and police records.

Defendants provided contradictory statements about what happened that night. Chris testified he fell more than five times, and that he was held down once, by Joe, but was mostly pulled up and held back by Dave. Grace's testimony backed up some of Chris's testimony, but she believed Linda handed the cord first to her mother. Other defendants recalled different details, some claimed to recall no details, and others were tripped up by police as having lied about their supposed recall. I used a combination of all the witness and victim statements, as well as police evidence, to re-create the scene, giving more weight to details that were confirmed by more than one witness. In some cases of conflicting information, I adopted the DA's theory of what had happened (for example, the DA concluded it was more likely that Linda handed the cord first to Bruce). During Sarah's trial, testimony got so specific as to include witnesses describing who was standing and sitting at what times, and which blows struck what parts of the body. The differing recollections made it a challenge to create a scene of what likely occurred, so I may have unknowingly written some actions out of order, or wrongly attributed some actions to certain individuals. There is no way to tell conclusively what happened that night, down to every detail. Even some who were present and cooperative with authorities said they were not in a frame of mind to remember things.

In the chapter titled, "Resurrection," quotes attributed to Traci Irwin are from Beverly Visser's recollection and may not be accurate word for word. The scenes involving Jerry's stroke and subsequent death are from Irwin family diary entries, texts, and emails; interviews with former church members; and police reports.

Some WLCC members, including the nine individuals convicted in this case, may have different recollections of events than others. I contacted every defendant in this case and offered each an opportunity for input. Only Bruce Leonard responded.